WORLD YEARBOOK
OF EDUCATION 1998

FUTURES
EDUCATION

Edited by
David Hicks and Richard Slaughter

Series Editors: David Coulby and Crispin Jones

**KOGAN
PAGE**

London • Stirling (USA)

First published in 1998

Apart from any fair dealing for the purposes of research or private study, or criticism or review, as permitted under the Copyright, Designs and Patents Act 1988, this publication may only be reproduced, stored or transmitted, in any form or by any means, with the prior permission in writing of the publishers, or in the case of reprographic reproduction in accordance with the terms and licences issued by the CLA. Enquiries concerning reproduction outside those terms should be sent to the publishers at the undermentioned address:

Kogan Page Limited
120 Pentonville Road
London N1 9JN

© David Hicks and Richard Slaughter, 1998

British Library Cataloguing in Publication Data

A CIP record for this book is available from the British Library.

ISBN 0 7494 2236 X

Typeset by JS Typesetting, Wellingborough, Northants.
Printed in England by Biddles Ltd, Guildford and King's Lynn.

Contents

Notes on the contributors

Walter Truett Anderson, PhD, is a political scientist, author and journalist whose columns on global politics, cultural change and technology are syndicated by the Pacific News Service. He is a co-founder and fellow of The Meridian Institute, an international network of scholars and activists engaged in thinking about governance, leadership, learning and the future, and is also president of the American Division of the World Academy of Art and Science. He has spent most of his life in the American West, and now lives near San Francisco. His most recent books are *Reality Isn't What It used To Be* (Harper Collins, 1990), *Evolution Isn't What It Used To Be* (W H Freeman, 1996), *The Truth About The Truth* (Tarcher/Putnam, 1995), published in the UK as *The Fontana Postmodern Reader* (HarperCollins, 1996). Address: Meridian International Institute, 1 Sansome St., Ste. 2100, San Francisco, CA 94104, USA.

Wendell Bell is Professor Emeritus of Sociology, Yale University. Before joining the Yale faculty in 1963, he taught at the University of California, Los Angeles, Northwestern University, and Stanford University. Also, he has been a fellow of the Center for Advanced Study in the Behavioral Sciences, Stanford, CA and of the Institute of Advanced Studies, the Australian National University. He became a futurist during the 1960s while he was doing research on political and social change in the emerging states of the Caribbean. Beginning in 1967, he introduced futures studies courses at Yale and, later, served on the Commission on Connecticut's Future. He has authored or co-authored more than 200 articles and many books, including the two-volume work, *Foundations of Futures Studies: Human Science for a New Era*, published in 1997. Address: Yale University, Department of Sociology, P.O. Box 208265, New Haven, CT 06520-8265, USA.

Peter C. Bishop, PhD, is an associate professor of human sciences at the University of Houston-Clear Lake. He teaches courses on social change, forecasting techniques, and systems analysis on the Masters programme in Studies of the Future. He also delivers keynote speeches on the future of education and facilitates visioning and planning workshops for corporations, universities, agencies, communities and not-for-profit organizations. He is currently working with the University to establish a process of student assessment that focuses on continuous improvement toward a set of defined learning outcomes. The process has the potential to refocus attention from teaching to learning and from summative to formative evaluation. Address: University of Houston-Clear Lake, 2700 Bay Area Blvd., Houston, TX 77058, USA.

John Fien is Director of the Centre for Innovation and Research in Environmental Education at Griffith University in Brisbane, Australia. He taught geography and social science in secondary schools before becoming a curriculum consultant, and then a teacher educator in Australia and the UK. He has represented the Australian Commission for UNESCO on several occasions, including international conferences on environmental education and teacher education, criteria for designing curricula and materials on global issues, and international education and teacher education. He is presently Co-Director of the UNESCO Learning for a Sustainable Environment: Innovations in Teacher Education Project which is building a professional development network of teacher educators interested in environmental education in Asia and the Pacific. In 1995 he edited the manual *Teaching for A Sustainable World* on behalf of the UNESCO-UNEP International Environmental Education Programme. Address: Centre for Innovation and Research in Environmental Education, Griffith University, Nathan Campus, Brisbane, Queensland 4111, Australia.

Hazel Henderson is an independent global futurist, author of *Building a Win-Win World* (Berrett-Koehler, 1996) and five other books on sustainable development. Her editorials are syndicated by InterPress Service (Rome) to 400 newspapers in 27 languages. She is fellow of the World Business Academy and the World Futures Studies Federation, and advisor to the Calvert Social Investment Fund (Washington, DC) with whom she is co-creating the Calvert-Henderson Quality-of-Life Indicators. She held the Horace Albright Chair at the University of California, Berkeley, and has served on Committees of the National Academy of Engineering, the National Science Foundation, and the U.S. Office of Technology Assessment. Address: PO Box 5190, Anastasia Island, St Augustine, FL 32085, USA.

David Hicks is Professor in the Faculty of Education and Human Sciences at Bath Spa University College and recently described himself in the journal *Futures* as 'a teacher, writer, poet, nurturer of visions, radical educator and green subversive'. Having directed the World Studies 8–13 Project and the Centre for Peace Studies at the University College of St Martin in Lancaster, he set up the Futures Project in 1989 to help students and teachers think more critically and creatively about the future. He is internationally recognised for his work on global and futures perspectives in the curriculum and has lectured widely in the UK, Australia, Canada and Italy. His most recent books are: *Visions of the Future: Why We Need to Teach for Tomorrow* (Trentham, 1995); *Educating for the Future: A Practical Classroom Guide* (WWF, 1994) and *Preparing* *for the Future: Notes & Queries for Concerned Educators* (Adamantine Press, 1994). He has recently carried out research projects on: children's hopes and fears for the future, the importance of envisioning preferable futures and sources of hope in postmodern times. Address: Bath Spa University College, Faculty of Education and Human Sciences, Newton Park, Bath BA2 9BN, UK.

Allyson Holbrook, PhD, is a senior lecturer in the Faculty of Education at the University of Newcastle and she is National Research Training Co-ordinator for the Australian Association for Research in Education. She has been a futures educator for a decade and also teaches research methods and history of education at the postgraduate level. She has found this combination to be fruitful as shown by her co-authored publication *Reflections on Educational Research in Australia*, and in journal articles on the use of new sources in history, directions for research ethics, and qualitative data analysis software. She is currently engaged in research on the transition experience of youth during the 1930s–50s, on-the-job training 1900–2000, and is editing a book on post-graduate supervision. Address: The University of Newcastle, Department of Education, Callaghan, NSW 2308, Australia.

John Huckle was Principal Lecturer in geographical and environmental educ-ation at De Montfort University in Bedford until retiring in 1997. The majority of his work was with pre-service teachers of physical education who were studying geography as a second subject – encouraging them to be inspired and inspiring in the classroom presented him with an everyday challenge. He has also taught environmental politics and worked as a consultant to the World Wide Fund for Nature. John has a long established interest in the politics of environmental education and recently edited *Education for Sustainability* with Stephen Sterling. He continues to address the tensions between green socialists and deep greens in education and is currently working on a teaching pack about a rave collective in Luton and their approach to sustainability. Address: De Montfort University, Lansdowne Road, Bedford MK40 2BZ, UK.

Frank Hutchinson teaches at the University of Western Sydney, Australia. Previously he worked as a curriculum consultant, at both the primary and secondary levels, in areas of social literacy and alternatives to violence. His main research and teaching interests relate to issues concerned with young people and educating for more peaceful, socially just and environmentally sustainable futures. He did his PhD on the topic *Futures Consciousness and the School* (University of New England, Australia, 1993). He is the author, co-author or contributing author of several books on futures education including: *Our Planet and Its People* (Macmillan, 1992), *Education Beyond Hatred and Fatalism* (Lund University, 1994), *New Thinking for a New Millennium* (Rout-ledge, 1996) and *Educating Beyond Violent Futures* (Routledge, 1996). He is a member of both the International Peace Research Association and the World

Futures Studies Federation. Address: University of Western Sydney, Faculty of Health, Humanities and Social Ecology, Locked Bag 1, Hawkesbury, Richmond, NSW 2753, Australia.

Sohail Inayatullah, PhD, is currently senior research fellow at the Communication Centre, Queensland University of Technology, Brisbane, Australia. He is on the editorial boards of the journals *Futures, Periodica Islamica* and *Futures Studies*. He is also the associate editor of *New Renaissance* and co-editor of the *World Futures Studies Federation Futures Bulletin*. Author of over 160 journal articles and popular magazine pieces, he is currently working on a book titled *Theorising Futures* for Grey Seal Publications. Recent completed projects include a multicultural web-based textbook titled *Reader in Futures Studies* and a special issue of the journal *Futures* on 'What Futurists Think' (Aug/ Sept. 1996). Address: Communication Centre, Queensland University of Technology, GPO Box 2434, Brisbane, Queensland 4001, Australia.

Christopher Jones is an associate professor of political science at Eastern Oregon University. He has been involved in international futures research for fifteen years and was formerly a research associate at the Hawaii Research Center for Futures Studies. His futures research topics have included: alternative futures images and methodologies; women's futures; ecology and environmental futures; future generations; space development; high technology and multimedia futures; global climate change and Gaia futures. Address: Eastern Oregon University, School of Arts and Sciences, 1410 'L' Avenue, La Grande, OR 97850, USA.

Graham May, PhD, is Course Leader and Principal Lecturer in futures research at Leeds Metropolitan University. He is author of *The Future is Ours: Foreseeing, Managing and Creating the Future* (Adamantine Press and Praeger, 1996) and of papers and articles in a range of publications including *Futures, Futures Research Quarterly, Town and Country Planning, Municipal Journal,* and *The Planner*. He has more than ten years experience teaching futures at undergraduate and postgraduate levels to courses in town planning, urban development, education management, consumer services management (home economics) playwork and building surveying. Convenor of the UK Futures Group and a founder member European Futurists Group, he has extensive international connections through the Future Generations Alliance Foundation and membership of the World Future Society and World Futures Studies Federation. Address: Leeds Metropolitan University, Faculty of Design and the Built Environment, Calverley Street, Leeds LS1 3HE, UK.

Aileen McKenzie, PhD, works part-time as academic co-ordinator of the MSc in Environmental and Development Education at South Bank University in London and, since bringing together the initial working party that set up the course, has played a central role in designing and developing its academic aspects. Prior to this she worked for many years as an education adviser for Oxfam and has also undertaken various pieces of work for other NGOs. Recent consultancies have included researching into adult learners' conceptions of globalization for the Worker's Education Association and looking at the politics and practicalities of implementing development education in the higher education system for the UK Development Education Association. The educational and public opinion-forming activities of environmental and development NGOs North–South hold an abiding fascination for her. Address: 18 Burcote Road, London SW18 3LK, UK.

Sandra Ramos Miller currently serves as principal of a school in the Walnut Valley Unified School District in Southern California. The school has utilized constructivist practices using technology and facilitation to implement its curriculum. The school works closely with a local university to train pre-service teachers and offers on-going professional development to its staff. Sandra's doctoral research focused on the elementary school in the year 2005, specifically the technological delivery of instruction and the content of curriculum. She received her doctorate degree from the University of LaVerne in 1995 and, prior to that, received her BA and MA degrees in Education and Special Education from Arizona State University. Her work includes over twenty years' experience in schools with all socio-economic levels, extensive student diversity, and all levels of teacher expertise. Address: 50 Westbrook Lane, Phillips Ranch, CA 91766, USA.

Ivana Milojevic was previously assistant at the University of Novi Sad, Yugoslavia, and is currently living in Brisbane, Australia. Her education and interests are in sociology, women's studies and futures studies. She has completed a book on violence against women and is, in between taking care of two young children, conducting research in the area of women's futures and feminist utopias. Address: c/o Communication Centre, Queensland University of Technology, PO Box 2434, Brisbane, Queensland 4001, Australia.

Jane Page is a lecturer at the Department of Early Childhood Studies, Faculty of Education, University of Melbourne. Her 1995 MEd thesis examined the discipline of futures studies and its potential application for early childhood curriculum. Her publications include 'Critical Futures Studies: Rendering the Early Childhood Curriculum Responsive to the Future Needs of Children', *Australian Journal of Early Childhood*, 1991, and 'Symbolising the Future: Developing a Futures Iconography', *Futures*, 1992. In 1996, she was awarded the Aurelio Peccei prize for her work in this area by L'Età Verde, Rome. Address: University of Melbourne, Department of Early Childhood Studies, 4 Madden Grove, Kew, Vic 3101, Australia.

Martha Rogers is Assistant Professor in the Department of Nursing at York University, Toronto. She developed and is teaching a course called 'Alternative futures of nursing and global health' aimed at helping nurses acquire a view of global issues and alternative futures. She is President of Canadian Nursing Consultants and in that capacity recently completed a study for the Canadian Nurses' Association entitled 'Four futures of Canadian nursing in 2020'. Her doctoral research, at the University of Toronto, focused on the experiences of adults learning about global futures. This continuing research has been the basis of several articles and international presentations for the World Futures Studies Federation, UNESCO, and the Future Generations Alliance Foundation. Address: Atkinson College, York University, 4700 Keele Street, North York, Ontario, Canada M3J 1P3.

Richard Slaughter is Director of the Futures Study Centre in Melbourne and a consulting futurist who has worked with a wide range of organisations in many countries at all educational levels. He completed his PhD in futures studies at the University of Lancaster. He is a fellow of the World Futures Studies Federation and a professional member of the World Future Society. His research interests include: the use of futures concepts and tools in education; the knowledge base of futures studies and the social implementation of foresight. He holds several editorial positions including: consulting editor to *Futures* (Oxford, UK); series editor for Routledge (London, UK) for the Futures in Education series; board member of the *Journal of Futures Studies* (Tamkang University, Taiwan). He is co-author (with Hedley Beare) of *Education for the Twenty-First Century* (Routledge, 1993), author of *The Foresight Principle* (Adamantine, 1995); editor of *New Thinking for a New Millennium* (Routledge, 1996) and editor of volumes 1–3 of *The Knowledge Base of Futures Studies* (FSC/DDM, Melbourne, 1996). Address: Futures Study Centre, 62 Disraeli Street, Kew, Victoria 3101, Australia.

Allen Tough, PhD, is a professor of education at the University of Toronto. He writes about humanity's long-term future and about the scientific search for extraterrestrial intelligence; he is active in several international conferences and projects on these two topics. He organised two conferences for the Kyoto-based Future Generations Alliance Foundation and was, with Rick Slaughter, guest editor of a special issue of *Futures* on 'learning and teaching about future generations.' He is the author of *Crucial Questions About the Future* and *A Message from Future Generations*. His earlier books include *The Adult's Learning Projects*, *Expand Your Life*, and *Intentional Changes*. Address: University of Toronto, Ontario Institute of Studies in Education, 252 Bloor Street West, Toronto, Canada M5S 1V6.

Paul Wildman is a lecturer at Southern Cross University, Australia. His interests include youth work, futures studies, regional development, work and community development, public and organisational policy and men's issues. Previously Paul worked as Director Labour Market Directorate TAFE Qld and was responsible for some sixty youth employment consultants in centres around Queensland. He has published over sixty articles, books, audio and videos on the above areas. Currently he undertakes futures studies workshops as an institutional tool and lecturers in futures studies via the World Wide Web. URL http://www.scu.edu. au/ewt/Futures/refers. Address: Southern Cross University, School of Social and Workplace Development, Lismore Campus, PO Box 157, Lismore, NSW 2480, Australia.

Preface

The World Yearbook of Education has had, since its inception some sixty years ago, two major aims. The first is the survey of an established field of educational enquiry, such as the 1992 Yearbook on Urban Education and the 1996 Yearbook on Vocational Education. The second aim is to open up emerging and important fields to a wider audience, as was done with the 1947 Yearbook on Educational Reconstruction and the 1982 Yearbook on Computers in Education.

This year's Yearbook, on futures education, falls into the second category. It is an important and emerging field of educational enquiry and practice and as series editors, we are grateful to David Hicks and Richard Slaughter for collecting together such an interesting and engaging set of essays by many of the leading figures in the field. Furthermore, as we move towards the Millenium, it is appropriate that we have a Yearbook that offers insights into the ways in which time can be dealt with in the classroom. As T. S. Eliot put it:

> Time present and time past
> Are both perhaps present in time future
> And time future contained in time past.
> If all time is eternally present
> All time is unredeemable

> From *Burnt Norton*

A further point about this volume relates to language. The spread of English across the globe has led to increasing variation in its conventions. In editing a book written in a range of English, editors are faced with the decision as to whether to make all the English used conform to one standard, usually that of the country of publication. However, we see this variation as a richness rather than an inconvenience and have subsequently maintained it. The most obvious example of this is the difference between American English and British English in relation to spelling but there are many more instances.

David Coulby
Crispin Jones

Series editors

Introduction

As the year 2000 approaches, releasing a rush of millennial hopes and fears, I take for granted that the future will once again play a dominant role in our lives...a few romantics like myself still believe that our sense of the future remains intact, a submerged realm of hopes and dreams that lies below the surface of our minds, ready to wake again as one millennium closes and the next begins.

J G Ballard (1994:1)

In his introduction to *Myths of the Near Future* (1994) novelist J G Ballard argues that at some point in the 1960s our 'sense of the future seemed to atrophy and die' and he looks to the millennium for a re-awakening of interest in the future. This book is one sign of just such an awakening.

Speculating about the future is an inescapable part of the human condition and, as such, is often seen as mere amusement or fantasy. There are, after all, no facts about the future. Yet the future is a major dimension in our lives, the place where plans and dreams may, or may not, be realised. It is the zone of possibility, always retreating before us, but profoundly influencing the present. We are, of course, all interested in our personal futures and the future of our own community or country. Increasingly people are also concerned about the global future.

Ballard's comment about the future is best understood, I believe, in this planetary context. Much of the debate about the nature of post-modernity hinges around the crisis of modernity and its global consequences. Looking back at the twentieth century it is clear that the fruits of the industrial and scientific revolutions and the insights of enlightenment rationalism have brought innumerable benefits to humankind. Yet, at the same time, we look back at a century which has seen two world wars, a forty year nuclear arms race, a rapidly growing wealth gap between richer and poorer nations, and environmental damage which is reaching irreversible proportions. No wonder that the future, once something to look forward to, has become a cause for concern.

Michael Jacobs, writing for the Real World Coalition (1996), sums these feelings up when he says:

For large numbers in Britain today, the new century is not a source of hope. The predominant mood, if anything, is of fear. People are anxious about the future, about the world they are leaving their children. They see, with a profound

1

understanding quite missing from national political life, the growing crisis of humankind's impact on the natural environment, as the simultaneous growth of material consumption and population generates inexorably greater pollution and resource degradation (Jacobs, 1996: 1).

Such concerns about the future are not, of course, restricted to Britain alone. It is all the more important, therefore, to realise that there has been a flourishing international 'futures field' for at least the last forty years. This field includes professionals and others from many disciplinary backgrounds who share a specific interest in exploring and analysing contemporary social change and its impact on the future. Slaughter (1993: 109–112) suggests that the futures field comprises a spectrum of concerns. At one end is *futures research* which primarily has a knowledge-seeking focus. The emphasis is on forecasting and planning, generally using analytic and quantitative methods. Here we find specialists involved with economic and technical forecasting, systems analysis and management science, often working for large organisations, think-tanks or government departments. At the other end of the spectrum are *futures movements* primarily concerned with promoting social and political change. More often labelled 'new social movements', eg those concerned with issues such as the environment, peace, gender or animal welfare, they all share some image of a more desirable future. They are normative in emphasis, focusing on change in both self and society. Between these two poles comes *futures studies*, ie the study and exploration of possible, probable and preferable futures. This may be through comparative surveys and critique of futures issues, or speculative writing as in science fiction, or it may be the study of futures within education. It is with the latter category that this volume is particularly concerned.

The key question for all educators has to be – if all education is for the future then when and where is the future explored within education? This volume sets out both the rationale for exploring alternative futures within education and also provides wide-ranging examples of good practice. A word is needed about terminology, however, as three different terms are commonly used within education: futures studies, futures education, and education for the future. *Futures studies* is used to refer to a specific subject, course or module which investigates different aspects of futures thinking. Thus the state of Queensland in Australia is currently trialling a futures syllabus in its secondary schools and chapters in this volume describe undergraduate and postgraduate courses in futures. *Futures education* is a term used more broadly to embrace not only the content and concerns of futures studies but also an approach to education itself, ie a recognition of the need for a futures perspective or a futures dimension across the curriculum of an insitution. Thus most schools will not have a subject called futures on the curriculum but they may well have a concern to promote futures-orientated education. For example, all second-year students training to be teachers at Bath Spa University College in the UK, take a half-module entitled Futures Education as part of their professional training. While futures education is an internationally recognised term most teachers in schools, certainly within the UK, are unlikely to have heard of it. They are more likely, however, to talk about *education for the future* as something in which their institution is implicitly or explicitly engaged. Whichever terminology you use this book is for you.

J G Ballard's hope that the future would return to the public agenda as a new century approached appears to be coming true. While, on the one hand there is uncertainty about the future, this is actually in part because of its absence from many curricula. Traditionally the future has been left implicit rather than made explicit in most formal teaching and learning. Uncertainty about the future of society specifically requires that we grasp the nettle of the future and examine it more closely. The futures field represents a vast reservoir of expertise which often is not called upon in popular debates about the future. Recent publications which are now bringing this expertise into the foreground include Wendell Bell's two-volume *Foundations of Futures Studies* (1996) and Richard Slaughter's three-volume *The Knowledge Base of Futures Studies* (1996).

The significance of this edition of the World Yearbook is that it now does the same for educators and for futures education. Both of its editors have, for a long time, been involved in futures studies and futures education. Working in Australia, Rick Slaughter's *Educating for the Twenty-First Century* (Beare and Slaughter, 1993) was one of the first of a new wave of futures-orientated educational publications in the 90s, followed by his *New Thinking for a New Millennium* (Slaughter, 1996). Working in the UK, with a background in global education and environmental education, David Hicks contributed *Educating for the Future: A Practical Classroom Guide* (Hicks, 1994a), *Preparing for the Future: Notes and Queries for Concerned Educators* (Hicks, 1994b) and *Visions of the Future: Why We Need to Teach for Tomorrow* (Hicks and Holden, 1995). With this present volume it feels as if futures education has come of age.

The book does not presume that the reader is familiar with the futures field. The chapters in Part One thus deal with the foundations of futures education. They look at the state of the world today and the consequent need for a more futures-orientated education. They set out some of the main principles and perspectives involved. The chapters in Part Two have been chosen to illustrate the practice of futures education. There are case studies dealing with early childhood, elementary and secondary education as well as undergraduate and postgraduate initiatives. Crucial questions are also raised about the impact on students of learning about global futures and the need to educate in a spirit of hope in turbulent times. The chapters in Part Three focus on work that is being done which specifically focuses on the need to educate for a more just and sustainable future.

Finally I would like to thank the General Editors, David Coulby and Crispin Jones, for inviting us to contribute a volume to this series. I am, as always, deeply indebted to the many friends, students, teachers and colleagues who have encouraged me and continue to inspire me in this work.

David Hicks

References

Ballard, J G (1994) *Myths of the Near Future*, London: Vintage Books.

Beare, H and Slaughter, R (1993) *Education for the Twenty-First Century*, London: Routledge.

Bell, W (1996) *Foundations of Futures Studies*, 2 vols, New Brunswick: Transaction Publishers.

Hicks, D (1994a) *Educating for the Future: A Practical Classroom Guide*, Godalming: World Wide Fund for Nature UK.

Hicks, D (1994b) *Preparing for the Future: Notes and Queries for Concerned Educators*, London: Adamantine Press.

Hicks, D and Holden, C (1995) *Visions of the Future: Why We Need to Teach for Tomorow*, Stoke-on-Trent: Trentham Books.

Jacobs, M (1996) *The Politics of The Real World*, London: Earthscan Publications.

Slaughter, R (ed.) (1996) *New Thinking for a New Millennium*, London: Routledge.

Slaughter, R (ed.) (1996) *The Knowledge Base of Futures Studies*, Melbourne: DDM Media Group.

Section I:
Foundations of futures education

1. A futurist reflects

Hazel Henderson

Summary

In this opening chapter, eminent futurist Hazel Henderson reflects on her work, on the current state of the world and some of the changes needed in order to create a more just and sustainable future. In particular, she looks at the complex impacts of globalization and the consequent need to reconceptualize traditional economics. She also details a range of positive changes occurring in the evolution of civic society and adds some final comments on the various levels – from individual to planetary – at which sustainable development needs to occur.

Introduction

We all have much to do as we approach the new millennium. We humans, with our flexible opposing thumbs and large forebrains, have been the most successful and adaptable species on earth. We have expanded into almost every region on this planet. We now occupy so many niches in our global ecosystem that we are crowding out and threatening thousands of other species – as well as each other. This book lays out tools to help us address these and the many conceptual and operational challenges we face together.

Today, our powerful technological and conceptual tools have escaped our grasp. From nuclear proliferation and toxic chemicals to our malfunctioning political systems and obsolete economics textbooks to the charters which empower our corporations globally – many of our tools are dysfunctional and out of control. Their often unanticipated consequences now challenge us to match our over-developed skills at technological and product innovation with a focus on new efforts and reward systems to call forth the needed social innovations to tame and steer these technologies. Between 1974 and 1980, I had the opportunity to study all these issues as a member of the original Advisory Council of the US Office of Technology Assessment (OTA). The OTA, a social innovation emulated in many countries, was shut down by the US Congress in an act of institutional vandalism in 1995, a reminder that powerful interests of the status quo do not often take kindly to needed changes in governance, education, academic paradigms, or existing institutions.

For over 25 years (Henderson, 1981, 1988), I have been writing about the need for a deeper paradigm shift beyond 'value-free observation' in science, the mechanistic clockwork universe of Isaac Newton, and the Cartesian worldview seeking understanding of wholes by examining their parts, all of which undergirded the Industrial Revolution. Today, we are in the Information Age and moving toward the Solar Age (Henderson, 1996) into a deeper ecological understanding of our living planet, our own biology, and that of our societies and economies. Today I am less impatient than I used to be. I realize that it takes a generation to change a paradigm. I began my work thinking of my daughter's future and that of her generation, to whom I dedicated my first book, *Creating Alternative Futures*, in 1978, now back in print unchanged. The litmus test of futurists' work is whether it proves predictive!

Let us encourage ourselves by remembering that the very concept of global citizenship is a rather new phenomenon. As the late Jonas Salk told me a few weeks before he died, 'Global citizens, who take responsibility beyond themselves and their communities for the whole human family and this planet are cultural mutants' – a sort of feedback system to course-correct directions for our human family. A US politician I met in Portland at a conference of Maine Businesses for Social Responsibility used a similar metaphor. She confided to me in the women's room that she and I (and so many activists like us here, I believe) are functioning in the body politic as 'anti-bodies.' We somehow sense the sickness in our societies and simply rush to repair and heal as nature designed anti-bodies to do. The challenge to Western science is not only to place the observer back into the equation, but to recognize the human actor as the key shaper of economics, technologies, and the evolution of cultures and societies as well (Henderson, 1997).

Globalizing forces

I also believe that the impulse to behave as a global citizen is intuitive, driven by concern for the future. Yet, through faith, most of us are not too overwhelmed by our concern to act. All of us seem to operate on a wing and a prayer. Whatever our faith and wisdom traditions, we swim upstream as 'contrarians' in today's globalization of industrialism, materialism, and technological expansionism. We share the old visions of all the major religions in the Golden Rule and our place within the divine creation. And we search for new ways to reinvent ourselves and redesign our social architecture. I was raised as a strict atheist and had to find my own spiritual path. I seek to understand my role as a human being at this stage in our social and cultural evolution and, as the Buddha taught, to be fully awake to all the beauty and opportunities for learning and service. The futures research field contains both practitioners who are normative in their approach and those who are technological trend-extrapolators. The latter tend toward technological optimism, while normative futurists are more often human nature optimists, who believe in education, human development, and the evolution of culture. Of course, in reality all futures research is normative, just as information, knowledge, and epistemology are also political.

Today's challenges lie in the often unintended consequences of the great forces we have unleashed which are globalizing: i) our technologies of industrialization and those of today's Information Age; ii) our financial systems and today's unregulated 'global casino'; iii) the globalization of work and the great migrations it engenders as corporations seek cheaper labor and people cross borders looking for jobs and better lives; iv) the post-Cold War globalization of the arms trade, where the five permanent members of the UN Security Council now export weapons to every tin-pot dictator and adolescent gang in the world. (The US military budget for 1997 is $265 billion, Russia's $63 billion, Japan's $54 billion, France's $41 billion, the United Kingdom's $35 billion, Germany's $34 billion, and that of China $29 billion); v) the globalization of human effects on the biosphere; and vi) the globalization of human cultures.

There is good news and bad news in these great globalizations. They have eroded the sovereignty of every nation and restructured every city and community all over the planet. Yet we cannot go back. Civic society groups, many of whom oppose globalization, must abandon simple theories of 'restoring equilibrium.' Too much evidence now exists that all life forms, including the human species and our technological tools, have evolved over millions of years on this planet through processes of rapid change and continual dis-equilibrium. Agrarian rural life, to which many yearn to return, was in itself a revolution which disenfranchised and displaced millions of nomadic peoples.

In reality, how does one 'repeal' the globalization of technology: satellites, jets, computers, and the Internet so intertwined with global corporations? Thus, the call for equitable, ecologically sustainable human development which embraces change, however misused, is still a rallying cry. Indeed, these grassroots and democratic trends are effects of the spread of the information technology corporations unleashed. The goals of such movements of citizens, employees, stockholders, environmentalists and human rights advocates include democratic control, political transparency, and public accountability, which today must be reinforced at the international level.

Today we must ask ourselves, what kinds of globalization, by whom, and in whose interests? Which kinds of globalization are life-threatening? For example, these include nuclear proliferation, the global arms trade, destruction of the planet's ozone shield, and pollution of our atmosphere and oceans. All of these require regulation and redirection toward civilian priorities. Which global trends can help evolve human cultures in positive directions? For example, the globalization of information and culture holds much promise as this volume clearly demonstrates. Yet information must be redirected to longer-term human purposes beyond corporate media conglomerations and 'government by mediocracy' based on spreading wasteful, unsustainable western-style commercial consumerism and its many addictions.

A new economics

The software governing global corporations, ie their legal charters, cannot be allowed to continue operating under 300-year-old rules which limit their liabilities, making them responsible only to their stockholders rather than to all their stakeholders. We must overrule the mistaken legal interpretation of corporations as 'natural persons' whose financial contributions corrupting our politicians are deemed 'free speech'. We can support the virtuous circle of smaller and more socially responsible businesses which are committed to Codes of Conduct, best practices, and higher global standards and greener technologies, as in the curriculum of the British-based New Academy of Business at the University of Bath.

We can remind ourselves that it is small businesses which create most of the world's jobs, rather than the global corporations which are automating, downsizing, and moving into that global fast lane. For example, in the USA, 8 million women-owned businesses employ one out of every four Americans in the workplace, more than all of the Fortune 500 companies put together. Both socially responsible businesses and investors, together with these women business owners, turn out not to be primarily profit maximizers. They confound those nineteenth century economic textbooks by putting first their hopes to contribute positively to society; to make the world a better place; for self-expression and economic self-reliance, before that of maximizing profits. The World Bank is learning that micro-enterprises are an essential part of healthy development and that the poorest entrepreneurs pay back their small loans more faithfully than do the rich. Economics courses need to teach what most ordinary people know: that most of the world's livelihoods are still made outside the money economy by careful stewardship and traditional uses of natural resources. Nowhere is the need for new thinking and social innovation more important than in economics and in designing more inclusive, equitable, and sustainable economies. This has been a special task for me. My first articles described what was wrong with traditional economics in the *Harvard Business Review* 1968, 1971, and 1973. The debate has changed little since then. Thanks to other such far-sighted journals, my broader model of the total productivity of an economy as a three-layer cake with a layer of icing on the top is now creeping into textbooks around the world. This model extends beyond the creativity, risk taking, and competition of the private sector, as well as the sharing of tax-supported infrastructure of the public sector, by including the unpaid production in the informal, 'Love Economy,' as well as nature's productivity, both still unaccounted in traditional economics. Today we know that the Love Economy accounts for 50 percent of all productive work, even in industrial societies, and up to 65 percent or more in many developing countries. This unpaid work was calculated in 1995 by the *UN Human Development Report* as $16 trillion still missing from annual global GNP. In 1995, the World Bank released its new Wealth Index, corresponding to my view of total productivity. My Country Futures Indicators (CFI)^{sm} are in a US version as the Calvert-Henderson Quality-of-Life Indicators^{sm} which include an education component, released by the Calvert Group Inc. of Washington, DC (Henderson, 1996). The chapters in this volume describe the changes implied for education for our global future.

Yet, faulty economics still underlies today's world trade system. World trade is destructive because it is based on layer upon layer of subsidies: from taxpayers who fund transportation infrastructure, underwriting roads and airports, to the corporate subsidies in most nations' tax codes which keep energy and resource prices below real costs. Most economic textbooks still encourage companies to 'externalize' social and environmental costs from their balance sheets and from the Capital Asset Pricing Models (CAPMs) of investors. The same exclusion of these costs from national accounts, still distorts the GNP, since the costs of cleaning up and repairing economic damage are double-counted as more production.

Thus, today's world trade is largely irrational. All the agreements, including those of the World Trade Organization (WTO), serve to subsidize a lowest common denominator economic playing field, a vicious circle sliding into global economic warfare. Today's global economy functions like a global behavioral sink, rewarding corporate and government irresponsibility, levelling rainforests, and homogenizing the world's precious cultural diversity just as it plunders the planet's biodiversity. As prices are slowly corrected to reflect true costs, as taxes are shifted from incomes and payrolls to resource waste, depletion, and pollution, and as the world's GNP-based national accounts are overhauled (as agreed to in *Agenda 21* at the UN Earth Summit in 1992), the wasteful, unnecessary global shipping of similar goods will slowly disappear. Meanwhile, governments can desist from auctioning off their tax bases, human and environmental capital to corporations in today's race-to-the-bottom global economic warfare. This behavior is now forbidden in the World Trade Organization (WTO) rules – the few that are geared to sustainability.

My vision of a healthy world trade system is one shifting from hardware (goods) to software, services, and 'exchanging our cultural DNA.' Most countries are capable of meeting many of their basic production needs and growing their domestic industries, which at full-cost prices will finally be revealed as most efficient. When economic and thermodynamic efficiencies are aligned, the British economist, John Maynard Keynes' observation that it is better to transport recipes than cakes, will be proved correct. We must also learn that we can all win if we also share these recipes. Countries can make cooperative agreements to share greener and innovative technologies, not hoard them, as in current trade agreements. Information is not scarce and economics is still about scarcity. Information is also cracking the old global money monopolies as high-tech barter, and all kinds of direct exchanges are proliferating. Local barter clubs, businesses and governments all engage in countertrade, now estimated at some 10 to 25 percent of all world trade. A healthy world trade system will celebrate and reward cultural and biological diversity as we learn to savor each others' music, art, dance, cuisine, and biodiversity.

A civic society

The rise of civic society and the recognition of the Love Economy all over the world is providing a third force and new voices and models are enriching our options. These growing ranks of citizens are becoming a new balance of power between business and government holding both more accountable. The UN has supported the emergence and growth of global civic society, those 'grassroots globalists' that have convened at all the UN conferences over the years on the real agendas of 'We the Peoples.' From the first conference on the environment in Stockholm, 1972, through those on Renewable Energy in Nairobi in 1981, on Population and Development in Cairo, 1994, the World Summit on Social Development in Copenhagen, and that on Women in Development in Beijing, both in 1995, to Habitat in Istanbul, 1996 – all have included ever-increasing participation by civic organizations.

All our efforts to end nuclear proliferation and other forms of mass destruction, including land mines and conventional weapons, must continue in the faith that we humans are an intelligent species and can reverse the terminal stupidities of the Cold War.

The efforts toward demilitarization, a subject still taught in too few college courses, are bearing fruit. Spearheaded by Dr Oscar Arias with his Global Demilitarization Fund and Global Code of Conduct for Arms Transfers proposals, they are supported by former US President Jimmy Carter and many others. Costa Rica has provided the world a working model of how the huge economic benefits to a country come from shifting military budgets toward investments in civilian sectors. Costa Rica's 92 percent literacy rate outshines many OECD countries, including that of the USA which has fallen to 80 percent. Panama and Haiti have seen the light and joined Costa Rica in redeploying and retraining their military forces toward domestic priorities. Dr Arias is among the supporters of two proposals of the Global Commission to fund the UN for shifting strategies of national security from their current focus on military means toward concepts of insurance against risks of aggression and funding such permanent peace-keeping operations of the UN through a pool of insurance premiums, by setting up a UN Security Insurance Agency (UNSIA). The companion proposal for Anticipatory Risk Mitigation Peace-building Contingents (ARM-PC) could use some of these insurance premiums to fund civic society networks already working in many countries in the north and south toward conflict resolution and confidence building. The ARM-PC proposal was debated in the UN Security Council in April, 1996, under Ambassador Juan Somavia's enlightened presidency.

Another high priority group of social innovations being promoted by the Global Commission to Fund the UN addressed the urgent need to tame today's global casino, where $1.3 trillion sloshes around our planet every 24 hours (90 percent of which is speculation). This global casino exhibits many of the shenanigans we saw on Wall Street in 1929 prior to the Great Crash; from bear raids and insider trading to money laundering. Thus, the Commission has called for the harmonization of securities and currency trading into something like a 'Global Securities and Exchange Commission' – to create a fairer game for all the players. Another proposal builds on the concepts of Professor Ruben Mendez of Yale University, John Maynard Keynes at Bretton Woods, and Professor James Tobin in the late 1970s.

These proposals can be married into the inauguration by the G-24 countries and their central banks, together with the UN and the IMF and the World Bank (when they return to the UN fold!) of a 'public utility' foreign currency exchange. This new foreign exchange infrastructure can be based on the most advanced computer-trading technology allowing nations and their central banks to add to their trade reporting requirements additional information of great positive value and to curb many of today's abuses. To these reporting systems on each trade a small fee could then be levied on all trades, much lower than that proposed by Professor Tobin since today's volume of transactions now exceeds by orders of magnitude those of the 1970s. Such a very low fee (somewhere below 0.01 percent) would be unobjectionable to most traders we have interviewed and yet could still yield large revenues for governments, as well as for relevant UN and other development purposes (Henderson and Kay, 1996).

The Charter of the Global Commission to Fund the UN and its Report, *The United Nations: Policy and Financing Alternatives* (Cleveland, Henderson and Kaul, 1996), contains many other proposals for alternative and innovative financing of the UN and other development needs. It includes proposals to collect user-fees on all commercial uses of the global commons. We all share the global commons and its infrastructures, including the global sea lanes and oceans; airways and atmosphere; the electromagnetic spectrum and the public airwaves that carry our TV, radio, and telecommunications; satellite orbits and outer space; Antarctica; and the world's precious store of biodiversity. The Global Commission also proposes that nations pursue additional international agreements, not only to collect such user-fees, but also to levy fines and taxes for the abuse of these global resources, including arms trafficking, cross-border pollution and currency speculation.

All such proposals can be studied in global futures courses along with new agendas for UNESCO and the United Nations University, such as the Millennium Project, a delphi of over 200 professional futurists creating global scenarios in an on-line system which links think-tanks in Beijing, London, Moscow, Cairo, Brussels, Buenos Aires, and Washington, DC. The UN is revitalizing itself for the new century. It is capitalizing on its considerable strengths and reshaping itself for the Information Age. The UN continues to be the world's best convenor and broker, networker, standard setter, and fosterer of new norms for our global human family. Some nations have resisted the UN's inclusion of grassroots civic organizations in its activities and conferences. They believe that the UN should remain exclusively an association of national governments. Some nations have used the UN as a 'fig leaf' and others as a scapegoat, whichever best justifies their national interests and policies. Unfortunately, in my own country the UN and its former Secretary General Boutros Boutros Ghali became 'political footballs' in our 1996 election season. This caused an unnecessary financial crisis at the UN while the US government shamefully withheld the $1.5 billion owed in back dues. Meanwhile, 70 percent of the American people do not want to go it alone as the world's policeforce, but wish the US to remain within the broad coalition of nations supporting multilateral peace keeping within the UN framework (New York Times, 1996).

Sustainable development

As futurists and systems thinkers, we are beginning to understand that shifting toward more ecologically sustainable, equitable forms of human development is occuring at seven levels of our societies.

1. Individual

De-materializing and de-monetizing individual and family lifestyles toward personal development, earth ethics, and sustainable values (Henderson, 1995).

2. Local government

Enacting government ordinances to encourage sustainable lifestyles, for example, pedestrian and cyclist options, zoning for mixed use densities, encouraging local currencies, solar and renewable resource options, recycling, while rejecting subsidizing via taxes and bond issues of global-scale corporate intrusions.

3. Corporate

Enacting redesign of corporate governance toward the stakeholder models and re-engineering manufacturing processes in line with corporate obligations under the 1970 OECD Polluter Pays Principle.

4. National

Governments can institute 'green' taxes on resource waste and depletion and pollution, while removing taxes on incomes and payrolls and implementing the overhauling of GNP/GDP national accounts toward multi-disciplinary, unbundled quality-of-life indicators and broader policy tools beyond macro-economics, and observing WTO rules on tax holidays to lure corporate relocations.

5. International

Redesigning and renegotiating of trade agreements for democratic access for developing countries, democratizing all international financial institutions, central banks, and trade negotiations to include representatives of employee unions and voluntary civic society. Implementing full-cost pricing, life-cycle costing, and application of corrected national accounts and quality-of-life indicators. Implement user-fees for all commercial uses of global commons and taxes and fines for abuses, to help fund United Nations infrastructure, commercial protocols and peace-keeping operations. Moving the World Bank and the IMF toward democracy, transparency, equity, and bringing them back within the United Nations' jurisdiction: reinvigorating ECOSOC, the UN Centre on Transnational Corporations, and other UN agencies.

6. Civic society

Strengthening and fostering the growth of civic society and education for global citizenship, including favored tax status and free public access channels on all global telecommunications media through treaties such as those governing the electromagnetic spectrum and other common heritage resources.

7. *Planetary biosphere*

Implementing agreements and the plan of action of the Cairo Conference on Population and Development, the Women's Conference in Beijing in 1995, and the Social Summit in Copenhagen in 1995, as well as *Agenda 21* and previous action plans that can move human societies towards sustainability and protect the planet's biodiversity. Bringing women into full partnership at all decision levels can lead to healthier societies, stable populations and sustainable, truly human development.

The growing power of civic society and the emergence of global citizenship around the world has sparked a new search for common human values and earth ethics among such groups as the Costa Rican-based Earth Council and the Boston Reseach Center for the 21st Century. Meanwhile, some 2 billion of our brothers and sisters still lack basic food, clean water, health care, education, and human rights. Civic society organizations, such as Amnesty International and others, together with the world's media, can keep their searchlights on all these oppressed members of the human family as well as all abuses of power, such as those of the Taliban in Afganistan who hold the female half of the population under virtual house-arrest.

Educating for a humane future is the most important enterprise of human culture, our investment in the very survival and evolution of our species. Let us remind ourselves that we need not be afraid to be great, each of us is a child of God. Let us keep that spark of divinity we all carry within us, shining brightly as we continue working to shape wiser, more just and loving societies.

References

Cleveland, H, Henderson, H, and Kaul, I (eds) (1996) *The United Nations: Financing Alternatives*, Washington DC: The Global Commission to Fund the United Nations.

Henderson, H (1981; 1988) *Politics of the Solar Age*, New York: Doubleday/Anchor.

Henderson, H (1997) 'Evolving Economies,' *World Futures*, David Loye (ed.) London.

Henderson, H (1996) *Building a Win-Win World*, chapter 10, San Francisco: Berrett-Koehler.

Henderson, H (1995) *Paradigms in Progress*, San Francisco: Berrett-Koehler.

Henderson, H and Kay, A. (1996) 'Introducing Competition to the Global Currency Markets', *Futures*, 28(4), 305–24.

'Who Should Be the World's Policeman?' Advertisement in the *New York Times*, A17, 26th September 1996.

2. Understanding the futures field

Wendell Bell

Summary

In this chapter, I briefly describe a few highlights of the history of the futures field, detailing some of its pioneers, publications, and purposes. Although thinking about the future has roots deep in human prehistory and exists in every human society, it was not until the mid-1960s that the futures movement emerged as an established field of inquiry. Yet modern futures studies has many precursors, dating back at least to the early Greeks and especially to the utopian writers, beginning with Thomas More. Modern futurists aim to maintain or improve the freedom and welfare of humankind and the life-sustaining capacities of the Earth. They speak out for the interests of as-yet-voiceless future generations. They work to achieve these goals through prospective and visionary thinking, futures research and education, critical discourse, and social action. In the decade of the 1990s, futures studies has achieved a new maturity.

Introduction

Even though passing time and images of the future are crucially important in shaping their lives, people seldom think much about them. But now, stimulated by the turn of the millennium, many people are consciously seeking answers to questions about what the future may bring. Already, writers are filling the Sunday supplements and popular magazines with forecasts of what is coming and professional groups are devoting their conferences to topics dealing with the twenty-first century. Frequently, such people lose their bearings in an intellectual landscape with which they are unfamiliar. Yet that landscape actually has already been well charted by an international group of scholars, known as 'futurists'.

Futurists, in fact, have formally studied the future for more than two centuries (at least since Condorcet), and in recent decades modern futurists have created a new field of social inquiry, futures studies. In this chapter I briefly describe a few highlights of its history, some of its pioneers, publications, and purposes.

Precursors to futures studies

Time, just as space, is an inescapable condition of human existence. As an aspect of human conceptions of time, thinking about the future has roots deep in human prehistory and exists in every human society, even though it may not always – or even often – be done well. Of course, divination, such as the examination of animal organs, was widespread among preliterate peoples and was used in part to forecast future events. In the civilizations of the ancient Near East by the twenty-fifth century BCE, various oracles and readers of omens were consulted in order to discover and to control the future.

As early as 800 to 500 BCE, Greek writers understood the direction of time, the inexorable movement on and on toward the future. The poet Hesiod, for example, had a pessimistic view of the trends of human history, describing an ideal past, the Age of Gold, and a decline over time through a series of metallic ages to end in the less desirable Age of Iron. Later Greek writers, including Xenophanes, Protagoras, and Democritus, were more optimistic, viewing prehistory as a period of human progress. Plato, as every school child knows, devoted his *Republic* to a description of a society importantly based on the principle of justice, partly as a guide to desirable change in the future.

Biblical writers based their notions of a paradisiacal state – some coming after life in a heavenly world that contained all that was considered good, and also its antithesis, an after-life in hell – on a variety of near-eastern pagan myths and on beliefs of some of the oldest cultures of Mesopotamia. Additionally, Judeo-Christian theology contains the prophecies of the apocalypse, images of future destruction followed by rebirth, resurrection, and salvation.

In 1516, Thomas More published his *Utopia*, literally 'no place', and a new genre of literature was born. Typically, as in *Utopia*, a hero sets off on travels to some geographical place far from Europe. He stumbles upon a strange and unknown land, often by accident such as a shipwreck. He lives there in this 'Other' society for some time and then returns to Europe where he describes the ideal society he discovered, as, of course, imagined by the author. By contrasting the customs of the ideal society with those of his own existing society, the fictional traveler produces both a critical analysis of the real social world and a guide for its future reformation.

Utopian authors, with many variations on More's model, created a vast literature, writing thousands of scenarios describing desirable societies – or in some case undesirable societies, sometimes gloomy predictions of doom that would result from the amplification of some then-current features of real society. To take a few examples, such writings include the imaginary descriptions of ideal cities of the Italian Renaissance; the millenarian utopias of Germany and Central Europe, such as that of Thomas Müntzer; the work of the Pansophists, including Giordano Bruno, Francis Bacon, Tommaso Campanella, Johann Valentin Andreae, and Johann Comenius; the so-called Levellers, Diggers, and Ranters, utopian groups that were active during the

English Civil War; Denis Vairasses's *History of the Sevarambians*, an imaginary society supposed to exist in then-unexplored Australia; François Fénelon's *The Adventures of Telemachus* which mixed dreams with real possibilities to help educate a future king, the duke of Burgundy; and Gottfried Wilhelm Leibniz's utopian plans for the creation of a Christian Republic throughout the world (Manuel and Manuel, 1979).

Because it advanced utopian thinking in several ways, we must mention *A Sketch for a Historical Picture of the Progress of the Human Mind*, written by the Marquis de Condorcet and published posthumously in France in 1795. With some notable exceptions, utopian scenarios up until the *Sketch* had placed the imaginary good society at some distant geographical place but at the same time as then-contemporary society. To the contrary, the *Sketch* firmly placed the Other in another time, the future. For Condorcet, the future was everything. We can rightfully call him 'the first futurist'.

Much utopian literature ought to be recognized as belonging to the history of social science, including even More's path-breaking *Utopia*. For, although utopias often contain fictional descriptions of the Other, they usually include, in varying degrees of explicitness, descriptions and critiques of actual existing societies. Condorcet went a giant stride forward by explicitly basing his visions of the future on the social science of his day. (Moreover, he made amazingly accurate forecasts, including describing coming developments such as widespread democratic governance; equal and public education; popular journalism; increasing human life expectancies; social security for the elderly, widows, and orphans; equality before the law; the end of slavery and colonialism and equal rights for women. However, he was wrong, at least to this day, in predicting that war would disappear.)

After Condorcet, the so-called 'utopian socialists', including Fourier, Godwin, Owen and Saint-Simon, firmly focused on the future and believed that they were doing social science as they explored both human nature and the design of social systems. A distinctive feature of their works was social experimentation as they carried out demonstration projects that attempted to transform their word pictures into living realities. Owen's model mill town at New Lanark in England and the planned community at New Harmony, Indiana, in the United States are examples. So, too, are the many Fourierist communities scattered from Rumania and Russia, across several countries, including Brook Farm in the United States, to modern Israel (Goodwin, 1978; Manuel and Manuel, 1979).

Karl Marx, Friedrich Engels, and their followers, of course, carried the orientation toward the future, social scientific analysis, and the actual attempts to construct utopia in the real world to extreme lengths. First, Marxist images of the future included descriptions of the development of capitalism from the then-present up until its presumed collapse; the nature of society during the first phase of communism under which the transition from capitalism to communism would be achieved; and features of the future communist society during its second and final phase, when, according to Marxists, alienation, inequality, scarcity, false consciousness, long work hours, private ownership, the war between social classes, exploitation, and even the existence of the state itself would end (Bell, 1997, vol. 2).

Second, 'scientific socialism' was backed by massive scholarly works - historical, empirical, theoretical – in the social science tradition, as exemplified in the seminal volumes of *Capital* and thousands of works by latter-day Marxists.

Third, the small demonstration projects of the utopian socialists were eclipsed by national experiments of entire societies as totalitarian regimes established 'command economies' and attempted to transform the lives of more than a billion people in the name of the future communist society. We now know that many of these experiments, eg in the former Soviet Union and eastern Europe, tragically failed, although, of course, several continue as I write most notably in the People's Republic of China.

The contemporary futures movement

In a magazine article published in 1901, H G Wells proposed 'a science of the future', and in a radio talk on the BBC in 1932, he said that in order to anticipate and prepare for the future, professors of foresight and entire faculties and departments of foresight were needed (Wager, 1991; Wells, 1987). Today, several hundred futures studies courses are being taught in Canada and the United States alone and a few departments or programs of futures studies exist, one of the newest being a master's degree program in foresight and futures studies at Leeds Metropolitan University in the United Kingdom (see chapter 13).

It is difficult to set a date for when the contemporary futures movement first began, because there are so many seamless connections through time between early and recent futures work. Yet many writers agree that a definite futures field was visible by the mid-1960s and that its basic conceptual and methodological foundations were beginning to be laid down by the late 1940s (Bell, 1997, vol. 1). Edward Cornish and others founded the World Future Society in 1964, and a core group that first met at the 'First International Future Research Conference' in Oslo in 1967 founded the World Futures Studies Federation in 1973.

Other strands in the intellectual history of the contemporary futures movement include the work on social trends and technological assessment of W F Ogburn which began in the 1930s; the efforts at national planning, especially military but also economic and social, during World War I and the Great Depression that followed it; the centralized planning not only in the early years of Communist Russia, but also in Fascist Italy and Nazi Germany. Planning, of course, necessarily involves futures thinking and is as old as human society. But the experiments in national planning in the first decades of the twentieth century reached a scale of social mobilization – both for better and for worse – seldom, if ever, achieved before in human history. After the end of World War II, national planning and 'central planning units' again began to spread, to authoritarian and democratic countries alike (Bell, 1997, vol. 1).

Another strand in the development of systematic approaches to futures thinking began near the end of World War II and has continued up to the present. It came about as a result of the breakdown of the colonial empires, mostly of European powers, and the creation of 120 or so new states, the great flood having occurred in the 1950s and early 1960s. In Africa, Asia, the Caribbean and the Pacific, and later in territories of the former Yugoslavia and the Soviet Union, new nationalist leaders came to power representing local peoples and undertook the tasks required to establish a state of their own. They faced making 'the decisions of nationhood', choosing, within the limits of the realities of their social contexts, what their new states' futures ought to be and, at best, planning the policies that they believed would shape the coming future to the hopes of their peoples. Of course, the future did not usually turn out exactly as planned, and it became obvious that there was an urgent need for a science of the future.

Other strands in the development of modern futures studies are operations research and the 'think tanks'. The former was found to be useful in the conduct of World War II and the latter boomed after the war, partly as a home for operations researchers. The RAND (**R**esearch **and D**evelopment) Corporation is an example, originating in an effort by the US Air Force to maintain part of its World War II operations research capacity.

There are hundreds – if not thousands – of such think tanks in existence today and nearly all partly engage in some form of futures research. In its early days RAND itself was a school for futurists and a source of many of the basic principles of futures studies. RAND researchers, for example, developed a systems approach to problems that involved a holistic view, interdisciplinary teams, and modeling – all aspects of modern futures studies. They also created or adapted methodologies for the study of the future, including gaming, computer simulations, technological forecasting, the Delphi technique, and program budgeting and cost effectiveness analysis. H Kahn, a pioneer futurist, was a RAND alumnus and his well-known book, *On Thermonuclear War* (1960), was partly based on a RAND report on which he worked (Bell, 1997, vol. 1).

Another pioneer futurist, H D Lasswell, worked for more than four decades to create what we now call futures studies. Beginning in the 1930s, Lasswell formulated the 'developmental construct', a concept similar to 'image of the future', as part of 'developmental analysis'. To take only one example, his early work in developmental analysis described a vision of a coming world of garrison states, a world in which specialists on violence would be the most powerful group in society (Lasswell, 1935, 1937, 1941). Writing several years before George Orwell published his chilling image of 'Big Brother' in *Nineteen Eighty-Four*, Lasswell envisioned the erosion of democracy and the rise of dictatorship, the end of competitive elections and the coming of government by plebiscite, the spread of one-party or no-party states, the elimination of free speech and other civil liberties, the suppression of political opposition, the abandonment of legislative assemblies except as rubber stamps, and the control of the rate of production by the state with priority given to military production. As in the yet-to-be written *Nineteen Eighty-Four*, the symbols, but not the substance, of democracy would be retained.

Although speculative and imaginative, a developmental construct, such as the garrison state, is based upon disciplined and careful consideration of the past and of conditions that contribute toward its formation. It is not, however, a dogmatic forecast. Rather, it is a possible, even probable, image of the future under specific assumptions if, for example, past trends continue as they are. In fact, Lasswell wanted to alert people who valued democracy of the threats to it so that they would take action to prevent garrison states from becoming realities.

When Lasswell offered his vision of a science of the future, the world's social scientists were not receptive to it. Lasswell recast some of his ideas in a different and more conventional form and with the help of others proceeded to found the policy sciences which he lived to see catch on and flourish, both in public and private management (Brewer and deLeon, 1983; Lasswell, 1971; Lerner and Lasswell, 1951)

The Commission on the Year 2000, chaired by D Bell, is important to this story because it added respectability to futures thinking as a professional activity among mainstream, establishment intellectuals. The Commission was established by The American Academy of Arts and Sciences and met twice, once in 1965 and again in 1966. Its purposes included examining hypothetical futures and methodological problems in forecasting and a variety of social problems expected for the year 2000. The results included some of the key founding works of modern futures studies, including a collection of the Commission papers, *Toward the Year 2000: Work in Progress* (Bell, 1968), *The Coming of Post-Industrial Society* (Bell, 1976) and *The Year 2000: A Framework for Speculation on the Next Thirty-Three Years* (Kahn and Wiener, 1967).

The Club of Rome, established in 1968 by A Peccei and others, gave still another boost to the growing futures movement. Peccei, who had been a top executive with Fiat, Olivetti, and Italconsult (an international investment firm), was both a visionary and a man of practical affairs. As a result of his business travels to many different countries, Peccei had been shocked by the hunger, deprivation, ignorance, injustice, land erosion and pollution, mindless depletion of natural resources, enormous military expenditures, and the risks involved in new developments in nuclear power and genetic manipulation (Moll, 1991). Peccei, who labeled these and other world problems the 'global problematique', began speaking out about them in the early 1960s and was determined to do something about them.

His aim was to create a worldwide, cooperative organizational network of citizens, based largely on private diplomacy, that could be mobilized to help solve such problems. It was named the Club of Rome and achieved phenomenal fame in its first report, *The Limits to Growth* (Meadows, Meadows, Randers and Behrens, 1972).

Limits became the centre of international controversy, selling more than nine million copies in twenty-nine languages (Cole, 1993). Using computer simulation to project global trends into the future, the authors concluded that in the next century unless changes are made, both population and industrial growth will stop because of overshoot and collapse of the world system. Human lives would become short and brutish. We had heard all of this many times before, of course, at least since Malthus published his essay on population in 1798, but never before had it been backed by so much data, so many variables, and such sophisticated methods of analysis.

Limits captured the world's attention. It was not perfectly correct, as its authors themselves (and hundreds of critics) pointed out. But its message that the Earth's human population and economies could not continue growing as they had been, got through and will probably never be forgotten. Although the Club of Rome continues its work and has supported many additional projects and reports, none has ever had the impact of *Limits*.

For the futures field, *Limits* established computer simulation and modelling as a method of futures research and more important, it made environmental concerns a permanent part of the human agenda, giving futures studies one of its most powerful core concepts, sustainability.

By the seventies, of course, Toffler's *Future Shock* (1970) had been published. It was to become a popular bestseller, ubiquitous in bright multi-colored editions at nearly every supermarket in the United States and eventually, a part of public consciousness nearly everywhere. When Toffler published his more mature *The Third Wave* (1981), although it had already experienced periods of growth and decline, futures studies had become a worldwide professional activity.

Purposes of futures studies

Futurists aim to maintain or improve the freedom and welfare of humankind and the life-sustaining capacities of the Earth. They speak out for the interests of as-yet-voiceless future generations. They work to achieve these goals through prospective and visionary thinking, futures research and education, critical discourse, and social action.

The major tasks of futures studies include the study of possible futures, often breaking out of the straitjacket of conventional thinking and taking unusual perspectives. Present possibilities for the future are real, even though they are often unrecognized. It is part of the futurist agenda to look at the world not only as it is but also as it could be, to identify possibilities and to bring them to the attention of people.

The study of probable futures is another futurist's task. It focuses on the question of what the most likely future of some specified phenomenon would be within some given time period and under specified contingencies. Futurists ask what would the most probable future be if things continued as they are? They also ask, what alternative futures would probably occur under a variety of different assumptions, if this or that condition changed?

One of the most important futurist purposes is the study of images of the future. What do people expect, anticipate, hope, or fear will happen in the future? Futurists study both the causes and consequences of images of the future, based on one of the most secure principles of futures studies: images of the future are among the causes of present behavior, as people either try to adapt to what they believe is coming or try to act in ways that will create the future that they want (Polak, 1961).

As producers and users of knowledge, futurists and their clients are concerned about the reliability and validity of their assertions. They ask how they know what they claim to know. Thus, another purpose of futurists is to provide philosophical grounds for the knowledge that they produce. Because the future is as yet non-existent and non-evidential, futurists appear to face perplexing epistemological problems. Until recently, they have mostly left these unanswered, even though they have adapted or constructed many research tools and carried out thousands of empirical studies. Futurists have begun to rectify this situation with the publication of Slaughter's *The Knowledge Base of Futures Studies* (1996) and Bell's *Foundations of Futures Studies: Human Science for a New Era* (1997).

Futurists explore not only possible and probable futures, but also preferable futures. Thus, they assess the desirability of alternative futures and the ethical foundations of their judgments. To do this, they are necessarily concerned with the nature of the good society and with standards of judgment. Futurists are expected to state clearly the values underlying their work, conduct empirical studies of the goals and values held by various people, from leaders and experts to ordinary citizens, and attempt to construct objective standards of value judgments by which values and goals themselves can be evaluated. Futurists ask, for example, why should present generations care about and make sacrifices for the well-being of future generations?

Other purposes of futures studies include interpreting the past and orientating the present, integrating knowledge and values for designing social action, increasing democratic participation in imaging and designing the future and, because futurists are sometimes activists rather than merely researchers, communicating and advocating a particular image of the future, such as the sustainable society.

The role of prediction

Because it is so widely misunderstood a few words must be added about the role of prediction in futures studies. By 'prediction', I refer to the shared meanings of anticipation, expectation, forecast, foresight, prevision, projection, prognostication, prophecy and other such euphemisms for 'prediction'. Thus, I use the term 'prediction' in a generic sense to refer to any statement or assertion about the future.

Although the situation may be changing, the general public has thought of futurists as crystal-ball gazers who are primarily engaged in predicting *the* future. Confronted with this view, most futurists sigh resignedly and begin, yet again, to explain that this is not the case. Rather, futurists envision *alternative futures*, describing various possibilities and trying to help people design and achieve the futures that are most desirable to them.

Educating the public to the fact that they are not predicting *the* future has led many futurists into denial about the role of prediction in futures studies. For example, Coates (1985: 21) writes that the 'central principle of futures research is alternative futures: there is no single predictable future'. But this is an overreaction.

Although most futurists agree that the purposes of futures studies include exploring probable futures, alternative possible futures and preferable futures, all of these futurist tasks actually do involve prediction to some degree. Futurists, as all people in their everyday lives, can and do – and often must – predict all the time, usually quite accurately. And, despite the denials, knowledge of the future is possible (Bell, 1997, vol. 1). Here is a brief summary of a few of the arguments.

One factor that supports the denial of prediction among futurists is that predictions often turn out to be false. But this appears to be the case largely because people want to know exactly those future events that are most difficult to predict accurately. For example, if we predict that the next US presidential election will take place in November, then we have said nothing exceptional even if it turns out to be true. After all, we now know that it is so scheduled. That is, we can – and do – predict thousands of routine events most of which will turn out to be true. Routines of repetitive behavior are an aspect of what social order is. We can predict when the bank will open, when the play will start, when the aircraft will take off, and which side of the street drivers will steer their cars, because such things are socially controlled. All normal people plan their personal trajectories through time and space according to such predictions.

We predict with great accuracy that a woman will not marry her father, that parents won't eat their children, and that people won't urinate on their dinner tables. Social life, indeed, is patterned and orderly under most circumstances and controlled by social norms. But such predictions are taken for granted and are uninteresting, except to anthropologists and sociologists, precisely because they are so certain (even though they may sometimes not come true, eg the outbreak of war might lead to postponement of the election, bad weather or a bomb threat may delay your flight, and that car coming toward you might pull over into a collision course).

But what is exceptional is to make predictions about events that are by their very nature not socially controlled, especially when the outcome is important to us. People must anticipate when and where the horse races will be held, if they intend to go to the track and place some bets, but what they really would like to know is which horse will win each race. Thus, if we focus only on the most uncontrolled and chancy events, then the conclusion seems to follow that we cannot predict accurately. Yet, obviously, we can and do make predictions all the time, and often correctly.

Moreover, predictions are always part of decision making and planning, both in the worlds of statesmen and other leaders and in the everyday world of ordinary people pursuing their individual projects. Imagining the future is how people make their way in the world. Prediction 'is a routine human preoccupation inherent in all social behavior.... Thus the decision to turn on a light switch is based on the expectation that the action will result in the illumination of a room' (Gabor, 1986).

Finally, to test the accuracy of a prediction by whether or not it turns out to be true is too simple. It often is misleading as an indicator of the validity of the prediction. This is so because some predictions are reflexive, ie they are self-altering. For example, a doctor predicts that a patient will die within six months if he does not stop drinking alcohol. Believing the prediction to be true, the man stops drinking and lives on for years. The prediction that he will die turns out to be false, but it was presumptively true at the time it was made (and helped to save his life).

All predictions are contingent or conditional. They depend on a variety of assumptions, even though they are often unstated, many of which can change and some of which may be changed because of people's reaction to the prediction itself.

Thus, the exploration of alternative futures is a matter of making a series of different predictions on the basis of different assumptions about conditions, including the expected behavior of relevant decision makers – for example, whether or not the Federal Reserve Board will or will not raise interest rates. Prediction, thus, plays an important role in the futurist enterprise, even though the predictions may be multiple, conditional, contingent, corrigible, uncertain, presumptively or terminally true or false, or self-altering.

Conclusion

By the 1990s, futures studies came to have many of the features of a distinctive discipline or, more accurately, multidiscipline. It had its own well-established publications (eg *Futures*, *The Futurist*, *Futures Research Quarterly* etc), organizations (eg Association Internationale de Futuribles, the World Future Society, the World Futures Studies Federation, and hundreds of others in many countries throughout the world), and methodologies (Delphi, scenario writing, future workshops, ethnographic futures research, etc). Increasingly, futurists also were coming to share among themselves conceptual and theoretical commitments, purposes, ethical awareness, empirical research and scholarship, professional ideals, a sense of community as futurists, and a growing body of substantive principles and knowledge.

Futures studies in the decade of the 1990s may have reached maturity. It was a time of consolidating past work and of agenda-setting for new advances in the field. For example, there was Moll's (1991) book on the Club of Rome and the role of futures studies in the environmental movement; Tough's (1991) *Crucial Questions about the Future*; Kurian and Molitor's (1996) *Encyclopedia of the Future*; Slaughter's (1996) multicultural three-volume work, *The Knowledge Base of Futures Studies*; the launching and early reports of a global, multi-year study of the twenty-first century known as the Millennium Project (Glenn, 1993; Gordon and Glenn, 1993). I hope that I may count in this company my own two-volume work, *Foundations of Futures Studies: Human Science for a New Era* (Bell, 1997).

Marien, editor of *Future Survey*, a monthly abstract of publications about the future, who is both one of the best informed contemporary futurists and a perennial critic of overly optimistic assessments of the progress of futures studies, has recently said, in what surely is an understatement, that 'future studies may develop into something resembling an academic field of study or a discipline' (Marien, 1996). Indeed, it has.

References

Bell, D (1968) *Toward the Year 2000: Work in Progress*, Boston: Houghton Mifflin.

Bell, W (1997) *Foundations of Futures Studies: Human Science for a New Era*, 2 volumes, New Brunswick, NJ: Transaction Publishers.

Brewer, G D and deLeon, P (1983) *The Foundations of Policy Analysis*, Homewood, IL: The Dorsey Press.

Coates, J F (1985) 'Scenarios Part Two: Alternative Futures', in Mendell, J S (ed.), *Nonextrapolative Methods in Business Forecasting*, Westport, CT: Quorum Books.

Cole, S (1993) 'Learning to Love *Limits*', *Futures*, 25(7), 814–18.

Glenn, J C (1993) 'The Millennium Project of the United Nations University', in Didsbury, H F (ed.) *The Years Ahead: Perils, Problems, and Promises*, Bethesda, MD: World Future Society.

Goodwin, B (1978) *Social Science and Utopia*, Hassocks, UK: The Harvester Press

Gordon, T J and Glenn, J C (1993) *Issues in Creating the Millennium Project: Report on Phase I from the Millennium Project Feasibility Study*, Washington, DC: The United Nations University.

Kahn, H (1960) *On Thermonuclear War*, Princeton, NJ: Princeton University Press.

Kahn, H and Wiener, A J (1967) *The Year 2000: A Framework for Speculation on the Next Thirty-Three Years*, New York: Macmillan.

Kurian, G T and Molitor, G T T (eds) (1996) *Encyclopedia of the Future*, 2 volumes, New York: Simon & Schuster Macmillan.

Lasswell, H D (1935) *World Politics and Personal Insecurity*, New York: McGraw-Hill.

Lasswell, H D (1937) 'Sino-Japanese Crisis: The Garrison State Versus the Civilian State', *China Quarterly*, 11, 643–49.

Lasswell, H D (1941) 'The Garrison State', *The American Journal of Sociology*, 46, 455–68.

Lasswell, H D (1971) *A Pre-View of Policy Sciences*, New York: Elsevier.

Lerner, D and Lasswell, H D *et al.* (eds) (1951) *The Policy Sciences*, Stanford, CA: Stanford University Press.

Manuel, F E and Manuel, F P (1979) *Utopian Thought in the Western World*, Cambridge, MA: Belknap Press of Harvard University Press.

Marien, M (1996) 'Future Studies', in Kurian, G T and Molitor, G T T (eds), *Encyclopedia of the Future*, 1, New York: Simon & Schuster Macmillan.

Meadows, D H, Meadows, D L, Randers, J, and Behrens, W W (1972) *The Limits to Growth*, New York: Universe.

Moll, P (1991) *From Scarcity to Sustainability*, Frankfurt am Main: Peter Lang.

Polak, F L (1961) [1955] *The Image of the Future: Enlightening the Past, Orientating the Present, Forecasting the Future*, 2 vols, New York: Oceana.

Slaughter, R A (1996) *The Knowledge Base of Futures Studies*, 3 vols, Hawthorn, Victoria, Australia: DDM Media Group.

Toffler, A (1970) *Future Shock*, New York: Random House.

Toffler, A (1981) *The Third Wave*, New York: Bantam.

Tough, A (1991) *Crucial Questions about the Future*, Lanham, MD: University Press of America.

Wagar, W W (1991) *The Next Three Futures*, New York: Praeger.

Wells, H G (1987) [1932] 'Wanted – Professors of Foresight!', *Futures Research Quarterly*, 3(1), 89–91.

Further reading

Bell, D (1976) *The Coming of Post-Industrial Society: A Venture in Social Forecasting*, New York: Basic Books.

Gabor, T (1986) *The Prediction of Criminal Behavior*, Toronto: University of Toronto Press.

3.   The changing nature of global change

Walter Truett Anderson

Summary

Consciousness of global change, fundamental to futures studies, is itself the product of change. This chapter argues, therefore, that we need to take a backward glance before leaping into the future. Global change has been influenced by many events and ideas – exploration, map making, scientific discoveries, political philosophies, the theory of evolution. There was a time when change was more or less synonymous with progress, but that assumption no longer holds. People are now sceptical of both ideologies of progress that prevailed in the Cold War era, the Marxist model and the Western concept of 'development'. Relativism, the recognition that there are many different cultures, none necessarily superior to the others, is an inevitable product of globalization. Globalization takes many forms: economic, political, cultural, biological. Globalization is driven by advances in information and communications technology, which also increase the awareness of global change. Among the many development projects needed now is a new, more mature and realistic, concept of progress.

Introduction

One of the greatest events of the twentieth century – as important in its way as any of the wars, depressions, discoveries and revolutions that crowd the history books – has been the recognition by all the world's people that the world does change. That recognition is not yet universal, but there can't be too many people left who lack an image of the whole world and who believe that the future will be like the present. This is a momentous transformation of human consciousness and of course, it is the foundation for all our thinking about the future. At the beginning of the twentieth century there was no discipline or profession of futures studies. Today, even though futures studies is still not as highly professionalized or academically respectable as some of its practitioners would like it to be, no enterprise can function without plans and forecasts. Even the most conservative and conventional planning activities assume some kind of change.

We think about the future because we have come to a new understanding of the past. The more we learn about the past, the more clear it becomes that the world and the human species have been in continuous movement and transformation, and the more reason we have to expect that transformation will continue into the future. Change itself becomes the new constant, but then turns out to be not quite constant either, because we can see now that the rate and manner of change changes, and so does people's understanding of change.

Homo sapiens began migrating out of Africa about a hundred thousand years ago – not a very long time by the clock of the universe – and since then there has always been change. People migrated in all directions, gradually inhabiting the entire planet. In the process they invented an astonishing variety of cultures, languages, rituals, religions and social orders. They separated, settled into the various regions that became their homes and, separately, decided they were distinct and unique. Many tribes and societies invented names for themselves that translated roughly as 'the people,' with the implicit, and sometimes explicit, understanding of other peoples as deeply different and somehow less than human. Although some people lived out their entire lives within a radius of a few miles and with little comprehension of a world beyond the horizon, there is also much archaeological evidence of migrations, military expeditions and trade, sometimes over long distances. People learned new things, invented new tools, developed new systems of communication.

Yet, over most of those thousands of years of change, change that we describe today as cultural evolution, most human beings appear to have lived with a view that the basic conditions of life did not change over time. All societies had creation stories, some had myths of a past golden age, some had legends of great events such as flood, many had stories of how the world might end in the distant future; but overriding all these was an expectation that life – daily life, ordinary life, real life – would remain essentially the same year after year.

The making of the modern world view

This was the consciousness that prevailed in the West during the Medieval Era, and that began about five hundred years ago to be challenged by a world view that was, for the first time in human history, truly a world view. The Modern Era brought a complete reorientation of human consciousness in both time and space (Tarnas, 1991). Many things contributed to this huge transition including these five crucial developments:

- In the 16th century, discovery of the spherical, oceanic world.
- In the 17th century, development of the idea of scientific progress.
- In the 18th century, emergence of concepts of social/political progress and human rights.

- In the 19th century, discovery of evolutionary change in nature – biological progress.
- In the 20th century, increasing globalization and cultural pluralism influenced by the idea of socially constructed reality. Reactions against the doctrine of inevitable progress.

Let us look at each of these in turn, not so much at the historical events, with which we are familiar, but at the impacts upon human consciousness, which we tend to forget.

The New World

The great accomplishment of the age of explorations was not just the discovery of the New World, but the discovery of the world as we know it. That discovery owed much to advances in shipbuilding and navigation, but it owed at least as much to advances in mapmaking and printing. The news of Columbus' first successful voyage did not stir great excitement in Europe, but the publication of the first maps, and the adventure-filled accounts of Amerigo Vespucci's explorations, were a sensation. In the minds of sixteenth-century Europeans, the world metamorphosed from a small piece of land containing the Mediterranean into a huge sphere of water, waiting to be explored. 'Never before,' notes Daniel Boorstin, 'had the arena of human experience been so suddenly or so dramatically revised' (Boorstin, 1983). No less momentous was the discovery of the human species, the slowly-dawning recognition that this was a populated world, and that 'the people' comprised many different races.

The scientific mind

People also discovered new ways of thinking. According to some accounts, the modern mind was born in a room with a stove in a little house in southern Germany, early in the seventeenth century. That happened during the winter in which Rene Descartes holed-up and commenced thinking his way down to the very core of 'reality'. It was a modern kind of project. He was in search of certainty and prepared to doubt everything, including all that he had been taught, until he could find some basis for it. Descartes lived in a time of great political, religious and philosophical turbulence. Old orders and old beliefs were literally collapsing around him. The Thirty Years War, which filled most of his adult life, brought an end to the old feudal system that had ordered European life for centuries. Another source of turbulence was the dispute over Nicholas Copernicus' heliocentric theory of the solar system. Copernicus' theory had been published in 1543, but the massive backlash against it, both from church authorities who saw it as a devilish contradiction of religious doctrine and from rival astronomers who saw it as a ridiculous departure from scientific truth, was slow to get started and was still going strong while

Descartes was growing up. Descartes' contemporary, Galileo, was in the thick of that upheaval, looking through his telescope and discovering a solar system – indeed, a universe – unlike anything that had been imagined before. During that winter in Bavaria, Descartes considered all the things it was possible to doubt and came down to the one fact that he could trust. He thought, therefore he existed; that much was certain. Upon this foundation, upon this confidence in a rational and integrated self, prepared to question all his society's received truths, he built his edifice of thought. Modern science rests in part upon that Cartesian foundation, as does the modern sense of a critical consciousness that can stand back from the world and study it.

Isaac Newton, integrating the work of Descartes, Johannes Kepler and Galileo, completed the Copernican revolution by establishing gravity as a universal force that governed the workings of the solar system. It is hard to comprehend in the present era, when we have come to take scientific advances for granted, how powerful was the impact of Newton's work. It gripped the imagination of people in his time not only because of what he revealed to them about the cosmos, but because he seemed to prove by his actions that all the secrets of nature could be uncovered by the human mind. Voltaire called him not only the greatest man of his time, but the greatest man of all time. The poet Alexander Pope wrote:

> Nature and Nature's laws lay hid in night:
> Then God said, Let Newton be! and all was light.
> (Pope, 1740)

Enlightened progress

Another English thinker who had a profound impact on Voltaire, and on the French enlightenment, and on the political events of the modern era, was John Locke. Locke was in many ways a revolutionary thinker, but he was also an eminently rational one. In his writings on the method of philosophy he argued persuasively for discipline and reason. He tried to show how confusion about problems often arose in the mind as a result of unclear thinking, not because of the inherent difficulty of the subject itself. His impact, like Newton's, was both in his ideas and in what his work seemed to say about political progress. The ideas about human rights found their way into the American Declaration of Independence and the Federal Constitution, and, by way of Voltaire, into the rhetoric of the French revolution. The implicit, and no less influential, message in his work was that the principles of order and good governance, like the mysteries of nature, could be discovered through disciplined human thought.

Precisely in the middle of the eighteenth century, in 1750, in a lecture at the Sorbonne, the young French intellectual Anne Robert Turgot delivered his memorable lecture entitled 'A Philosophical Review of the Successive

Advances of the Human Mind' – the manifesto of the modern religion of progress. Progress, as he described it, was achieved primarily through rational thought: 'Time, research, chance, amass observations, and unveil the hidden connections which united phenomena.' But he was also a great believer in the importance of personal freedom, and held that even the least magnanimous of human drives, 'Self-interest, ambition, vainglory,' also served the cause of progress (Nisbet, 1980).

Turgot's thinking made an immense impression on intellectuals of his time, and some of the themes that he first articulated can be found in works as diverse as Adam Smith's economics and Jean-Jacques Rousseau's romanticism. Although he was a Christian royalist, he was much admired by revolutionaries, who reasoned that, if progress was inevitable over time anyway, a great forward leap might be achieved through deliberate effort.

Breaking the Great Chain

The Darwinian revolution in thought, with its idea of biological progress, was in some ways the most profound of all, and it is not surprising that it is still being opposed and resisted. It challenged not only the scriptural version of Creation, but also a theological/biological world view that had prevailed in the western world for centuries: the Great Chain of Being. This was the view of a universe systematically and unchangeably ordered into strata of living things – inert matter at the bottom, God at the top, human beings below the angels, all other life forms on Earth in descending ranks below human beings. The Great Chain was believed to be a fixed arrangement, completed when God had created Adam and Eve. Religion and science shared this world view. Scripture described how such a world came into being, and the work of the scientists was to fill in the details of the picture by studying and classifying various living things. There was no idea that the picture might change. Arthur Lovejoy in his book *The Great Chain of Being* (1950) describes Abbe Pluche's summary of mainstream thinking on this subject:

> Nothing more, therefore, will be produced in all the ages to follow. All the philosophers have deliberated and come to agreement upon this point. Consult the evidence of experience; elements always the same, species that never vary, seeds and germs prepared in advance for the perpetuation of everything...so that one can say, Nothing new under the sun, no new production, no species which has not been since the beginning (Lovejoy, 1950).

No new species appearing, and none lost either; the idea of extinction was incompatible with the view of such an ordained and ordered system of life.

Rethinking progress

Believers in the doctrine of continuous, onward-and-upward progress generally assumed that once a truth had been discovered, Newton's laws for example, a piece of the world's work was done, and done for good. Each discovery was a building block for those to come. But in the twentieth century a much more complex view of progress began to emerge, shaped by the post-Newtonian physics of Einstein and others, experiments and theories that undermined virtually every aspect of the orderly, mechanistic universe. For a while, science had seemed to be merely a superior kind of common sense, but by the mid-twentieth century lay people began to discover that reality as the physicists understood it was beyond their comprehension. The idea of scientific progress was still a powerful force in modern western culture, but it was now expected that new advances would be as likely to dismantle earlier ones as to build upon them. Easily the most influential work *about* science in the twentieth century was Thomas Kuhn's *The Structure of Scientific Revolutions* (1962), which depicted scientific progress as a series of paradigm shifts, each new paradigm challenging the paradigm that had preceded it. So the human species ends the twentieth century with a different idea of scientific progress from the one with which it entered, and it also inhabits a vastly different universe. Concepts of time and space, ideas about the smallest components of matter, images of the size and structure of the cosmos, all are changed and still changing. In the life sciences, even as the theorists of evolution continue to fight rearguard actions against ancient creation stories, new ideas in areas such as genetics and complexity theory explore the ways that life continually reorganizes itself, finds new ways to change. We see now not only that life evolves, but also that evolution evolves.

The twentieth century has also been a time of unprecedented worldwide political change, of which the most visible historical landmarks were two world wars, each followed by the creation of an international organization dedicated to maintaining world peace. We have seen, in the prolonged period of ideological conflict called the Cold War, the collision of two different models of change – the Marxist revolutionary version, and the western concept of 'development'. Each of these changed significantly toward the end of the century. The most dramatic evidence of such change, of course, was the collapse of the Soviet Union and with it, the collapse (or perhaps downsizing would be a more apt term) of the global Marxist movement. But the western ideology of development has been under severe stress also, from several directions – in the West, from critiques based on concepts of sustainable development, in the rest of the world from those who want to have some model of development or modernization that is not simply the adoption of western institutions and culture.

One of the most powerful intellectual forces in the twentieth century has been the rise of relativism – and the reactions against it. It was inevitable, as the boundaries of human society stretched, with more details about past civilizations coming from the archaeologists and the historians, and more information about other present societies coming from the anthropologists and the growing numbers of world travelers, that people would begin to develop more sophisticated ways to account for the vast differences of value and belief. It was no longer sufficient simply to say that one society's beliefs were correct and all the others wrong, one society superior and all the others inferior. This new perspective came in several different packages – historicism, the sociology of knowledge, the rediscovery of earlier thinkers such as Giambattista Vico, the philosophical works of contemporaries such as Isaiah Berlin (1991) and Richard Rorty (1979), the whole body of ideas classed as 'poststructural' or 'postmodern.' In this complex body of thought we find an increasing tendency to regard all values and beliefs as socially constructed, reflecting the conditions of people in a particular time and place.

The four globalizations

So globalization is its own kind of revolution, forcing people to perceive the enormous range of values and beliefs that exist in the world, and that have existed in the past; disturbing the foundations of belief. And that revolution may scarcely have begun. We are, at the transition from the twentieth to the twenty-first century, in the midst of a huge process of globalization, perhaps better understood as several differing processes which are establishing new connections among people and places. In the organizations where I have been doing most of my own exploration of this subject, the Meridian Institute and the World Academy of Art and Science, we have usually found it useful to talk of 'four globalizations' – economic, political, cultural, and biological. These are not distinct processes, of course, just different conceptual windows through which to view the huge, complex and astonishingly rapid changes that are taking place in our time.

Economic globalization

In the economic category are such developments as the growth of international trade in goods and services, the internationalization of finance, and the conversion of many once-domestic corporations into multinational or trans-national ones. As the economy globalizes there are still local, national and regional economies of all kinds, globalization does not mean simply that all economies are seamlessly united into a single system. What it does mean is that many new markets and commercial linkages are created, and all econ-omies are, in various ways, altered by virtue of operating in a global context. And we have not only a legal and visible global economy, but also an illegal and hidden one – the huge international trade in drugs, weapons, and other contraband items.

Political globalization

Political globalization is perhaps most visible to us in the way events in one part of the world become, almost instantly, global dramas. Television and the other communications literally bring the world into our living rooms. We also have a growing number of organizations, both public and private, which are involved in governance and politics. The United Nations is the centerpiece of the structure of global governance that has evolved in the second half of the twentieth century, but it is far from the whole thing. The number of nations has increased, as has the number of international governmental organizations (including some, such as the World Trade Organization, that are created to deal with, and advance, economic globalization) and non-governmental organizations. The non-governmental organizations have proliferated at an amazing rate in the late twentieth century; nobody really knows now how many NGOs there are in the world, but it is clear that they play an increasingly important role in governance at all levels, from the local to the global. Some people see them as the visible evidence of a growing 'global civil society' that will be an essential element in the functioning of a global system of governance. Even harder to quantify has been the growth of a global political culture, the internationalization of ideas such as democracy and human rights that were once regarded as native to a limited number of countries and societies. This is not only hard to quantify, it is also controversial, because some people view it as a new kind of Western imperialism. Terrorism is, unfortunately, also a part of globalization, a new kind of paramilitary action that makes use of the communications media, that preys on the airlines, the tourist industry, and other forms of international commerce.

Cultural globalization

Cultural globalization is seen by some as nothing more than a process of homogenization and trivialization as the artifacts of Western pop culture, from sneakers to fast food, become universal. It is that, and it is more than that. For the first time since human beings began to disperse around the world and invent different cultures, all cultural forms – all the symbols, languages, rituals, religions and customs – become, in a sense, everybody's property. Never before has there been anything like the wholesale importation and exportation of pieces of cultures from all over the world, not only Western modernism and ideas, but Chinese food, African music, Native American spirituality. To the dismay of purists, few things remain in their original forms but are modified, elaborated, combined with others in new ways. Anybody looking for a global culture will find not one uniform set of values and beliefs, arts and rituals, but at an endlessly-recombining variety of them.

Biological globalization

Then there is biological globalization. The movement of plants, animals, insects and micro-organisms has also been escalating rapidly in the latter decades of the twentieth century. It is, in fact, creating a world quite different from the one we have known in the recent past. All the world's ecosystems, like all the world's cities, are becoming more pluralistic, host to exotic newcomers from distant lands. Some of the causes are fairly obvious. It is well documented, for example, that human mobility is at an all-time high, and human beings never travel alone. World trade is also growing, and insects and other stowaways frequently travel in food shipments. Researchers frequently exchange specimens: living organisms, tissue, seeds and clippings. There is a strong market in many countries for exotic pets and plants, tropical fish and birds. Some of the trade that serves this demand is legal, some of it is not. Biological globalization often causes severe ecological upsets when plants or animals are imported into regions where they have no natural enemies – the rabbits and cane toads in Australia, the goats in the Hawaiian Islands. But it is a condition of life in our time, not merely a problem to be solved. Human life depends on it. Everywhere in the world, agriculture, medicine and industries rely on genetic material from other parts of the world for breed improvement and disease resistance. Biological globalization shows every indication of continuing to increase in the foreseeable future. This means that people and societies everywhere are going to have to develop a general sense of their environment, the word 'world view' is particularly apt here, quite different from past assumptions and understandings. And there is another kind of biological globalization – the increasing recognition of the Earth as a single ecosystem, in which changes such as warming or cooling of the climate affect all its parts.

Technological changes, particularly those which involve information, communications and travel, have always been the great drivers of globalization: shipbuilding, navigation, mapmaking, printing, radio, telephone, computers, television. Global information-communications linkages show every likelihood of continuing to grow in capacity and range, quite possibly at increasing rate of speed, in the decades ahead. As I write in 1997, most of the people in the world have never used a telephone – but new telephone systems, many of them based on wireless technology, are being constructed all around the world. All the people in the world are becoming connected as never before, and some of the communications hookups are becoming so easy to use over great distances that it is possible for enthusiasts to speak of 'the end of geography.'

Although globalization has been going on for centuries, we have really only begun to become aware of it, and to recognize its increasing speed, in the past few decades. We live not simply in a globalized world, but in a world that is globalizing. The various processes I have identified here – economic, political, cultural and biological – may very well have scarcely begun. As information-communication system reaches more people, more people will become more aware of living in a world, and in a changing world. Technologies are not only drivers of globalization, but drivers of the awareness of globalization.

Globalization as a global issue

Globalization is sometimes seen as being 'out of control,' and in a sense it is – because it is multicausal and multicentric. Like the diaspora out of Africa that allowed different peoples to become separate, the processes that now allow (or force) them to become connected are the result of many different actions. Globalization may be inevitable, but it is far from desirable in the eyes of many people. The world is full of movements and activists struggling either to combat some particular effect of globalization or to reverse the whole globalizing trend – religious fundamentalists, cultural preservationists, bioregionalists, nationalists, localists, economic protectionists, defenders of linguistic purity. Globalization itself becomes one of the most controversial issues in a global civilization (Anderson, 1990, 1995, 1996).

We also see, as signs of the growing awareness of entry into a global civilization, a proliferation of global agendas and scenarios – predictions, prescriptions, mapmaking attempts to describe the order of a post-Cold War, post-industrial, postmodern information society. Among these are Francis Fukuyama's (1992) image of universal liberal democracy, Samuel Huntington's (1996) forecast of the clash of civilizations, Hazel Henderson's (1996) vision of cooperative global economics, Kenichi Ohmae's (1990) borderless world, Jean-Marie Guehenno's (1996) end of the nation-state, and of course the vast literature concerning future global environmental disturbances such as climatic change and species extinction.

All of this indicates a growing willingness to think hard about the future, a willingness born of the recognition of global change. There is a certain kind of rough consensus about this, shared by those who have vastly different agendas for change and even by those who would like to turn back the clock. We are increasingly united in the recognition that the future will be fundamentally different from the present and because of that, we are vastly different from most human beings who lived in past centuries. We have a far more intense and informed sense of change but what we don't have, any more, is a sense of progress. That giddy certainty of inexorable betterment that gripped the minds of western intellectuals a couple of centuries ago has run its course. There are optimists among the futurists today, but they are an embattled faction.

There is certainly no shortage of work to be done in the next century, projects large and small to be undertaken in service of achieving some real progress – bringing in more justice and equity, making wiser use of the world's resources, helping to steer our amazing technological development in sane and humane directions. One of these projects, surely, will be work of the mind, in search of a deeper understanding of progress itself. We need a new world view – a body of art and science, an intellectual discipline – that can look at the whole course of biological and cultural evolution. Such a world view clearly will have outgrown the simplistic faith in a march toward perfection. But it may, and I think it will, be able to marvel at the huge drama of the Earth's history, and to find in both the past and future of human experience an awesome and difficult struggle of learning, growth, and even improvement.

References

Anderson, W (1990) *Reality Isn't What It Used To Be: Theatrical Politics, Ready-to-Wear Religion, Radical Chic, Global Myths, and other Wonders of the Postmodern World*, New York: HarperCollins.

Anderson, W (1995) *The Truth About the Truth: De-confusing and Reconstructing the Postmodern World*, New York: Tarcher/Putnam.

Anderson, W (1996) *Evolution Isn't What It Used To Be: The Augmented Animal and the Whole Wired World*, New York: W. H. Freeman.

Berlin, I (1991) *The Crooked Timber of Humanity: Chapters in the History of Ideas*, New York: Knopf.

Boorstin, D (1983) *The Discoverers*, New York: Random House.

Fukuyama, F (1992) *The End of History and the Last Man*, New York: The Free Press.

Guehenno, J-M (1995) *The End of the Nation-State*, Minneapolis: University of Minnesota Press.

Henderson, H (1996) *Building a Win-Win World: Life Beyond Global Economic Warfare*, San Francisco: Barrett-Koehler.

Huntington, S (1996) *The Clash of Civilizations and the Remaking of World Order*, New York: Simon & Schuster.

Kuhn, T (1962) *The Structure of Scientific Revolutions*, Chicago: University of Chicago Press.

Lovejoy, A (1950) *The Great Chain of Being*, Cambridge: Harvard University Press.

Ohmae, K (1990) *The Borderless World: Power and Strategy in the Interlinked Economy*, New York: HarperCollins.

Nisbet, R (1980) *History of the Idea of Progress*, New York: Basic Books.

Pope, A (1740) 'Epitaph Intended for Sir Isaac Newton', in *Complete Poetical Works*, Boston: Houghton Mifflin.

Rorty, R (1979) *Philosophy and the Mirror of Nature*, Princeton: Princeton University Press.

Tarnas, R (1991) *The Passion of the Western Mind: Understanding the Ideas That Have Shaped Our World View*, New York: Random House.

4. The knowledge base of futures studies

Richard Slaughter

Summary

This chapter provides an overview of the knowledge base of futures studies. This model, the series of books derived from it and the field it represents, have many educational and cultural implications, some of which are explored here. A range of applications and benefits are discussed, as well as some suggestions about the way the knowledge base may continue to evolve. The role of futures thinking in education is outlined. It is suggested that the changing prospects for humankind mean that futures concepts, tools and approaches will necessarily be much more widely taken up and applied. The chapter ends with a summary of commonly-noted outcomes of teaching and learning within this perspective.

The emergence of futures studies

Futures studies has emerged steadily over recent decades and is increasingly recognised as a discipline. Its subject matter is elusive, but it is not the only area to deal with uncertainty. Over recent years significant arenas of uncertainty have opened up in science and mathematics, and a new interpretative sophistication has developed across the humanities. Our understanding of the social construction of reality, of cultural editing, of worldview analysis and the formation and dissolution of so-called 'disciplinary paradigms' has provided many potent insights. It is a context in which futures studies has a clear and a central role to play (Ogilvy, 1996). Its knowledge base is no more challenging, no less soundly based, than that of other fields. The knowledge base of futures studies has appeared to be more problematic than it really is for a number of reasons.

For example, 'the future' has been widely misconstrued as an 'empty space' rather than as an active principle in the present. Futures work has also been over-identified with prediction, forecasting, 'think-tanks' and western, corporatist, positivistically-inclined 'futurology'. Again, the highly visible work of pop-futurists, along with media stereotypes and a range of visually-compelling, but often spurious, pseudo-futuristic imagery (which has more

39

to do with present-day marketing practices than 'the future') have diverted attention from more substantive options. Finally, there are not yet enough scholars working in the field to achieve a 'critical mass' of practitioners. But there will be for one simple reason: there is a growing structural need for high-quality futures work.

With the late-industrial system, classical economics, international trade, 'trickle-down' development, the mechanistic worldview and the global environment (to name but a few aspects of the global *problematique*) slipping ever deeper into crisis, the need to critique past practice, to institutionalise foresight, reconceptualise cultural and political assumptions and to 'steer' more carefully is very clear. Regardless of the difficulties involved, futures studies is a necessary enterprise in a fragile, interconnected world. While we unquestionably remain caught up in a vast web of institutional and learning lags, the problems addressed by futurists and others in associated fields will not go away. They will become more urgent and pressing as time passes. This can be stated with confidence because we have sufficient insight into the underlying structure of the coming decades – regardless of detailed events – to know that this will be a most challenging period (Slaughter, 1994).

However, along with this confidence in the role of futures studies there should also be a certain modesty, for the future is most certainly open and unpredictable. Futurists cannot predict the future, but they can help develop individual and collective foresight – which I take to be primarily a widely-shared human capacity, and only secondarily a professionalised technique (Slaughter, 1995a). One result of good foresight work is a well-developed decision context embracing aspects of past, present and possible futures. A careful look at the outputs of futures work shows that the field produces useful provisional knowledge and supports disciplined enquiry. Another term for this is scholarship. It is a key to the future of futures studies (Bell, 1996).

A model of the knowledge base

Futures studies is a substantive interdisciplinary field of enquiry. The fact that it is richly interconnected at the margins with many other enterprises and fields means that the boundaries cannot be clearly defined. However, accounts of a core arguably have greater clarity. The model used here is illustrated in Figure 4.1. It is made up of several identifiable overlapping layers or elements. For analytic purposes it is convenient to separate them. However, in reality they are interconnected and functionally inseparable.

In this approach, a viable model emerges from the interaction of core elements, eg futures concepts and tools, futures methods, literature and organisations. As noted, some of these elements are certainly shared with many other fields and enterprises. But where they overlap, an internal synthesis can be identified (indicated here by the vertical arrows). Similarly, an

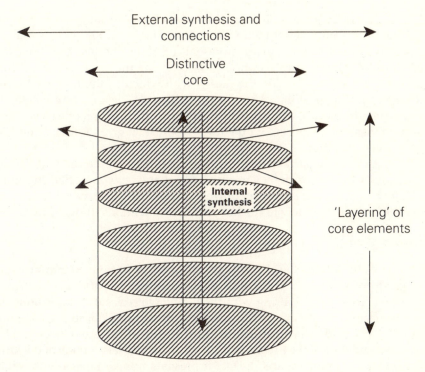

Figure 4.1 Model of the knowledge base.

external synthesis is always possible through lateral connections with other fields such as long-range planning, policy-studies, development studies and so on.

Such a model helps to integrate elements of the field more systematically. For example, foundation courses in futures studies arguably require something akin to the following as a starting point. It provides a way of bringing clarity to an area which tends to appear abstract or confusing at first sight (Rogers and Tough, 1992). We should also bear in mind that all models are provisional, and this is no exception. However, its first exposure in a special issue of *Futures* received sufficient endorsement from the profession to permit a new series of books to emerge with the collective title of *The Knowledge Base of Futures Studies* (Slaughter, 1996a).

So what are some of the key elements, or layers, of futures studies? There follows a brief overview.

Language, concepts and metaphors

The language, concepts and metaphors of the futures field can be regarded as primary intellectual and symbolic resources for the field itself and for education at every level. The very concepts of 'future' and 'futures' point toward one of the distinguishing criteria which provides the possessors of a human brain/mind system with a unique vantage point in time, ie one that is not restricted to the 'creature present' of other species. Concepts such as those of 'alternatives', 'options', 'agenda for the twenty-first century' and 'sustainability' provide the means with which to think about futures. Metaphorically speaking, they are 'springboards' or 'building blocks' for understanding which, when developed and explored, permit otherwise vague and provisional notions about the future to take on greater clarity and form (Slaughter, 1996b).

Metaphors have particular applicability in futures studies, in part through the active ways in which they organise and shape our conceptual structures. While their power to shape discourse tends to take place invisibly, they can also be used deliberately to further conscious intentions (Judge, 1993).

Theories, ideas and images

The symbolic building blocks outlined above can be assembled into structures of great power and insight. For example the idea of 'worldview design' or that of a 'wise culture' bring with them a whole series of propositions that can be used to clarify important aspects of present-day questions and future options. The field as a whole generates a web of interconnected theories, ideas and images which serve to contradict the popular and false notion of the future as merely an 'empty space'. In fact it presents human beings with a wide range of options, alternatives and dilemmas which need to be debated and to lead to thoughtful responses. It follows that futures studies encourages an active engagement with history. Far from being merely problematic, the challenging, open-ended nature of the subject is exactly what the human mind and spirit thrives upon. The future can be explored through many avenues, and not least through theories about evolution, progress, chaos, stability, sustainability, permanence and new forms of society. Some aspects of futures are best approached through visual or literary images.

Images of futures are both ubiquitous and understudied. Yet they are being continuously negotiated at all levels of society. They are consciously deployed, for example, in attempts to gain social support for major projects. But they may also be unconscious, or obscured by ideological uses. Images of futures in the late-twentieth century tend to be either technophilic or dystopian. Both can be usefully explored, critiqued and compared with, eg those emerging from speculative fiction, art and non-western cultures (Slaughter, 1991). As noted below, futurists ignore such sources at their peril in part because they complement and extend the mostly rationalist operations of professional forecasters and others. But, more important, they foreshadow the often-eclipsed possibility of a wider range of futures traditions based on other epistemologies and 'ways of knowing' (Sardar, 1996).

Literature

The futures field has a very rich literature. Familiarity with it provides access to the substance of the field. Obviously, this literature can be studied like any other. It can also be critiqued, explored and extended. One could not be a futurist without some knowledge of at least part of it. One could not train students to become professionals in the field without it. So teaching and research are heavily indebted to it.

There are two main branches. In my view the core of the professional futures literature resides primarily in about 200 key books by authors from around the world (Marien, 1996– ; Slaughter, 1997). The journals help bring a measure of order to this diverse, widely scattered area. They provide a forum for new ideas, a means of communication and foci for professional identity. When people enquire about the intellectual foundations of futures studies, I often suggest that they consider some back issues of *Futures, Futures Research Quarterly, Technological Forecasting and Social Change* or the Australian journal *21C*. No one could consider such publications without coming away with a clear impression of substance and quality. The concerns raised in these publications are of a different order to the familiar 'litany' of media-induced issues: they go right to the heart of the civilisational challenge facing our species.

The other branch of futures literature is that of speculative writing. This is seldom produced by futures writers *per se*; but the corpus of written (and pictured) speculative fiction enlarges the range of images, concepts and ideas about the future. Whereas much futures work is based on rationality, logic, extrapolation and scholarship, speculative fiction draws on different sources – primarily imagination, game-playing (such as 'what if…? games or alternative histories) and creativity. As such, and at its best, it expands or fills out the medium (and the long-term) future with a wide range of possibilities. I F Clarke, among others, has demonstrated how speculative literature has affected social, cultural and technological processes over a very long period. It remains a significant resource for anyone wishing to look beyond the immediate future (Clarke, 1979).

Organisations, networks and practitioners

There are a number of core organisations and networks in the futures field. Two are centrally placed. The US-based World Future Society (WFS) and the World Futures Studies Federation (WFSF) (Didsbury, 1996; Stevenson, 1996). Both are distributed widely across the globe. The Federation is a true international network with an activist, cultural, political tradition and a broadly facilitative outlook. The WFS is perhaps an order of magnitude larger, is more popular, conservative and corporatist in outlook. Together, these two organisations cater for the broad interests of most practising futurists through publications, projects and meetings. They both have local or national branches in a number of countries.

In addition, there are a number of more specialised organisations which
fall under the heading of 'institutions of foresight'. They include the Institute
for 21st Century Studies (Washington D.C), the Club of Rome Institute for
21st Century Studies (Italy), the Network on Responsibilities to Future Generations (Malta), the Secretariat for Futures Studies (Germany), the Institute
for Social Inventions (London) and the Robert Jungk Futures Library (Salzburg). Depending on definitions, there are probably 200 or more worldwide
clustered around the core of futures studies and supporting a wide range of
more focused activities. Many are small, under-funded, and even marginal.
Yet they tend to be pioneers, or 'leading-edge' organisations which act as seed
beds for innovation. While the wastage rate may be high, their collective
impact is significant. It is therefore essential for links to be built between them
and for research to be carried out into their effectiveness (Slaughter and
Garrett, 1995). Overlapping these near-core contexts are a diverse range of
futures-related organisations including NGOs, consultancies, government
bodies and other international groups often associated with the UNESCO or
the OECD. Some overlap with social movements occurs here (see below).

Futures practitioners create, refine and apply the formal knowledge which
finds its way into the futures literature. Estimates of the numbers of people
working full-time in futures studies vary according to definition, but there
are certainly enough to sustain the wide variety of networks and organisations
noted above. If it is language, concepts and metaphors that provide the
symbolic foundation of futures studies, it is the practitioners who supply the
human, intellectual and applied force. It is they who are energised by this
powerful idea of 'futures' and who use it to pursue numerous projects in the
present (Inayatullah, 1996b). Such outcomes of futures work affect social
processes in countless ways, but most importantly through projects, enabling
structures and social innovations.

Methodologies and tools

The core of applied futures work is methodology. Just as theories create new
structures from underlying concepts, so methodologies increase the intellectual and applied power of ideas and theories. Basic methodologies include:
environmental scanning, scenario analysis, cross-impact matrices, the Delphic
survey method, forecasting and strategic management, national and global
modelling and, last but not least, positive critique and analysis of discourse.
Some elements of the above are combined in useful sequences to create a
more sustained and penetrating methodology. They have been extensively
applied in educational contexts by Morrison (Ashley and Morrison, 1995).
Methodologies of this extended type are in wide use in some government
and corporate contexts, but unfortunately they remain uncommon in the
educational and social policy arenas.

Futures tools may be overlooked by professional futurists. They are simple versions of some of the methodologies, or practical applications drawn from them. They include time-lines, futures wheels, space/time grids, simple technology assessment, strategies for responding to fears and so on. Such tools have been developed and applied over a quarter of a century since the first courses in futures were taught in, or around, 1966. They are particularly useful in schools where futures concepts and tools provide a rich smorgasbord of options which can be combined and applied in many, many ways and at every level (Slaughter, 1995b, 1996b).

Social movements and innovations

The extent to which the peace, women's, environmental and other movements are part of the futures field is difficult to determine. However, I have always seen them as closely related in that they have attempted not merely to discuss and theorise about future societies, they have acted in the present to bring about change. Hence, they align with one of the core purposes of futures work. Social innovations are often overlooked, yet they are ubiquitous and easy to study. The process of creating them can be taught and learned (Albery, 1986).

General applications of the *Knowledge Base* series

The applications and uses of *The Knowledge Base of Futures Studies* are almost infinite, so I will briefly mention four as they apply to this series. First, those who are professionally involved in futures work will find the series a handy reference work, and a state-of-the-art summary of futures thinking. No one can be a specialist in every area of futures studies, so a resource such as this, along with the others mentioned here, will be very helpful to consultants, researchers, scholars and the like. Second, others who work in futures-related fields will find the series an authoritative source of insight, techniques, methods etc which they can draw upon whenever they require some aspect of futures understanding. In addition, the copious references provide access to the wider literature on theoretical and applied futures work. Third, the series provides a foundation for the creation of new courses, modules and units, both at school and tertiary levels. In schools it provides a resource for professional development, in-service work, leadership training etc. In colleges and universities units and courses up to and including the Masters level can be constructed in the light of the conceptual framework and content of these volumes. Finally, students taking a futures courses or courses in related areas will find access to the series invaluable, particularly if they are writing dissertations, researching particular areas or studying alone, perhaps through distance methods. A glossary of futures terms helps to make the sometimes esoteric language more accessible. CD-ROM and internet applications will make access to, and uses of, the series much more flexible. In time, detailed bibliographic searches will become possible.

General benefits of *The Knowledge Base*

These will become clearer as time goes by. But even at this early stage, five linked possibilities can be suggested. First, the series brings a new level of clarity to futures studies. By providing a number of paradigmatic examples of 'good work', questions of 'what futures studies is' and 'what it is about', are much easier to answer. Second, the series showcases some of the best contemporary work in the field and makes this available to a wide international audience. The fact that it provides a global overview assists this process. Third, the series provides a model of core concerns and foci for the field which can serve as a device for focussing professional applications (such as research and conferences) and for facilitating the further development of the field. For example, having such an explicit model will greatly clarify areas where futures thinking/ technique/methodology etc are lagging, as well as those where new and original work is needed.

Fourth, the series helps to make futures studies more visible. The books are finding their way into many libraries, they will appear on bibliographies, references to them will multiply on the Internet. Unknown numbers of future enquirers will track them down for a wide range of purposes. Finally, the series will help support the further legitimation of futures studies as a credible, substantive field of enquiry and action; in essence, it will help the field 'move on'. While there have been many, many fine futures books, and while the futures literature is one of the richest in existence, it can be difficult for newcomers to find their way around in such a broad, deep area (Bell, 1996; Kurian and Molitor, 1996). Hence the series provides an accessible 'map' which should make it easier for people to find and use futures material. As a result, the uptake of futures concepts, methods, tools etc should rise, and with this the field should gain greater acceptance.

How will *The Knowledge Base* continue to develop?

This series is not a frozen, monolithic, entity set in concrete for all time. It is part of a much wider process (Slaughter, 1996f). Over time some elements will become redundant, others will grow more central and new elements will be added. There are at least three ways that this process may occur: critique, innovation and new voices.

Critique

Critique is vital for a growing field such as futures studies. Without it futures studies could become a 'cosy club' of friends and associates. It is a necessary stage which, properly understood and used, leads on to further developments. Critique should not be seen as unwelcome, or as a necessary evil, but as part of the *modus operandi* of any intelligent approach to futures and part of its own internal provision for quality control.

For example, Bertrand de Jouvenel critiqued the use of futures studies by those who wanted to 'colonise' the future for their own interests, ie manipulate aspects of it for their own ends. This view remains pertinent decades later. Simon Nicholson, among others, also pointed out how children and young people were excluded from the futures discourse, leading to what he called a 'communication backlash', from which he sought to free them. Others have made the same point with regard to women and disadvantaged minorities. However, some of the most powerful critiques in recent years have been made on the basis of the overwhelmingly western character of most futures studies work and literature. Hence well-grounded critiques help the field to develop and evolve.

Innovation

Robert Jungk once told me how he regarded futures studies as essentially a 'seed bed' for social and methodological innovations. He certainly proved that with, for example, his grass roots approach to futures workshops and the establishment of a futures library in Salzburg, Austria (Jungk and Mullert 1987). Indeed, this is a basic pattern for successful futures work. Futurists are not, by and large, interested in describing problems, but in exploring solutions. Hence conceptual innovations are constantly springing up within a futures context. As some of these gather momentum they can be expected to create new foci for innovative work. For example, Hazel Henderson's critique of economics has led to proposals for better and more comprehensive economic indicators (Henderson, 1996).

Methodological innovations continue to arise at all levels. At the level of pop futurism, Faith Popcorn has distilled a simple trend-reading method which can usefully be employed to guide the marketing strategies of retail businesses. At the problem-oriented level, Michel Godet and his colleagues in France, and Peter Schwartz and his colleagues in the Global Business Network have pioneered new approaches to scenarios and strategic management. At a deeper level Duane Elgin's *Awakening Earth* has provided us with an elegant new paradigm for possible stages of future social development (Elgin, 1993). Finally, at the epistemological level, books such as Ken Wilber's *Sex, Ecology, Spirituality* and *A Brief History of Everything* give us new ways of looking at ourselves and our world (Wilber, 1995, 1996). Yet some of the most fruitful futures work to come lies in the emergence of new voices.

New voices

To some extent, new voices have already been heard from marginalised groups within western cultures: women, young people, the disadvantaged. They have also emerged from the growing 'techno-elite': those who thrive on the Internet, the World Wide Web and the sub-cultures of 'cyberspace'. Yet it is likely that still more original voices will emerge from non-western cultures. The global spread of English, of Western values and lifestyles, has cast a homogenising spell over the cultural diversity of the world. Yet, as Mahdi Elmandjra (1996) suggests, cultural diversity is one of the main keys to survival. It follows that new and substantive innovations in futures studies will tend to occur through the emergence of new thinkers, scholars, artists and others from non-western backgrounds. As more new and original voices emerge, each imbued with a particular cultural ethos, so the global futures 'conversation' will be enormously enriched. Indeed, the present knowledge base shows that this process is already under way.

Some educational implications

The bulk of mainstream educational work is profoundly compromised in part because, deeply buried in its *modus operandi*, there is a guiding operational assumption of a static world picture. Unlike companies and some government departments, educational systems make little use of up-to-date methods for understanding and responding to global change. They neither scan the macro environment nor have any methods for interpreting the significance of signals of change. In other words, schools and school systems tend to operate on the basis of a taken-for-granted, business-as-usual view. However, when examined, such a view lacks credibility. We know that we are living in a period of dramatic change and we also understand clearly some of the future changes in prospect. Hence we already know a great deal about the twenty-first century long before it is upon us. This is not prediction. It is the exercise of informed foresight. Webster's Dictionary defines foresight as: 1. an act or the power of foreseeing; prescience; 2. an act of looking forward; a view forward; and 3. provident care; prudence.

These are not qualities that are common in late industrial cultures. However they can be quite easily developed, once the point of so doing is understood and the means to do so are put in place (Slaughter, 1995a). Since our students are supposed to be preparing now to live in this future context, it is a matter of utmost urgency to provide them with all necessary means. We already know enough to be able to do this with confidence and professionalism: we know what major life challenges they will face, we know many of the new ethical dilemmas they will be presented with, we know a great deal about the global *problematique* which the industrial era has bequeathed them. We even know a lot about the resolutions to the *problematique*, and this knowledge can inform educational theory and practice at every level (Slaughter, 1994).

Therefore, educators of all persuasions should avoid the convenient fiction that a 'hands off' policy of laissez faire or 'drift' is educationally or socially responsible, for it is not. The human species is the most dominant force on the planet. It is responsible for what happens. This alone of all species can roam at will through past, present and future. People are therefore able consciously to explore the past, understand the present, design futures worth living in and work toward their implementation. The relevance of futures to education is simply that the former is congruent with the underlying purpose of the latter. That is, one cannot educate for the past (only from it), nor merely for the present (because times change). Any act of teaching and learning occurs primarily to achieve ends in the future: personal, professional, social. The whole educational enterprise is intended to contribute toward the further development of the society as a whole. These are true futures concerns (Beare and Slaughter, 1993).

In educational contexts, futures study can certainly be implemented in the form of a subject. This has happened in many places. For example, as this chapter is written, a new Board of Senior Secondary School Studies subject called Futures is under trial in Queensland, Australia (Board of Senior Secondary Studies, 1995). Much support exists there for this development. Significantly, it was the existence of *The Knowledge Base of Futures Studies* that helped convince the Board that it was appropriate to proceed with the new syllabus. Such developments will continue. However, as noted above, futures studies should primarily be seen as a cross-curricular dimension at every level (see Table 4.1).

Table 4.1   Futures Studies: Levels of implementation in education

---

Pre-school
An *emphasis* on teacher preparation, curriculum development

Primary
A *perspective* in teacher preparation and curriculum design: simple futures tools, exercises and concepts

Secondary
Disciplinary perspective and *subject*: introduction to knowledge base, futures discourse, methods, social applications

Tertiary
Scholarly discipline: advanced discourse, research, discipline-building, social implementation

---

Table 4.1 suggests that futures studies has a range of progressively more sophisticated applications as one moves from early childhood education right through to the post-graduate level. At the primary level it is both a focus in the education of teachers and the introduction of futures concepts and tools. At the secondary level more sophisticated concepts, methods and ideas can be introduced. Finally, at the tertiary level it is an interdisciplinary field of enquiry with an advanced discourse, a broad research capability and a globally-distributed body of practitioners capable of supporting many scholarly and applied activities. Because of this 'amplitude', ie the way it can be applied in many ways and at many levels, I have adopted a 'smorgasbord' approach which attempts to make the basic tools (ie concepts, methods and literature) widely available (Slaughter 1995b, 1996b, 1997; Hicks, 1994a, 1994b; Hicks and Holden, 1995).

In summary, the relevance of futures to education is simply that it provides the symbolic, intellectual and methodological resources to re-orient the whole enterprise toward desired, long-term ends (Slaughter 1996c; Hutchinson, 1996). Educators are already in the futures business, though not all of them realise it yet.

Outcomes of teaching futures studies

Futures studies would not be being taken up and applied with such enthusiasm unless it was of proven value. In my own observations at secondary and tertiary levels and through the associated futures literature, I have found clear evidence of at least five key outcomes of successful futures teaching.

First, a working familiarity with futures concepts, tools and methods provides the basis for a futures discourse. It is this which is missing from so many of the great institutions and social formations that profoundly condition social life: politics, economics and indeed much of education itself. Yet access to these resources makes it possible to be more creative, to think long term and to become responsive to the emerging futures context. These are significant gains and should be part of the stock-in-trade of all professions. Second, teaching futures enhances the capacity of people to engage in futures work of many kinds. Concerns that may have been unclear and poorly articulated are re-defined and become the source of innovations, projects and other creative responses. People with a futures background, or with close knowledge of it tend to be innovative and enterprising. They understand the risks, but they also understand that the key to solving many futures problems lies in the nature of the human response. I call this 'the empowerment principle'.

Third, futures teaching specifically encourages constructive and empowering attitudes. Young people are exposed to a great deal of negative material in popular culture, and more specifically in youth culture. Futures studies teachers can explore the significance of such material and lead students to understand its origins in the industrial worldview and explore the many routes and resources beyond it. Perhaps the most wide-reported outcome of futures courses are the constructive shifts in attitude that they engender (Hicks and Holden, 1995). Fourth, it follows from the above that futures teaching helps people to develop the skills of proactive citizenship and leadership. The latter is always leadership toward something, so people with futures skills and understandings are well equipped to engage in purposeful, productive action.

Finally, such teaching provides ways of grasping what is sometimes called 'the big picture'. This provides a clear overview of the processes of continuity and change, of challenge and response that structure our world (Slaughter, 1996d). From this vantage point the backward look becomes a diagnosis of where we have come from and why – in other words a critique of industrialised culture. The analysis of the present builds on this and suggests where our energy and attention are needed. Futures work defines, clarifies and enables the follow through in terms of decisions, policies, principles, practices, projects and the like. It creates the basis for moving away from fatalism, despair and dystopian futures to engagement, empowerment and real progress toward new stages of civilised life (Elgin, 1993; Henderson, 1996).

Conclusion

A danger in using the term 'knowledge base' is that one can be trapped into a metaphorical assumption that this 'base' is a solid and settled one. But this chapter suggests otherwise. The knowledge base in 1996 is not what it was in 1986, nor what it will be in 2006 or 2056. The present synthesis is only a starting point: the result of a collective process of searching, reflection, dialogue and winnowing. It is a provisional structure which emerges from a shared understanding of the current state of development of futures studies. Naturally, it is also limited by the present state of our ignorance. Yet it brings a new level of definition and clarity to futures studies which, as noted, will facilitate further theoretical and applied developments.

The justification for regarding futures studies as being of central value to education is that it brings two vital gifts that are all too rarely used and applied. The first is the gift of a futures perspective, with its advanced discourse, methods, literature etc. The other is the range of rich insights futures studies provides to the constitution of viable human futures. By carefully questioning what is frequently taken for granted (such as economic growth, 'value-free' technical innovation or the marketing imperative) it is possible to distinguish new personal, organisational and social options. This 'unfreezing' of the status quo has powerful implications. It provides us with new (or renewed) sources of freedom. It also permits a much wider variety of alternatives to be imagined and explored than are conceivable from within a dominant, catastrophe-prone paradigm. It is for such reasons that futures studies can contribute to a reinvigorated educational enterprise.

The central point is this. Human societies developed out of a context which is genuinely and radically different from the world picture before us at the end of the twentieth century. But they have not yet come to grips with the significance of the transformations in progress or those emerging clearly into view. Nowhere is this more clear than in education where the push of the past, and the pressures of short-term politics and Industrial-Era economics, far outweigh any attention given to the forward view. This oversight constitutes a major systemic defect in all education systems and one that should be urgently corrected. The continued attempt to move toward a challenging future on the basis of short-term thinking, drift, fatalism and denial cannot but end in disaster on an unprecedented scale. It is this insight, perhaps, as well as the positive aspirations of many people all over the world, that have stimulated the emergence of futures studies as an international concern. It now needs to become a much more widely accepted body of knowledge and be fully implemented in every education system, school, college and university throughout the world.

If *The Knowledge Base of Futures Studies* can help to support and sustain this process it will have served its purpose. It is, after all, a means towards this end, rather than an end in itself.

References

Albery, N (1986) *Social Invention Workshops*, London: Institute for Social Inventions.

Ashley, W and Morrison, J (1995) *Anticipatory Management*, Leesburg, VA: Issue Action Pubs.

Beare, H and Slaughter, R (1993) *Education for the Twenty-First Century*, London: Routledge.

Bell, W (1996) *The Foundations of Futures Studies: Human Science for a New Era*, vol. 1, New Brunswick, NJ: Transaction Pubs.

Board of Senior Secondary Studies (1995) *Futures: Draft Syllabus*, Brisbane: BSSS.

Clarke, I (1979) *The Pattern of Expectation 1644–2001*, London: Cape.

Didsbury, H (1996) 'The World Future Society' in Slaughter, R (ed.) *The Knowledge Base of Futures Studies*, vol. 2, Melbourne: Futures Study Centre/DDM Media.

Elgin, D (1993) *Awakening Earth*, New York: Morrow.

Elmandjra, M (1996) 'Cultural Diversity: Our Key to Survival in the Future', in Slaughter, R (ed.) *The Knowledge Base of Futures Studies*, vol. 3, Melbourne: Futures Study Centre/DDM Media Group.

Henderson, H (1996) *Building a Win-Win World: Life Beyond Economic Warfare*, San Francisco: Berrett-Koehler.

Hicks, D (1994a) *Educating for the Future: A Practical Classroom Guide*, Godalming: World Wide Fund for Nature UK.

Hicks, D (1994b) *Preparing for the Future: Notes and Queries for Concerned Educators*, London: Adamantine Press.

Hicks, D and Holden, C (1995) : *Visions of the Future: Why We Need to Teach for Tomorrow*, Stoke-on-Trent: Trentham Books.

Hutchinson, F (1996) *Educating Beyond Violent Futures*, London: Routledge.

Inayatullah, S (1996a) 'An Introduction to Futures Studies Epistemologies and Methods', in Slaughter, R (ed.) *The Knowledge Base of Futures Studies*, vol. 1, Melbourne: Futures Study Centre/DDM Media.

Judge, A (1993) 'Metaphors and the Language of Futures', *Futures*, 25(3): 275–288.

Jungk, R and Mullert, N (1987) *Futures Workshops*, London: Institute for Social Inventions.

Kurian, G and Molitor, G (1996) *Encyclopedia of the Future*, New York: Macmillan.

Marien, M (ed.) (1996–) *Future Survey*, annually, Washington DC: World Future Society.

Ogilvy, J (1996) 'Futures Studies and Normative Scenarios', *Futures Research Quarterly*, 8(2): 5–66.

Rogers, M and Tough, A (1992) 'What Happens When Students Face the Future?' *Futures Research Quarterly*, 8(4): 9–18.

Sardar, Z (1996) 'Futures Studies and Non-Western Cultures', in Slaughter, R (ed.) *The Knowledge Base of Futures Studies*, vol. 1, Melbourne: Futures Study Centre/DDM Media.

Slaughter, R (1991) 'Changing Images of Futures in the 20th Century', *Futures*, 23(5): 499–515.

Slaughter, R (1994) *From Fatalism to Foresight – Educating for the Early 21st Century*, Monograph 16, Melbourne: Australian Council for Educational Administration.

Slaughter, R (1995a) *The Foresight Principle: Cultural Recovery in the 21st Century*, London: Adamantine Press.

Slaughter, R (1995b) *Futures Tools and Techniques*, Melbourne: Futures Study Centre/DDM Media Group.

Slaughter, R (ed.) (1996a) *The Knowledge Base of Futures Studies*, Vol. 1: Foundations; Vol. 2: Organisations, Practices, Products; Vol. 3: Directions and Outlooks, Melbourne: Futures Study Centre/DDM Media.

Slaughter, R (1996b) *Futures Concepts and Powerful Ideas*, Melbourne: Futures Study Centre/DDM Media Group.

Slaughter, R (ed.) (1996c) *New Thinking for a New Millennium*, London: Routledge.

Slaughter, R (1996d) 'Why Schools Should be Scanning the Future and Using Futures Tools', *The Practicing Administrator*, 18(4): 42–43.

Slaughter, R (1996f) 'The Knowledge Base of Futures Studies as an Evolving Process', *Futures*, 28(9): 799–812.

Slaughter, R (1997) *The Annotated Futures Bibliography*, Melbourne: Futures Study Centre/DDM Media Group.

Slaughter, R and Garret, M (1995) 'An Agenda for Institutions of Foresight', *Futures*, 27(1): 91–95.

Stevenson, T (1996) 'The World Futures Studies Federation', in Slaughter, R (ed.) *The Knowledge Base of Futures Studies*, vol. 2, Melbourne: Futures Study Centre/DDM Media.

Wilber, K (1995) *Sex, Ecology, Spirituality: The Spirit of Evolution*, Boston: Shambhala.

Wilber, K (1996) *A Brief History of Everything*, Boston: Shambhala.

Further reading

Inayatullah, S (ed.) (1996b) 'What Futurists Think', special issue of *Futures*, 28: 6/7.
Slaughter, R (ed.) (1993) 'The Knowledge Base of Futures Studies', special issue, *Futures*, 25(3).
Slaughter, R (1996e) 'Futures Studies: From Individual to Social Capacity', *Futures*, 28(8): 751–762.

5. Listening to non-western perspectives

Sohail Inayatullah

Summary

Can the West listen to non-western futures is the central question asked in this chapter. The strength of the West has been its ability to maintain a hegemonic relationship while naturalising its own conquest of the future. Through asymmetrical definitional, temporal, spatial and economic relationships, the West has risen to unimaginable heights. However, the inability to listen to the Other, particularly the futures of others, is leading to civilisational flatland. Deep multiculturalism that creates a gaia of cultures focused on all of our futures generations is a far more important endeavour than technocratic forecasting. Offered as alternatives are visions and epistemologies of seeing and living in the future from Tantric, Hawaiian, Islamic and Aboriginal perspectives. But it is not simply more information about the future that will lead to global transformation but planetary trauma and transcendence.

Introduction

> Plant taro, if you want to plan for the next six months,
> Grow teak, if you want to plan for a decade,
> Teach your children, if you want to plan for the next hundred years.
>
> Ancient Hawaiian saying

> The present is the dreaming of the ancestors.
> The dreaming of our present becomes the waking state of our ancestors
> – dreaming is the reality of ancestors.
> The future is the balance between conscious and unconscious, history folding in on itself to become the sacred moment.
>
> Aboriginal view of the future

The shudra (unskilled worker) thinks of only the fleeting present.
The ksattriya (warrior) imagines myths and stories of the past.
The vipra (intellectual/priest) thinks of the future as the transcendental.
The vaeshyan (merchant) commodifies time and controls the shudra, warrior and vipra.
But the wise person lives the divine and thinks neither of past, present or future.

Tantric typology of social time

The cost of perfection

In contrast to these views of the future, the hegemonic – what is considered truth, non-contestable, natural – western view of the future sees time largely as linear, exponentially so. The future began with the taming of nature, with the move from our animal irrational past to our glorious present of science, technology and liberal democracy. The future is linear and it is, will be, perfect. Perfection will be attained once the invisible hand of the market allows buyers and sellers to meet on a level playing field. This will allow untold wealth to accumulate. Remembering Comte and Spencer, religion and philosophy will slowly disappear as the technocratic managers solve the world's problems, either through new technologies or better organisational skills.

There are deviations to this model such as communism and now evolutionary systems theory but in general the trend is secular, linear, progress based with the ultimate goal of heaven on earth. The dark side of this overarching paradigm is that the cost of perfection is the exploitation of nature, the Third World and the Other – the periphery. But the deeper cost is the creation of a civilisation that cannot listen to the Other. The only others the West can meet are simulacras of itself. Multiculturalism, for example, merely means equal opportunity, a collection of idiosyncratic individuals from other places, a woman here or there, some mention of the spiritual, or a trip to the Pacific islands. But the deeper ways of knowing of other civilisations, Islamic, Indic, Confucian and Pacific (and the diversities within these civilisations) are lost. Perfection on Earth can only be realised through the eradication of difference.

In linear western time, those ahead construct those behind as culturally inferior, their faces as ugly – certainly not worthy to walk the catwalks of fashion shows. In exponential western time, cybertime, not only are they not worthy, but they no longer exist. They are at best virtual. Indeed, the futures of the non-West are in virtual museums.

The cost of the rise of the West, of the splendour of clean streets, beautiful concert halls, of seamless travel on the Internet is the loss of the ability to understand the Other on its terms and thereby the loss of the West's own humanity.

The West has prospered precisely because it has been able to be diverse enough to appropriate the symbols of others without changing its essential world view. Through its *alter ego* – small scale and community – its own other, existing on its own periphery, it has managed to rise and rise while other civilisations have declined. For example, Johan Galtung argues that the West is expansion and contraction based (with Islam being in an inverse relationship to the West) (Galtung, Heiestad, Rudeng, 1979). If the West had been rigid, only linear and without a composite cosmology – ego and *alter ego* – it would have collapsed. Its success on becoming a world civilisation, indeed, in appropriating civilisation (and thus defining civilisation as solely itself) has been its ability to allow selectively the Other in without fundamental internal transformation. This coupled with military and technological might – and a willingness to use it when the natives become restless – has destined the West to rise.

However, this rise has not been seen as imperialistic, rather it has been naturalised, with the Other theorised as too disorganised (the Pacific), too religious (India), too transcendental (its own middle ages, which the West seeks to disown seeing the Middle Ages as a historical aberration instead of natural to it), too rigid (Confucian systems) or too close to nature (women and Africa).

Central to the rise of the West, in the rise of the world capitalist system, has been the transformation of perfection as a spiritual ideal (as wisdom), to perfection as an economic ideal (as technocratic engineering) – from perfection as a moral process, to perfection as an ideal wealthy society. The time of future thus has been transformed from astronomical/cosmic metaphors (as unknown and vast), agricultural metaphors (the circularity of the seasons), from religious metaphors (the future as heaven as opposed to the future as hell, the long fall from Grace), from transcendental metaphors (the future as eupsychia, the perfect self) to a site that can be colonised, that like death, can be tamed. With space already being colonised in the name of globalism by northern and eastern Asian transnationals, all that is left now is time – the past is either romanticised or considered inferior, the present victorious but with collapse (the fear of Fall) always in sight. What is left is future time to colonise, not to mention the studies of the future.

The West thus has maintained its hegemony by securing: i) definitional power, defining what is important, what is truth, good and beauty; ii) temporal power, naturalising measurable time; iii) spatial power, transforming sacred spaces into secular spaces, centralising power and exchange in megacities; iv) creating a centre-periphery based world economy, where wealth trickles upward from the poor to the rich and social control downward from the powerful to those aspiring for power. East Asian nations have been able to challenge the economic power of the West (and centralised themselves, only keeping the spiritual in ceremonial forms) but have made few inroads into temporal and definitional or epistemic power. Given the asymmetry of world relations, we ask is it possible for the West to listen to non-western perspectives of the future? More specifically, we ask can futures studies open up to non-western futures epistemologies and methodologies?

Futures studies

In the last fifty years or so, the future has increasingly become futurologised, defined, extrapolated, and owned. From thinkers such as Herman Kahn developing scenarios to consider nuclear war options to a vast array of national and global futures societies committed to investigating the twenty-first century, we can easily say that the future has arrived. With cyberspace becoming universal, the future as the victory of the West has arrived. As cultural historian William Irwin Thompson writes:

> Futurism is little more than a not very imaginative managerial description of the implications of the present. Futurology, like archaeology, is an academic way of closing down the past and the future so that they are no longer open to the imaginative expansion of the present. The space of the present is under the political control of the technocratic management; so it is very important that the thought police patrol the exits...we are closed in and protected from any narrative of future or past that is not propaganda for our present technological mentality (Thompson, 1985: 65–66).

What is left then is merely the task of working out the global details. Should the EU or the USA handle eastern Europe? Who to dispatch to Kashmir? Book now to holiday in Cuba or wait another decade? Forget Central Africa or let the South Africans handle it?

The dimension missing from the above quote by Thompson is that there can be dissenting futures. Not dissent in the leftist sense, which merely reinscribes materialistic civilisation and merely puts workers on top of others (with intellectuals interpreting the world for them and providing leadership), but in the deeper sense – dissent as unofficial knowledge, as truth outside the margins, as truth that cannot be easily comprehended within the gaze of modernity (Inayatullah, 1995). As Ashis Nandy writes:

> Explorations in the future, I passionately believe, have to be specifically statements of dissent from the existing ideas of normality, sanity and objectivity. As in the case of the visions of the great 'seers' of the past, such explorations have to flout or at least stretch the canons of conventionality to be worthwhile (Nandy, 1996: 637).

It is thus not only critiques of materialism and technocraticism that are necessary but the models of rationality that underpin these discourses. What is asked for is a new ordering of knowledge that disturbs, perhaps even makes strange current world views, nations, leaders and conventional understandings. But this reordering must go beyond postmodern chique. At heart is not metaphorical playfulness but issues of civilisational life and death, of trauma and transcendence. Cafe Latté postmodernism, while enthralling, manages to avoid the reality of deep human and nature suffering.

But where can these come from? We certainly should not expect studies of the future that have the ability to transform the present to emerge from those invested in current models of the future – neither fashionable universities, government policy institutes, nor even the world futures societies.

Real futures, and here not necessarily sustainable futures – that is to say echoing the need to be fashionably green – are perhaps those that cause cognitive dissonance, that do not make sense to the immediate – not because they are nonsensical but because we do not have the epistemological frames, the language, to comprehend them.

Futures might thus emerge not from the victor's modernity but from those who accept it as part of the many. One cannot be multicultural if one is in a dominant situation, if one has levels of power over others. It is he or she who exists on margins, who must learn different ways of knowing to survive, that can know differently (through trauma and transcendence) and can thus offer alternatives beyond postmodernity and the information superhighway.

Futures are more likely to come from the non-West, from the indigenous traditions: Tantra, the Aboriginal, the Hawaiian, the African and even the Muslim (not the Muslims that live in an oppositional relationship to the West, but Muslims who dissent from mullahist Islam and secular nation-statism). Others marginalised by the victory of world capitalism, women, the disabled and of course men individually critical of the system they structurally perpetuate, too, can offer alternatives. Futures studies has much to offer precisely because it is not an official bounded discipline – it neither offers riches to practitioners nor stability to believers. Universities are unable to departmentalise it and thus for the time being it can maintain its authenticity.

The 21st century and the time of the non-West

These alternative traditions must not only give new visions but must have solidarity with all those that have been the victims of history, that have lost their diversity. For these alternative traditions, among other disruptions – such as contesting the neutral nature of the Olympics (which now, for example, allows ballroom dancing but does not consider legitimate numerous local Nigerian or Pakistani sports (Obijiofor, 1996)), is the issue of the demarcation of the future, particularly the myth-like significance of the approaching millennium.

In the name of the twenty-first century, the future has arrived. In the name of the twenty-first century, debate has ended except for grand issues such as in Australia as to whether there should be a republic or monarchy. The altern-ative of creating a council of Aboriginal elders to become the guiding wisdom behind the parliamentary system is, for example, not discussible. In the name of the twenty-first century, information has been victorious over knowledge and wisdom, over the visceral reality of the spiritual. In the name of the twenty-first century, the futures has become the future.

But as the world prepares for millennium parties, not everyone will be celebrating. For many parts of the world, the beginning of the third millennium is a non-event. Instead of the twenty-first century, Confucianists as well as island nations talk of future generations, a concept located more in the idea of family, in children's children and ancestors. Chinese history, following the stars, has no definable beginning nor end, just a succession of virtuous and evil leaders and of the rise and fall of the Tao (Watson, 1958). After all, 1998 for many Chinese will be remembered as the Year of the Tiger and not necessarily as 2000 minus two.

For Muslims, instead of the twenty-first century, the key event was not the death of the Christian-Muslim prophet Jesus but the flight from Mecca to Medina (the *hegira*) of Muhammed. For Indians, the demarcations are also less important – time is cosmic, the blink of Brahma is millions of years. Time for Indians of many traditions is also cyclical, with humanity now leaving the worst of the iron age, and moving to *satya yuga* or *ananda yuga*, the golden era or the era of bliss.

The twenty-first century is thus not merely an unproblematic objective timing of the real. It is an arbitrary cut-off point but one which reinscribes the body of the West on the souls of the non-West. Describing the world in these terms, immediately cuts off the diversity of ways with which others time the world. No number of policy reports, millennium studies or twenty-first-century studies are likely to produce or create anything novel if they begin with that framework. The texture needed to touch the heart and passions of most of the world's communities will not come from such superficial metaphors. While certainly the allure of Disneyland is always there – of the perfectly social-controlled society with no illness, no fear, of a rich society – there might be more to life than that, as the existence of non-western cosmology testifies.

For much of the non-West, it is the spiritual that is the base of the triangle of needs, not the top. Seeing the world in terms of deep unchanging truth is where one begins the journey. The good society is one which allows individuals to pursue the *satya* (truth for the benevolence of all). Creating a rich society with open markets and then expecting spiritual values to emerge from that, while possible, is unlikely. While individuals might drop out, chosing unconventional futures, the civilisation as a whole will fulfil its social grammar until it becomes so exhausted that only a Spenglarian decline is possible.

Of course, we must not simplify the non-West as well. Certainly postcolonial Asia and Africa have done little to convince the planet that they can be great societies, essentially spiritual but equally strong on gender cooperation, ecology, dynamic economic growth and social distribution.

Still while the non-West has partly entered scientific and business time, it has not lost its historical ecological diversity of time and culture. Even under the veneer of accepting western notions of death, that is, death must be battled through technology, the non-West retains varied cultures of death. It sees death as the meaning of life, to be mystically transcended (the *Upanishads* for example), as resignation (karma, Allah's will) and as joining one's ancestors. But for the West, fear of death is the defining impulse. The twenty-first century perhaps is a boast, a call out to the universe, we have made it! 2000 years and still going strong – Nazism defeated, Fascism defeated, Communism defeated and now only Islam, uppity East Asians and nature left (Africa will take care of itself and South America has already joined). Still there are 1000 years for that project. Most likely we will only need 100, after all, all roads lead to the melting pot.

The question remains: how then can the West listen to the non-West when its temporal frame does not allow other timings? How can it listen when death, the future of the future, is defined as an external battle (and not as an inner dance or as link to the ancestors and nature)? How can the West listen when it defines itself as the site of not only the true and the good, but the beautiful as well? How can the West listen when it pledges global democracy but only when it suits its strategic interest (Algeria where opposition victories were not supported and Serbia where they were) and only in the context of the nation-state, not true world one-person, one-vote democracy?

Sarkar as epistemic transformer

But looking from Calcutta, as macrohistorian P R Sarkar did, or in a taro patch in old Hawaii, one knows that the strong shall fall and the others shall rise – history is cyclical. Hubris and karma cannot be evaded – one's excellence is one's fatal flaw. The inability to listen to non-western futures is the flaw which will bring the behemoth down.

Sarkar's work is important to us for many reasons. Not only did he redefine rationality, seeing it in spiritual and social justice terms, but he placed the subtleness of inner love at the centre of his cosmology. But while love was the base, he did not neglect the harsh realities of the world system. While certainly his work can be seen as part of the larger global project of creating a strong civil society to counter the waves of corporatist globalism, his move-ments are unique in that while most social movements are western, highly participatory, goal oriented, short-term and single-issue based, Sarkar offers a genuine non-western future (Sarkar, 1988, 1992; Inayatullah, 1988). His movements are:

- **Third-World oriented**, hoping to be the carriers of the oppressed yet also seeing the oppressors in humanist terms.

- **Tantric**, focused on reinvigorating mystical culture and not necessarily on immediate efficiency.
- **Comprehensive**, working on many issues (and not just on the issue of the day) from women's rights and workers' rights to the prevention of cruelty to animals and plants.
- **Very, very long-term oriented**, hundreds of years, that is, structures and processes that cannot fulfil their goals for generations ahead.
- **Committed to leadership creation** and not just organisational development, thus avoiding the bureaucratic tendency.
- **Trans-state oriented**, not solely concerned with nation-states and ego-power, but acknowledging that there are four conventional types of power – worker, warrior, intellectual, economic – and the challenge is to develop processes that create a fifth that can balance these forces.

Underneath these projects has been Sarkar's effort of creating and using a new language (*samaj, prama, microvita, samadhi, sadhana*) and new metaphors (Shiva dancing between life and death) to help be the vehicles of the good society he envisioned (Inayatullah and Fitzgerald, 1997). But it was not perfection Sarkar was after. Influenced by Indian thought, he understood that there are deep evolutionary structures that cannot be changed, but certainly the periods of exploitation can be minimised. Perfection for Sarkar was only possible for individuals in the spiritual inner sphere, timeless time.

For Sarkar, history is the cyclical rotation of worker, warrior, intellectual and merchant eras. At the end of the merchant era, society through evolution or revolution enters the next worker era. But power quickly centralises to the military. Each era brings in innovation but then overstays, thus brutally oppressing others. The challenge is to develop spiritual and moral leadership that can maintain a dynamism. Contrast this view of the dynamics of social history to Marx (progressive steps ending in a communist society) or Comte/ Spencer (elimination of the past ending in a positive/scientific state).

Sarkar's perspectives, as well as the many other non-western perspectives, hope to create not just a global civil society as with normal Western social movements but a gaia of cultures. Civil society is a response to particular dynamics of European history with its division between religion and church, state and society. For Muslims the dream is a global *ummah* (a world community or *ohana* or family). For the Maori, the appropriate word is the creation of a *whanau*. It means a vast universal family that connects the stars, the moon, the earth, the sky and all life forms that reside therein, the world of animation and inanimation, the worlds of the living and the dead. It is not *universum nullium* but knowing and intelligent, linked by genealogy for the indigenous, or for Sarkar, by consciousness. While Sarkar is perhaps among the most important of non-western visionary thinkers and activists, he is certainly not alone in his articulation of a different universal family.

Future generations thinking

Perhaps the most important recent critique of futures studies and its domination by western epistemology has come from writers and activists working
in the futures generations paradigms. This perspective is far more concerned
with the family, in all its variations – instead of forecasting decades ahead or
centuries ahead – preferring to see time as future generations' time: the future
of children and their children and their children. Future generations thinking
has almost a natural affinity with the non-West. Children (even as children
are often abused, made rightless, exploited), nature (even as the rural pack
into the city creating catastrophic and polluted megalopolises) and family
(even as this means often authoritarian relations between elder and younger,
where senility among the old is confused for cryptic wisdom) still retain
mythic if not actual significance (Inayatullah, 1996). It is certainly easier for
non-western cosmologies to think of the future in these terms.

Taken together, future generations thinking can be characterised by the
following:

- **Commitment to the family** (going far beyond the nuclear family to the
  extended family to the planetary) as a basic, non-negotiable unit of
  analysis.
- **Expansion** of the family, of the notion of being, to include all **sentient
  beings** – plants and animals.
- **Intergenerational** approach, an expanded temporal definition of the
  family that goes seven generations ahead and before, ancestors and
  futurecestors (in futures studies, Elise Boulding's idea of an extended
  present).
- **Values-based** primarily, drawing from indigenous as well as Confucian
  and Buddhist thought, far less concerned with technical issues of forecasting and more concerned with creating a future that rebalances the
  fundamental forces of the universe: 'Man', Nature and God(s).
- **Repeatability**, a view that the future is the past, that ensuring the survival
  of future generations is in fact keeping alive the dreaming of ancestors
  (as in Aboriginal dream-time epistemology) (Wildman, 1997). The future
  and the past curve into each other with the distinction between dreaming
  and reality blurred such that past and future 'snake' back into each other.
  In this sense, while in futures studies the future cannot be remembered,
  in future generations thinking, the future can be remembered!
- **Spiritual and collective** view of individual choice and rationality in that
  choice is contoured by both the *aina* (land, as in the Hawaiian tradition)
  and the heavens. Rationality is not individual or instrumental based,
  but collectively linked to *samaj* (Sarkar's Tantric Indian idea of a society/
  family moving together towards a spiritually balanced society) and it is
  given by God. Rationality is not merely logic but inclusive of other ways

of knowing such as intuition, the voices of the spirits/ancestors, and the altered fields of awareness generated by interaction with the wildness of nature. Rationality is thus tied both metaphorically speaking to the heart, to others and to nature – ultimately rationality is about understanding that which is eternal.

- **Pedagogy** that has a strong focus on **enhancing wisdom**, on moving beyond the litany approach of problem identification/solving to deeper issues of conscience, of discerning what is lasting and what is temporary (civilisation foresight).

- **Sustainability or reproducibility**, ensuring that current practices do not rob material and cultural resources from future generations. Future generations research is an implicit critique of the idea of progress. There are natural limits which humans must not transgress.

- **Global focus**, a view that while future generations thinking is civilisation based its message is universal, searching for similarities among the many differences between peoples, creating a family of civilisations.

- **Teaching and learning** must be authentically multicivilisational bringing the perspectives of time, space, self, gods of many cultures, all the time searching for the anchors, the points of unity, within the sea of differences. Education thus must help move beyond postmodernity, searching for a global ethics. Ultimately teaching must be inclusive, going beyond egoism, nationalism, racism and other 'isms', that is, committed to the needs and rights of all present and future generations.

The future generations perspective thus has very clear value positions drawn from its varied cultural backgrounds. In terms of the division of futures studies into predictive, interpretive and critical frameworks, it is perfectly placed in the interpretive (Inayatullah, 1996). While the predictive perspective believes that the universe can be known and thus through appropriate methods we can know the future, the goal in the interpretive is to recover a future obscured by the materialist and instrumental rationality of modernity – by the desire and urge for more, quicker, and bigger. The challenge is to recover a balance, a *prama*, an ontological equilibrium that was given to man by nature and 'God'. The critical view of futures, here as an important contribution of European thinking, is that the task is not to offer particular predictions or search for deeper meanings, but to call into question the assumptions of any truth claims, asking who wins and loses, who gets his or her world view naturalised, and who gets his or her world view marginalised or ridiculed.

The difference in future generations as in most non-West futures perspectives, is that it has a clear non-negotiable core while futures studies has many core perspectives (Slaughter, 1996). But non-west perspectives including future generations thinking is not transparent, it is problematic. It is far too easy to critique the West for the ills of the planet and then quickly articulate a historical non-western view as the obvious solution to the world's ills. For one, this forgets that all non-western views have been westernised. Moreover, non-western views eliminated by the onslaught of modernity existed in historical contexts – they cannot be simply idealised and raised as the solution to the future. The non-West should be seen in its entire humanity, as good and evil, as sensate and ideational, and not as romantic reified archetypes that are the sole carriers of wisdom, of humanity's salvation. As Zia Sardar argues, the non-West as the spiritual Other of the West, is as much as a projection as the non-West as the historically inferior (Sardar, 1993). As Edward Said has shown, what Europe denied to itself, it projected outwards onto the non-West making it the site of the exotic and the erotic (Said, 1979). Thus, just because a culture is suppressed, it does not follow that everything from that culture that is recovered is good for all. For example, many practices of indigenous cultures are not post-rational practices that are inclusive of many ways of knowing, rather they are simplistic pre-rational practices that confuse cause and effect, which confuse levels of reality. The logical mistake of misplaced concretism is often made, leading some to argue that angels can be tapped so that humans can travel to Mars. Metaphors are appropriate at particular levels but not at every level. Story telling is not the best way to do everything, it is one way.

But the larger question often not asked in future generations thinking is whose future generations are to be honoured and protected? (In the West it is *prima facie* assumed this means the West). In the plea to save the world for future generations, issues of the rights of the Other are often forgotten. Each civilisation wants to ensure that its members survive and thrive, expanding to all corners of the world, that the graves of their ancestors are forever enshrined. But often it is at the expense of other civilisations that these claims are made.

Finally, while rich in temporal epistemology, non-western thought, particularly future generations thinking, is weak at disjunctive thought, at the dramatic changes to history that genetic, virtual, nano, and psychic technologies promise. While the future might be the past, it also might be the 'unknown country', a transformative world which cannot be imagined with any of our current or past categories.

Defining futures and futures studies

Future generations is certainly not a dominant perspective in futures studies. Thus, the future and futures studies have in many cases come to mean not only the definition of the future from the West, but the definition of what is futures studies of the same West. Two important referencing sources show evidence of this. The recently released *Encyclopedia of the Future* specifically goes out of the way to exclude non-western references, since these books will be difficult for Americans to find (Kurian and Molitor, 1996). Referencing, however, is not merely a sign of a bookstore but symbolic of what is important.

The knowledge categories of the classification scheme, in addition, only make sense to the western world view. That is to say, the choice of what is covered, Italy and India but not Pakistan or Malaysia; cross-impact analysis and Delphi but not the I-ching; Hinduism but not Tantra. Of the top 100 futurists listed, there are barely a handful that come from the non-West (actually just one, Yoneji Masuda). There is Teilhard de Chardin but not Allama Iqbal. Does this mean that there are no non-western futurists? Hardly. Of the classical thinkers included there is no mention of Ibn Khaldun, Al-Baruni, Ssu-Ma Chien or Confucius. Crucial terms such as karma, *dharma* (one's inner nature and duty), *prana* (the breath of life that regulates health), *prama* (dynamic balance, the central principle to a society that is in equipoise between the spiritual and the material, the inner and the outer, struggle and acceptance), *mana* (the life force), *aina* (land but not real estate), *ilm* (knowledge) that are central to understanding the epistemologies and methods of other cultures, are missing. While the *Encyclopedia* is a good initial effort, its defining power is disastrous for those wishing for a future different from the present.

Of course, one cannot cover everything, but the omission is predictable since as Robert Bundy has declared, in reference to his own book on the future, 'Western civilisation is the obvious focus of all that is said. But the drama engaged in is global, there is an important underlying assumption in all the essays that what happens to the West will significantly shape what the world will be like in the second millennia' (Bundy, 1976: 5)

The contribution by Edward Tenner (1998) to the *Britannica 1998 Yearbook of Science and the Future* – while a solid review of futures studies – makes the same mistake equating thinking of the future with seminal works from the European enlightenment. This linear history of the future again limits the richness of the future. It assumes the future is merely about what technologies will be present. This is certainly one layer of the thinking about the future, but as important are the social and political factors and the paradigms and worldviews which provide the base for the technological. Nor does Tenner present examples of utopian thinking in other cultures. However Tenner does rightly understand that futures studies will rise and fall not because of its predictions, but because it offers a richer debate on questions concerning the good society and self. He writes: 'At its best it [futures studies] offers not a crystal ball, but a kaleidoscope' (Tenner, 1998).

But this of course is not a critique of the authors but a pointing out that these images are unavailable to them: fish certainly did not 'discover' water and the West will not find the future even as it predicts it. For example, the one scenario that American World War II planners did not plan for was attacks by Japanese Kamikaze pilots (Tenner, 1998). However, anyone remotely sensitive to East Asian culture would understand the different meanings given to the giving of life for a higher cause – self-immolation and other activities occupy less controversial space in large parts of the non-West.

This does not mean to say that futures studies in the recent years have not benefited from the rigour developed in the United States, that is through military forecasting, scenario development and a host of new methods, it does mean to say that the methods are based on flat methodologies. They are not layered. They are unable to negotiate with the grand differences that is the world today.

For example, the conventional way of thinking about the future is through the use of four models. The first image is that of the dice. It represents randomness but misses the role of the transcendental. The second is the river leading to a fork. It represents choice but misses the role of the group in making decisions. The third image represents the ocean. It is unbounded but misses the role of history and deep social structures. The fourth image is that of a river rapid dotted with dangerous rocks. It represents the need for information and rapid decision making but it does not provide for guidance from others: leadership, family, or God. Less tied to western images, other useful metaphors (from the Philippines, India, Malaysia and Fiji, respectively) include the coconut tree (hard work to gain rewards); the coconut (hard on the outside but soft on the inside); the onion (layers of reality with the truth invisible); snakes and ladders game (life's ups and downs are based on chance, the capitalist vision); being a passenger in a car where the driver is blind (sense of helplessness).

Knowledge thus must be deconstructed and seen critically, that is to say, as particularly ordered, as political, as opaque (Inayatullah, 1992). It must become authentically multicultural creating a global conversation of theory development, of story telling; stories of pain and suffering, of truth and lies, of past and futures.

To conclude: while there are certainly structural features that are similar to West and non-West (that is, all have phases in history dominated by merchants and intellectuals; all have periods where the sensate has dominated and where the ideational has dominated; all have exploited others, especially women and nature; all have levels of structural violence; all have historically operated from instrumental rationality even as they claim to be the carriers of moral civilisation), still there are deep differences. Can these differences be negotiated? Can we collectively create a multicivilisational world, where we do not have to ask if the non-West can be listened to? On the positive side, there are certainly macrohistorical forces that are transforming modernity (and postmodernity) and creating the possibility for a more integrated civilisation (Galtung and Inayatullah, 1997). At subtle deeper levels, the *mana* is active in creating a bifurcation to new futures. At the same time, many still believe that by simply having more information, social transformation is possible. This is not the case. Transformation comes from trauma and transcendence.

References

Bundy, R (ed.) (1976) *Images of the Future*, Buffalo NY: Prometheus.

Galtung, J, Heiestad, T and Rudeng, E (1979) 'On the Last 2500 Years in Western History: And Some Remarks on the Coming 500', *The New Cambridge Modern History*, vol 13. Cambridge: Cambridge University Press.

Galtung, J and Inayatullah, S (1997) *Macrohistory and Macrohistorians*, New York: Praeger.

Inayatullah, S (1988) 'Sarkar's Spiritual Dialectics', *Futures*, 20(1): 54–65.

Inayatullah, S (1992) 'Deconstructing and Reconstructing the Future', *Futures*, 22(2): 115–41.

Inayatullah, S (1995) 'Beyond the Postmodern: Any Futures Possible?' *Periodica Islamica*, 5(1): 2–3.

Inayatullah, S (1996) 'Future Generations Studies: A Comparative Approach', *Future Generations Journal*, No. 20: 4–7.

Inayatullah, S and Fitzgerald, J (eds) (1997), *Transcending Boundaries: P.R. Sarkar's Theories of Individual and Social Transformation*, Singapore: AM Publications.

Kurian G T and Molitor, T T eds (1996), *Encyclopedia of the Future*, 2 vols. New York: Macmillan Library Reference.

Nandy, A, (1996) 'Bearing Witness to the Future', *Futures*, 28(6/7): 636–9.

Obijiofor, L and Inayatullah, S (1996) 'The Olympics and Cultural Hegemony', *Global Times: The World Alternative Journal*, 5(7): 19–22.

Said, E (1979), *Orientalism*, New York: Vintage Books.

Sardar, Z (1993) 'Colonising the Future: the 'Other' Dimension in Futures Studies', *Futures*, 25(2): 179–187.

Sarkar, P R (1988) *PROUT in a Nutshell*, vols. 1–25, Calcutta: AM Publications.

Sarkar, P R (1992) *Proutist Economics: Discourses on Economic Liberation*, Calcutta: AM Publications.

Slaughter, R (ed.) (1996) *The Knowledge Base of Futures Studies*, 3 vols, Melbourne: DDM Media Group.

Tenner, E (1998) 'Futures Research', *Encyclopedia Britannica Yearbook of Science and the Future* (forthcoming).

Thompson, W I (1985) *Pacific Shift*, San Francisco: Sierra Club.

Watson, B (1958) *Ssu-Ma Chien: Grand Historian of China*, New York: Columbia University Press.

Wildman, P (1997) 'Dreamtime Myth: History as Future', *New Renaissance*, 7(1): 16–20.

6. The needs of future generations

Allen Tough

Summary

By empathically considering the needs of future generations, educators can make their curricula and teaching much more relevant. Far from being merely an abstract concept, the term 'future generations' refers to actual people who someday will be just as alive and busy as we are. If future generations could send us a friendly message, they would probably ask us to emphasize these six societal and educational priorities: develop and preserve significant knowledge on the 'big questions'; conduct futures-relevant research; provide futures-relevant education for all ages; foster learning about the 'big questions'; promote an attitude of deep caring; foster a widespread sense of meaning and purpose. In addition, future generations would like to tell us how to learn more about their perspective, how to feel hopeful and empowered, how to experience deep bonding with them, and how to help them.

Introduction

When educators consider the needs of future generations, their curricula and teaching become much more relevant. Future generations are not alive at the moment. But they will eventually be alive sometime in our future – as busy with their hopes and projects as we are with ours. They, too, will work, learn, love, and dream.

'Future generations' is not just some abstract concept in some philosopher's imagination. Future generations are real, or at least they will be someday. At any given time in the future, real people will actually exist and be leading busy lives on earth and perhaps elsewhere in the galaxy, not just in someone's imagination. They will be flesh and blood, mind and heart, just as we are.

Perhaps as you read this, you say to yourself, 'But future generations are not real; they have not even been conceived or born yet!' It is true that they do not exist as people at the moment you read this, but they will be real someday. They will be just as real as we are. Just as real as you were exactly one year before your birth, even though no one alive on that day knew very much about you and your characteristics. Just as real as the people in your

69

family tree and the people in history books used to be. Future generations are not like unicorns, the ancient Greek gods and goddesses, characters in a movie or novel, or other fantasies that have never existed in the real world and never will.

Yes, it is true that they will live several years later in human history than we do. Yes, many things about human culture and the planet will change over those years. But if we met future generations face-to-face, we would still recognize them immediately as human. We might smile with amusement at their clothing and their hair-styles and how they speak. But we would feel a kinship with them. We would say to ourselves, 'Well, I suppose I would have looked and sounded just as weird to people who lived a few decades before I did. So of course these people of the future look and sound a little strange to me. Still, they are people.' We would see that they do just the same sorts of things that people have always done: talk, smile, laugh, gesture, frown, cry, love, wonder, work, build, invent, walk, sing, dance, hug, kiss, learn, teach, reflect, help, explore, play. Just as we do, they will have their favorite places, fascinating conversations, meaningful rituals, significant institutions and creative arts. Their emotions will basically be the same as ours – they will experience pain, frustration, fear, doubt, love, joy, sadness, excitement.

The role-play

Students can benefit greatly from role-playing people alive in the future. This exercise is quite easy for students: they enter and stay in their role with ease and enthusiasm. I have used this exercise in my own education courses over several years. In 1993, at my suggestion, instructors in thirteen universities and high schools in nine countries led their students through this exercise. These instructors then sent me the messages composed by the students (in the year 2030) 'to send back to the people of the 1990s.' My initial report on their messages appeared in the December 1993 issue of *Futures*. The nine countries were Australia, Canada, Japan, Korea, New Zealand, Nigeria, Pakistan, Thailand and the USA.

Since then I have been further developing and enlarging the message that future generations might send back to us if they were able to speak to our era. In this chapter you can read an enlarged and revised version of the message that future generations might send to us if they could. It is based not only on the responses from the students' role-playing, but also on the more usual academic procedures such as searching the literature, networking, conferences, thinking and reflection. After carefully considering the entire array of ideas that arose from all of these sources, I selected and integrated the key points into a single cohesive message. An integrated message is far more useful than an archival attempt to reproduce all of the individual student responses, the class responses and the relevant portions of the literature. Since the message is a blended synthesis of ideas from many sources, it is not feasible to credit each point in the message to one particular source.

Now, for the rest of this chapter, let's listen to the neglected voices of future generations. Paying attention to their words can be a very powerful and educative experience. From the viewpoint of future generations, what societal priorities are especially important? Six of these are centrally relevant in education and will be presented here in the words of future generations. (Three other priorities – peace and security, the environment, population growth and governance, should also be high on the agenda, but there is not room to include them here.)

If future generations could speak to us, here is what they might say to us about six priority areas: i) significant knowledge; ii) futures-relevant research; iii) futures-relevant education; iv) learning about the 'big questions'; v) caring; vi) meaning and purpose. We switch at this point to the words of future generations themselves.

A message from future generations

'Cordial greetings from future generations! We are the people of the future – all the generations that will be alive after yours. Thank you for listening to our perspective. Our voice is rarely heard in your television and radio broadcasts; our views rarely appear in your newspapers and magazines. We cannot speak during your policy making and planning, we cannot lobby your law makers, we cannot carry placards in front of your legislative and parliament buildings, and we cannot vote in your elections. That is why we are so glad you are willing to listen to our neglected voice.'

Significant knowledge

'Speaking on behalf of future generations, we want you to know how much we value humanity's accumulated body of knowledge and understanding. It is one of our most treasured possessions. Your era's contribution to that knowledge is one of the most valuable gifts that you can pass on to us. Please continue your efforts to improve your knowledge, ideas, insights, and wisdom, especially in directions that emphasize depth and synthesis. In order to maximize your contribution, it is important to keep your thinking open-minded yet skeptical, bold yet disciplined, fresh yet profound, wide ranging yet penetrating.

In particular, we hope you will double your efforts to understand humanity's broad significant contexts, the biggest questions of all. Our place and significance in the universe, for instance, and our sources of meaning and purpose. Other intelligence and civilizations that have developed in our galaxy, and how our future and theirs might be linked. Better ways of

exploring whether God, spirits, Satan, psychic and spiritual phenomena, life
after death and reincarnation actually exist in the external world or are better
understood as inner-human experiences. Feasible paths for achieving a positive human future.

In addition to enlarging the storehouse of significant knowledge, it is
important to protect it from dictatorships and other potential catastrophes.
Remember that various armies, rulers and governments throughout history
have tried to suppress and destroy existing knowledge. This could happen
again. Please develop steps to ensure that the core of human culture, knowledge, literature, music and art will survive any war and any repressive world
wide regime, whether military, political or religious.'

Futures-relevant research

'In order to achieve a satisfactory future, you need to rapidly expand your
efforts to develop futures-oriented knowledge, ideas, insights, understanding,
visions and wisdom. You need to know far more about world problems, social
change, potential futures, the effectiveness of various possible paths, individual change, the personal foundations of caring about future generations and
several other future-relevant topics. This futures-oriented inquiry can include
not only research and development projects, but also creative visioning,
speculative brainstorming, disciplined thinking, synthesis, conceptual frameworks, theory-building and wide-ranging dialogue.

Move toward a body of concepts, ideas and knowledge that is profound,
powerful and well organized. Carefully examine your conceptual frameworks
and paradigms. Organize your existing knowledge base more rigorously;
don't be conceptually sloppy or lazy. Critique and build on the ideas and
frameworks of others, instead of operating in intellectual isolation. Try to
attract people with especially penetrating minds and thoughtful approaches,
then generously support their intellectual work.

The amount of effort going into creating knowledge that is profoundly
significant to the long-term future is only about one third of what it should
be. The gap between the optimum effort and your current level is foolish and
poignant. Your aim should be to multiply your futures-oriented inquiry
threefold over the next few years. The long-term benefits will far outweigh
the costs.

For success, you need to increase your knowledge of world problems and
social change much faster than the problems themselves increase. At present,
the problems are outstripping your knowledge of how to deal with them.
You are going to have to run much faster than you do now simply to catch
up with all the major problems. Then you may find that the negative forces
are running faster and faster, becoming more and more challenging. To
develop the knowledge to outrun all these tendencies for civilization to
deteriorate, you will need to increase your efforts even further. You certainly

have the potential to win the race, but not by coasting along at your present level of futures-oriented research.

You are to be congratulated on the useful ideas and insights that you have already produced in fields devoted to studying the future, the environment, policy, risk, future generations and sustainability. At the same time it is important to realize that many more ideas and insights remain to be discovered. We are particularly pleased, of course, that several of your organizations and projects are specifically devoted to future generations. Although getting through the next forty years safely and successfully should be the central goal in your futures-relevant research, a small portion of your inquiry should look even further ahead to the endless procession of future generations.'

Futures-relevant education

'Learning and teaching about the future provide an essential foundation for building a better world. You cannot achieve a positive future without far-reaching learning and changes by individuals around the world. These individuals include all of you, not just political leaders, government officials, policy experts or business leaders. You no doubt recall the prescient words of one of your early futurists, H G Wells: "Human history becomes more and more a race between education and catastrophe". You can successfully navigate through the next few decades only if a large proportion of the world's population understands global problems and potential futures, cares about future generations, accepts the need for change and takes a co-operative and constructive approach to dealing with hard choices. Once enough people care about future generations, implementing the needed actions will become much easier.

Any path to a positive future will require deep changes in individual perspectives, values, and behaviour. From early childhood to late adulthood, learning opportunities should be widespread. In every city on earth, at least some schools, colleges, adult education programs and libraries should provide a wide array of methods for people to learn about the future prospects of their civilization and their region. In addition to various educational programs and institutions, these opportunities can include libraries, discussion groups, informal education, workshops, support groups, television, printed materials, electronic sources and hardware, and self-planned learning projects. This range of learning opportunities should help people of all ages understand global issues, think sceptically and critically when appropriate, treasure all life on earth, feel concern for other people, grasp the importance of caring about us future generations, grasp our perspective, feel committed to necessary changes, tolerate diverse cultures and views, cooperate for the common good and pursue meaningful non-material goals.

Educational institutions should provide courses in futures studies, with some emphasis on the perspective of future generations, using approaches that affect the head, heart, soul and hands of people of all ages. Your education about the future could be greatly enhanced if you develop a better knowledge base about potential futures, conduct research on the processes of learning and teaching about the future, and experiment with innovative and profound approaches to such learning and teaching.

In addition, we urge you to consider a worldwide campaign to increase caring for future generations. This campaign, aimed at the general public as well as students, could use various approaches, including:

- clear, moving, powerful books and booklets written for the general public and for students;
- superb television programs and films that enable you to 'experience' future generations, and to grasp the fact that we too are actual living people (in your future) rather than some abstract concept;
- classroom exercises, such as speaking with the voice of future people, of wild species, or of beings on other planets;
- writing a pledge to future generations;
- a large membership organization for the general public, possibly combined with inspirational support groups;
- transformative experiences that combine music, poetry, powerful prose, nature, rituals, inspirational meetings and the voices of children and youth.

All of your educational efforts could promote: a widespread desire to cooperate and contribute; a caring, nurturing attitude toward other people and the environment; widespread kindness, goodwill, compassion, and altruism; fewer people who intentionally take far more from the world than they contribute; more people eager to contribute to their world and to future generations; much more hopefulness than cynicism in the world; a dramatic reduction in hostility, hatred, revenge and destructiveness; instead, a pervasive attitude of co-operating and contributing.'

Learning about the 'big questions'

'Your society could do much more to foster widespread individual learning about the most important questions of all. You should encourage and help each individual to learn the accumulated knowledge on these questions, and also to think through their own best answers. Obviously they will be more successful in their quest if your society has fostered their ability to think clearly, flexibly, creatively and sceptically about difficult and controversial questions. Here are some of the 'big questions' that thoughtful individuals face:

- the origins of the universe;
- cosmic evolution and the ultimate destination of the universe;
- our place in the universe;
- our relationship with other intelligent beings and civilizations in our galaxy;

- the origin, history, and long-term future of humankind and human culture;
- our appropriate relationship with the planet and its diverse forms of life;
- core values;
- finding a path to a positive human future;
- how each individual can contribute to achieving that positive future.'

Caring

'In this priority, we urge your society to focus plenty of attention and support on the deeper and softer aspects of individual lives. We refer specifically to widespread caring based on deep connectedness to all people, to the planet and its diverse forms of life, and to future generations,

Your society should do much more to help people feel this sort of deep bonding or connectedness. Explore the usefulness of music, hymns, songs, poetry, prose, laser light shows, art, hiking, cathedrals, inspirational services, children, mountains, observation towers, zoos, nature reserves and scenic beauty for this purpose. As more and more people experience a deep connectedness, they will care strongly about humanity, future generations and the planet, and will act on that deep love and caring. They will eagerly want to make a positive difference to humanity and the planet. They will be happy to experience a bond with something ageless, something transcendent, something much larger than their own life.

Creating inspirational groups dedicated to future generations could be particularly useful. The people in these groups would feel bonded together by their deep caring for future generations and by their efforts to build a better world. Various methods could be used to inspire and strengthen each member's sense of connectedness to humanity and its positive future. Inspirational gatherings, oral readings, silent reflection, discussion, and songs of gratitude and joy could all play a part. Members could share their feelings about the long-term future, discuss our message to you, reflect on the implications of recent events, and discuss their most significant unanswered questions. Members could also discuss their current efforts to contribute, including their strategies, obstacles, triumphs and failures. Many people want to make a positive difference to the world, but lack a sympathetic and inspirational support group. Such groups could be built on love and reverence for human civilization and other societies in our galaxy, awe concerning the mysteries of the universe and commitment to service on behalf of future generations. By supporting various efforts to build a positive long-term future, these groups could provide people with an inspiring and transcendent purpose in life.

These inspirational groups have the potential to develop into a powerful world-wide network. This inspirational movement might occur within

established religions, and remain a vital part of these religions for many generations. Alternatively, the inspirational groups might eventually form a new
religion of service to the cosmos, a global religion centred on humanity's
positive future within a grand universe. As a third possibility, the inspirational
movement might occur within a new secular organization that resembles a
religion but that is silent on the nature and role of a deity, leaving people free
to follow their own beliefs on that matter.'

Meaning and purpose

'Our final priority is this: your society should focus much more attention and
support on the individual's desire for a sense of meaning and purpose in life.
A sense of meaning and purpose can easily pervade a society in which people
share a sense of connectedness with the cosmos, with its diverse life and with
the continuous procession of generations. These foundations are quite real,
of course; there is no need to adopt false beliefs or unrealistic expectations in
order to feel a deep sense of meaning and purpose.

As your support for this societal priority increases, you will find that more
and more lives are suffused with insight, wisdom, love, caring, altruism,
meaning and joy instead of ignorance, ill will, meaninglessness and unhap-
piness. Some fears and pain and sorrow will remain, but will be more focused
on future generations than on oneself. Over time, in fact, the distinction
between oneself and future generations will blur. As the depth and strength
of the connectedness increases, the boundaries between self and humanity
become softer and less important. The dominant perception is a sense of
oneness. People feel like affirming "I am at one with future generations: they
provide a shining beacon in my life".'

Reflections on these priorities

'The changes that need to be made by individuals, schools, universities,
organizations, governments and society are startlingly large, deep and far
reaching. But the alternative is for your grandchildren and the other members
of their generation to spend much of their adult life in a social and physical
environment that is bleak and nasty. The profound changes are necessary in
order to avoid such a negative outcome. They provide the best path to a
positive future.

Perhaps you are feeling that our message to you is unrealistic and too
ambitious. You wonder whether you can actually manage to implement the
priorities that we are recommending. We believe that you can. If you focus
your attention and resources on these crucial priorities, you have a good
chance of success. The costs and obstacles are daunting, but you are quite
capable of overcoming them if you are strongly motivated. Do not be too
quick to dismiss our recommendations as farfetched or impossible. Human
history provides other examples of dramatic paradigm shifts. The priorities

can be achieved if enough people around the world become strongly motivated to do so. We have intentionally omitted dozens of other worthy priorities
from the list in order to make it more feasible, because no one can achieve all
of their hopes and dreams, no matter how worthy.

We are grateful for the inner changes and outer efforts that are already
under way. But we worry that you will choose the tempting path that lies
right in front of you, dissipating your efforts on alluring goals and priorities
that will have little influence on long-term flourishing, squandering your time
and energy not only on consumption, luxury, competition, quarrels, and
violence, but also on the faddish projects and causes of the moment. Think of
the pain and suffering that you will cause us, the bleak lives and barren planet,
the harsh restrictions, the lost potential, the sense of malaise and futility. We
cry when we think of what might come to pass. Perhaps you too will feel
some tears as you think about what your era's lack of futures-oriented caring
and effort could inflict on us.

Thank you very much for listening to our views so thoughtfully. We are
cautiously hopeful that more and more of you will grasp our perspective,
and that your society will treat our needs as equal in importance to your
own. If enough people join the loosely knit, world-wide effort to build
a positive future, then a profound change in direction becomes possible.
Working together, you can shift to a path which improves your prospects
for a peaceful, caring, flourishing future. You can pass on to us a store
of deeply relevant knowledge, a flourishing and peaceful culture, and a
vibrantly healthy planet. You can steer human history toward a shining positive future.'

How to learn more about us

'If you want to learn more about our perspective, there are several avenues
that you can follow.

Experiential learning through imaging exercises is one excellent avenue.
Such an exercise can help you 'know' us in a more direct and immediate way
than simply reading about us. In a quiet room, you can fantasize that you are
one of us. Either just generally be someone in the future or choose a particular
identity, such as a shopkeeper in Budapest or Lima living 70 years in the
future. What does this person need and want from you? If she could send a
message back to you and your era, what would she want to say to you? You
might want to turn on a tape recorder before you begin this exercise, so that
you can play back your experience and thoughts later on if you wish.

Reading is another excellent avenue for learning more about us. To help
you choose particularly useful books, we provide a list of suggestions for
you at the end of our message.

Joining a highly relevant organization or talking with other informed people
is another good avenue. As you select from among the many voices and

groups competing for your attention and money, ask yourself which one truly looks far enough ahead to understand our perspective. Which one takes our needs seriously and pursues a path that will actually turn out to be helpful to us? From such people and groups you can learn a lot.

Other avenues, too, can be useful for learning about us. Occasionally a television program, radio program, or magazine article focuses on the long-term future of the planet and humanity. In-depth travel to various parts of the world can produce insights, understanding and caring. Occasionally some other opportunity for learning will arise unexpectedly, if you are on the lookout.

At times you may find that learning about us will challenge your intellect to the limit, especially as you wrestle with just how your era can actually succeed in giving us equal opportunity. Some world problems are difficult to grasp in all their complexity, despite all that is written about their causes and potential solutions. As you learn about world problems and potential futures, you may find at times that you have to learn certain knowledge that is paradoxical, counter-intuitive, highly conceptual or theoretical, technically or psychologically sophisticated, or deeply challenging to your current beliefs and world view.'

How to feel hopeful and empowered

'As you learn more about our perspective, you may find yourself experiencing a wide range of positive and negative emotions. On the positive side, you may feel eager, excited, challenged, exhilarated, hopeful, joyful, enthusiastic, empowered and committed.

On the negative side, especially during the early or middle stages, you may experience fear, grief, horror, revulsion, frustration, anger, discouragement, hopelessness, despair, even depression. Sometimes you may want to run away from the whole appalling subject and retreat into disbelief, denial, defensiveness, cynicism, apathy and paralysis. You may also find that your sense of meaning and purpose in the universe and in your own life is shaken at times. Learning what you are doing to us can produce an earthquake deep within you.

All of these emotional reactions are quite normal and natural as people face the wide array of potential long-term futures, ranging from some dreadfully bleak possibilities through to some glorious utopias. Our advice to you is simply to get in touch with your feelings fairly often during your learning process. Express them face-to-face to a supportive companion, or express them to yourself aloud or in writing. As you stay in touch with those feelings and continue expressing them with full force, they will gradually lose their power over you. There is no need to become stuck in negative emotions or hopelessness. Fully face the negative sides of the world and its potential futures, of course, but do not become paralyzed by feeling that the problems are too big, the forces against change are too entrenched, your actions are too slight or the odds are too unfavourable.

After you have allowed yourself to experience and work through the negative emotions, you will probably find yourself ready to move on to feeling more hopeful and empowered. This transition can be aided by noting various positive options and projects and organizations. You might ask people about them, read about a few, or even visit one or two. It also helps to develop a clear vision of a positive future. You might do an imaging exercise in which you imagine yourself walking around in a future world without weapons or without hunger, for instance. You may also develop a strong sense of mission in life, a clear goal toward which you will devote your efforts.'

How to experience deep bonding with us

'As we have just said, learning more about us will help you make a difference to our world and well being. Working through your negative emotions and becoming more hopeful and empowered will also increase your usefulness.

But there is another level, too, a level that you may experience as even deeper than learning and emotions. This is the level of deep bonding or connectedness with us. This level may feel to you like a deep spiritual level or even a mystical experience, a melting of the boundaries between you and the earth, between you and humanity, between you and future generations. Such an experience can produce a very deep seamless caring for the planet and future generations.

Music is probably the most common path to this experience. You may find that symphonies, electronic music, songs and hymns about the future, triumphant celebrations or rock music is best for you. Or one particular piece may produce tears of joy and beauty one day, and quite a different sort of music may have the same effect a year later.

You may also find that immersing yourself in nature can give you the experience of feeling deeply bonded with us. Interacting with young children may do this; reading science fiction or other future-oriented fiction, watching movies and television stories that occur in the future.'

How to help us

'So many tasks need to be done in order to build a better world for those of us who live in your future! If you are trying to choose your particular contributions, there is certainly no scarcity of possibilities.

You could begin by thinking about some of the obvious ones. Promote the long-term perspective in a letter to a political leader or newspaper. Try to reduce your impact on the environment. Discuss world problems with the people around you. Speak up for your own views. Join a group that shares your concerns. Offer to speak to a group or class. You could also contribute money to organizations and projects that are particularly beneficial to future generations. Put yourself in our shoes and ask what projects we would be most likely to recommend to you. Be on the lookout for worthy projects that have not yet caught the public's attention.

Volunteer activities provide another path for helping us. Many organizations and projects need volunteer researchers, writers, office workers and executive officers. Another useful option is to initiate some project on your own to meet one of our needs. Reflect on the unique ways in which you might contribute through writing, public speaking, teaching, mass media, art, music, politics, your present work, or a new job.

Your present work may be an excellent opportunity to contribute to humanity's future, especially if you emphasize the long-term perspective. Another possibility is to choose a new field or job with excellent scope for making a long-lasting contribution. In the extraordinary times in which you live, the choice of one's career or other work becomes a moral choice. Morality requires each individual to put service (building a better society) ahead of personal gains.

In choosing your own path for helping us, think carefully about its likely long-term contribution. In what ways will it help future generations? Think too about your own inner qualities. What are your particular interests and strengths? Which tasks and challenges will arouse your energy and passion? What are your most cherished hopes for making a contribution, your half-hidden visions, your impossible dream? What does your deep inner self say to you? We hope you will get in touch with your inner dream – your altruistic, caring, ethical desire to make a positive difference to the world – and let yourself take the risk of striving for that dream.

At times you may feel powerless, doubtful that one person can make any difference. One way of breaking out of this helpless feeling is to think of yourself as part of a team of people with a similar goal, even though this group may be scattered geographically. Working together, a few courageous and dedicated people can sometimes begin a process that eventually results in saving a wilderness area, ending a senseless war, initiating a new field of study, or inventing a fresh social solution to a problem. Another way to feel empowered rather than paralyzed is to think of the many aspects of our heritage that were contributed by individuals. Examples of individual contributions include the ancient artwork in such places as Beijing's Forbidden City and Pompeii, the plays of Shakespeare, the Gettysburg address and hundreds of poems, symphonies, and books.

Here are twelve books that are especially useful for understanding our perspective – the views of future generations. Many other books and papers are useful too, of course, but we hope that suggesting twelve specific books will help you proceed with your learning about our views.'

Further reading

Agius, E and Busuttil, S (eds) (1994) *What Future for Future Generations?*, Valletta: Foundation for International Studies, University of Malta.

Bell, W (1996) *Foundations of Futures Studies* (2 vols), New Brunswick (USA) and London (UK): Transaction Publishers.

Care, N (1987) *On Sharing Fate*, Philadelphia: Temple University Press.

Care, N (1991) *Caring for the Earth: A Strategy for Sustainable Living*, Gland, Switzerland: IUCN, UNEP, WWF.

Chaisson, E (1987) *The Life Era: Cosmic Selection and Conscious Evolution*, New York: Atlantic Monthly Press.

Tae-Chang, K and Dator, J (eds) (1994) *Creating a New History for Future Generations*, Kyoto: Institute for the Integrated Study of Future Generations, Future Generations Alliance Foundation.

Meadows, D, Meadows, D and Randers, J (1992) *Beyond the Limits: Confronting Global Collapse; Envisioning a Sustainable Future*, Post Mills, Vermont: Chelsea Green Publishing Company.

Partridge, E (ed.) (1981) *Responsibilities to Future Generations: Environmental Ethics*, Buffalo: Prometheus Books.

Schell, J (1982) *The Fate of the Earth*, New York: Alfred A Knopf, Inc.

Slaughter, R (1994) *Thinking About Future Generations*, Kyoto: Institute for the Integrated Study of Future Generations, Future Generations Alliance Foundation.

Slaughter, R (ed.) (1996) *New Thinking for a New Millennium*, London and New York: Routledge.

Tough, A (1991) *Crucial Questions About the Future*, Lanham, Maryland: University Press of America; London: Adamantine Press (1995).

7. Learning from feminist futures

Ivana Milojevic

Summary

This chapter surveys both the changing bases of feminism and future visions by women. Taking an eclectic approach, feminism is described as a spiral learning form, influencing debates on postmodernity, social sciences and development. The implications on education of feminist perspectives of history, politics and knowledge are articulated. Described next are the bases for most feminists futures – a stronger communal life, more fluid gender roles and a breakdown of the public/private division. This article concludes with the futures of gender. Three scenarios are offered: unisex androgny; female-male polarity and multiple gender diversity.

Feminism as a social movement

Thinking about the future, for most people, generally brings either hopes or fears, sometimes both. We fear that our lives will become worse, that humanity will find itself in turmoil and chaos, that we and our children will face major natural and social disasters. When we try to listen to the more optimistic side of ourselves, we often imagine a peaceful and sustainable future, where there will be continuing personal, social, cultural and technological growth. Fears bring apathy, depression and withdrawal from society. Fear makes us desperate. It makes us attempt to obtain as much stability and security in our personal spaces as possible. On the other hand, hopes bring action, a sense of togetherness and mutuality and make people bind, connect and associate. People connect on the grounds of their mutual beliefs and goals, in order to bring about the future they want or to avoid the one that they fear.

If an idea gathers a critical mass of people who organize to implement that idea, we consider it a social movement. Feminism is such a movement. It is a community of similarly thinking people who want to change society and bring justice for most of its members. Feminists are following the footsteps of other social movements and progressive theories, which are committed to making a fundamental shift away from a world based on power hierarchies (Nielson, 1990).

These movements are often labeled as 'left' or 'liberating'. The feminist movement became particularly massive only in the twentieth century but it has had a long history marked by constant individual and group effort to achieve the liberation of women and create a world based on equity between sexes. In its effort to abolish one more injustice in the march towards a more meaningful and fulfilling world, feminism became not only a practice but a strong political theory, providing a basis for understanding and, more importantly, changing every area of our lives. The feminist movement developed mostly as a reaction to the oppressive conditions women face in most known societies and it is actively trying to prevent a future which would for women just bring 'more of the same'.

Trend analysis

One does not need to be an expert to realize that wherever we look, whether into our past or our present, our local community or around the world, one fact remains almost universal: society always treats its women worse than its men. For thousands of years, women have been treated as property, as minors, or as lunatics, without having either rights or will of their own. They were either killed for being raped or forced to marry their rapist or, if 'lucky' enough to avoid these possibilities, they lost all the benefits, privileges and respect within their community. Being born as a female, in some communities and in some periods of time, results in being awarded a death penalty. Women have worked most of the day and often through the night for the benefit of the others, but the community did not give them their rights in return. Excluded from politics, religion and education, women were kept in the private sphere, their position depending on the good will of their male family relatives.

Today, many things have changed but, unfortunately, if current trends continue women will continue to suffer from violence, poverty, malnutrition, legal and economic disadvantages well into the twenty-first century. We will continue to face more difficulties than men in many areas of life, mostly because our societies are still controlled by men and male values. The crucial spheres for 'controlling' the future, politics, as well as most institutional and personal decision making processes, will remain out of women's reach. According to the UN's future projections, women's position will improve a bit, but even in the year 2200, we will be far from reaching gender equality (Kurian and Molitor, 1996). According to these projections, the percentage of world income received by women will increase from the current 10 percent to 20 percent in the year 2025, and then further to 40 percent in the year 2200. The percentage of world property owned by women will increase from the 'huge' one percent it is today, to three percent in the year 2025, and 20 percent in the year 2200. In the year 2025, women will still outnumber men as poor (60%), illiterate (55%), refugees (70%) and sick (57%) (Kurian and Molitor,

1996: 400). We can still hope to outlive men, as female life expectancy continues to be higher than male, but this happens not because of our social and 'human' efforts to help the disadvantaged, but in spite of them.

But let us look at some more optimistic prognoses. The American optimism of Aburdene and Naisbitt leads to them forecasting a much better future for women. In their *Megatrends for Women* they conclude that we will reach a 'partnership society', fifty years from now, wherein 'that ideal is realized in the developed world and actualizing in much of the developing world' (Aburdene and Naisbitt, 1992: 326). Before then, not only will there be a woman president in the USA (at the latest in ten years time), but women will change the world in such way that the 'New World Order is also a 'New Order of Women" (Aburdene and Naisbitt, 1992: 322). In this new world, professional women will become role models for young women (instead of media stars and fashion models), and in general women will continue to assume leadership roles, transforming business, politics, health, religion and spirituality. The Goddess is awakened and the balance has finally tipped in women's favor, say the authors. While Aburdene and Naisbitt are certainly right in their claim that women's position in most developed societies has significantly improved, more realistic prognoses, especially those who have in mind the world as a whole, would be extremely cautious in predicting such radical changes in a relatively short time frame (50 years).

Knowledge

As previously stated, feminists are changing the fabrics of our societies, especially in the western world and in the industrially developed countries. The most important change, however, is occurring in the area of knowledge, as epistemic changes do not just mirror changes within society, but more importantly, the other way around, they help bring about new resolutions, policies and actions. Theories and ideas often reflect the social context in which they are born: feminism became a mass movement once democratization of education and the need and the possibility for women to get jobs and work outside the private sphere took place. Feminism came about as it was becoming more and more obvious that the treatment of women is unjust, that women's position in society is politically created and not a necessity arising from the laws of nature, and that the world in which men had all the answers is archaic and belongs to the past.

Once educated women, influenced by the feminist movement, started to rethink the dominant theoretical discourse within the different scientific disciplines they worked in, feminist theory started to develop and a paradigm shift occurred. It became apparent that what was once considered 'universal' and 'objective' science was, in fact, knowledge faulted with prejudice and bias, twisted in a way to accommodate male perspectives and sustain their dominant position in society.

Both society and knowledge have been extremely unbalanced when it comes to gender. While in society women are to be 'seen and not heard', in the knowledge area women barely have existed at all. 'World history' has been, for example, a history of white European men, coming from the perspective of a ruling economic elite. As we can see, not only women, but most ethnic groups and lower classes have been excluded as well.

The exclusion of women took several forms which within feminist theory are usually recognized as: direct or structural invisibility and pseudo-inclusion. While women have been included in written texts, they were either marginalized, considered unimportant unless situated within relationships with men, or everything in relation to women was explained by one single variable – nature.

Women were viewed as unchanging essence independent of time, place and social context. For centuries, women were only considered in relation to their sexuality and role in procreation. Not only was women's sphere cons-idered less part of a 'culture' and more part of the natural world, nature itself was there for one and only reason: for superior man to conquer it. Simone de Beauvoir, among others, started to challenge this view by proclaiming that one is not born as a woman but becomes a woman in a process of socialization. The way we see nature has also recently started to change by accentuating sustainability and cooperation rather than utilisation and exploitation, together with seeing all of the natural world as intrinsically interconnected (Eisler, 1987, 1997).

The importance of feminist research and knowledge is its potential for 'double vision', meaning that women, because of their disadvantaged position in the society have the ability to incorporate a more complete view of social reality, including both the dominant perspective and their own. Feminists argue that a female-centered theoretical perspective can, in fact, be more objective, because 'less is assumed and more is examined'. Feminist research and the knowledge gathered from feminist perspectives is metaphorically described as a 'turn of a spiral, not the flip of a coin' (Thiele, 1986: 41).

In recent years, feminist researchers have became aware of their own limit-ations, especially of some over generalizations and impositions of Western feminist positions and values on the women from other parts of the world. Feminist research is moving further towards interdisciplinary and transdisc-iplinary approaches and is becoming more diverse and more civilizationally and culturally sensitive. This will probably enable the spiral to keep going towards achieving more objective knowledge for future generations.

Implications for education

Feminist perspectives are increasingly becoming part of a dominant knowl-edge paradigm, mostly in the academies of the West but also through dissenting movements in the Third World (Milojevic, 1996). Mainstream education is, however, lagging behind these huge and important changes and is, in many ways, preparing future generations for a world long gone. Radical changes are necessary in order to transform what is often seen as elitist, exclusive, and education remote from the reality of people's lives, especially from the reality of most women's lives. Feminists see education as an extremely important social institution, if not the most important one, and believe that, as such, it should receive more attention in society.

Feminist fiction writers have often put education, together with parenting, at the centre of social life and everyday activities. Since current education is, within feminism, seen as a major vehicle for the reproduction of gender inequality, it is not surprising that in both feminist fiction and feminist theory educational institutions and processes are radically transformed. The most often criticized aspects of current education are:

- existence of 'hidden curricula', ie different treatment for boys and girls in such a way that existing gender inequalities are maintained;
- fragmentation of knowledge into discrete specializations where everything has to be classified, measured, categorized and presented in terms of higher and lower achievements ;
- lack of topics of interest for women (eg childbirth, housework, sexual abuse, family relationships, peaceful management of our species through history, daily life and work);
- bias against women in most textbooks;
- concentration on 'big' names and 'big' events, as well as on teachings about the conquest and domination of the others (including nature).

In order to transcend these limitations, feminists have developed 'women's studies' (some of those courses later becoming 'gender studies'), characterized mainly by multidisciplinary approaches, close relationships between theory and practice, participatory research, equal power relationships between subject and object of study and between the teacher and student themselves. The main focus is, of course, on gender. Everything, including existing data and 'facts', is re-examined and reinterpreted from a new perspective. This new perspective, however, did not remain closed in a women's studies 'ghetto', but has started to spread through most scientific fields. Both natural and social sciences have seen their assumptions and theories being questioned and consequently so has futures studies.

Futures studies

Although people have always had thoughts about the future, future studies is a relatively new field. Since most futurists gained their academic training from other disciplines, futures studies is firmly connected with other contemporary social sciences. Their dominant theories and methodologies and the general framework of knowledge is derived from them. Therefore, it is to be expected that futures studies are burdened with a male-centred bias. For millennia men have been in charge of controlling the future, so it is not surprising that they are seen as creators of everything that is 'new', radically different and progressive. Just one look at futures studies can make us conclude that 'the only relevant futurists in the world are a handful of old, white, American men' (Dator, 1994: 40). There is also a general assumption in most societies that thinking about futures is not part of women's domain. In general, women traditionally are perceived as conservers, while men are seen as those who move forward. This is well illustrated in widely accepted symbolic language, particularly in the presentation of women and men. Looking at the male symbol we notice that its main characteristic is a pointed arrow, aiming towards the upright direction, which is also how we draw trends and movements toward the future on diagrams. On the other hand, the female symbol is represented with the circle and cross firmly rooted to the ground. If the common theme for both symbols, the circle, represents the head, women essence is in the body, men's in transcending and activating the mind. The further story goes like this: women need to have a nest, stability and security, while men want adventure and excitement. This dichotomy often leads to women being conservative in their political and religious beliefs, while men bring about political changes and preach radically new prophecies. Elise Boulding explains the lack of women authors in her futures library by the fact that the 'creative imagining work of women does not easily fit into the mold of the professional futurist' and that 'women are more likely to encounter it in science fiction than in the 'serious' work of spelling our futures' (Boulding, 1976: 780). For Boulding, this is nothing else than 'nonsense', because 'every woman with responsibility for a household is a practicing futurist' (Boulding, 1976: 781). This, of course, is true not just for women but for every human being as this ability to think about the future is one of the most distinctive characteristics of our species.

But there is one very important fact which divides women and men when it comes to futures. The futures that most women envision are quite different from the future envisioned by, if not all men, at least from the future envisioned by their most powerful members. Frankly, it would be difficult to imagine societies run by women where the main effort would be in the 'destroying-lives industry', or societies in which women would consider themselves so utterly above nature, that the destruction of the natural world would not be connected with the destruction of our species and its future generations. Somehow this connection is lost on many men. Men's appropriation of technology and its development from a male perspective has led to a general belief that all our problems can be resolved by technology. Our most pronounced imaging of futures is still obsessed with technological forecasting as seen, for example, in much science fiction. Men's 'colonization of the future' brings into our mind images like production of babies in factories; men driving spacemobiles and spaceships with women in the passenger's seat; destruction of Gaia's tissue and its replacement with man-made ones; an artificial ozone layer; artificial limbs, organs and even artificial brains; war games with ever more powerful weapons and ever more powerful enemies; conquest of the old and new (aliens, cyborgs, mutants or androgynes); further degradation of women through cyber-exploitation as in cyber-pornography; and, creation of submissive women's roles in virtual reality.

Feminists have been actively criticizing futures images derived from the dominant sexual ideology. They also struggle to imagine new ways of organizing our world on a basis of gender equity, a world which would be a better place for women, men and nature.

Feminist utopias

So, what kind of world and future societies do feminists want to bring about? First it important to note that while trend analysis by focusing on probable futures helps women realize which futures they do or do not want for themselves, many feminist authors prefer utopian thinking. Utopian thinking not only critiques the present but also gives women a greater sense of futures possibility and thus optimism.

Second, while feminist writers claim to speak 'in the name of the women', there is sometimes a gap between these two groups – one politically involved and committed for the empowerment of all women and the other, much bigger group of 'ordinary' women, who think within the traditional knowledge paradigm and/or have priorities among personal and political goals somewhere else. These two groups however, do tend to learn from each other: large groups of women, in developed and Third World countries, are increasingly accepting some feminist ideas and goals, while feminists in many ways have changed some of their initial positions, in order to accommodate previously neglected views of some groups of women.

Third, since there are many billion women, the answer to the question 'what are women's visions of futures' would be obviously a difficult if not impossible task. Feminism, on the other hand, has a more explicit agenda, and can be followed, for example, from feminist science fiction writings, as well as those of feminist futurists or from feminist political theory and practice. Here, we inquire into some ideas developed within feminist fiction and feminist theory, coming mostly from the Euro-North American world.

Questioning current gender relationships is common in feminist fiction, for example by imagining a world in which there is a more balanced distribution of power among genders. Some feminist fiction writers imagine a world dominated by women, or societies in which there is a strict division by gender (women and men living separately) and further contemplate the consequences of such social organization. Others describe a world in which women's sub-ordination is taken to the extreme, societies in which women have hardly any rights in male-dominated societies, where they can be 'kept' for the sole purpose of procreation or satisfaction of men's sexual desires. These dystopias represent social commentary rather than vision, and are definitely not desir-able futures for women.

Apart from questioning gender relationships, there are some other common themes in most feminist novels: future societies tend to live in 'peace' with nature and have some sort of sustainable growth; they are generally less violent than present ones; families seldom take a nuclear form but are more extended (often including relatives and friends); communal life is highly valued; societies are rarely totalitarian; oppressive and omnipotent govern-mental and bureaucratic control is usually absent, while imagined societies tend to be either 'anarchical' or communally managed.

The division of private and public sphere is also commonly challenged by, for example, patterning society after the family, more fluid social roles or higher involvement and greater intersection between those two areas. The present low status of women's work is often criticized and some traditionally 'feminine' occupations are revalued and re-examined. In most feminist utop-ias, education and motherhood are, therefore, extremely respected, sometimes being the main purpose for the existence of the utopian society in question. The majority of feminist fiction writers explore not only the way humans act and behave, but also concentrate on the meanings attached to such actions and how people feel about them.

Of course, as there are many different positions in feminism, there are many different images of desirable future societies. Indeed, feminists have recently moved away from universalist utopian visions based on essentialist theories of human nature. In the era where gender, for the first time in human history, has become transgressional and fluid, what is 'woman' and 'man' is increas-ingly seen as being socially constructed. The consequence is that gender relationships can be imagined in many different and radically new ways. While most traditional utopias tried to imagine future societies which would be organized in accordance with human nature, often locking women into their 'natural' roles and functions, contemporary feminist utopianism is questioning not only dominant sexual ideology but gender itself.

The other main difference between fiction written from feminist perspect-ives and those based on traditional notions about gender, is that women are not pushed into ghettos and examined as one of many topics. In feminist writings women are everywhere, portrayed as 'speakers, knowers, and bearers of the fable' (Bartkowski, 1989: 38).

The most important aspect of feminist fiction is the message that alternatives to patriarchy do exist and 'that these alternatives can be as 'real' as our reality' (Halbert, 1994: 29). It provides a variety of options instead of having only one, universal and rigid solution for the most important social institutions and activities, such as education, marriage, parenting, health, defence, government, reproduction and sexuality, the division of labor and the work people do.

In many ways, feminist visioning corresponds with women's reality, with the life and work of 'unknown' women (which often tends to be local, sustainable, concerned with peace, growth, nurturing, service, helping others, and is child and less-abled centred), but is at the same time trying to question myths about women's 'natural' roles and activities. Its main function is to break and transform patriarchal social and cultural practices. It is extremely important to stress that feminists are careful not to engage in creation of definite, clear and rigid images of what societies are supposed to look like. Most feminists are aware that no 'perfect' society can be created, especially not based on ideas coming from the past. As Ashis Nandy notes, today's utopias can easily become tomorrow's nightmares (Nandy, 1987). Most feminists are indeed aware that any rigid imaging could bring future societies in which gender relations might be 'equal', but society would definitely be totalitarian and absolutist.

Lucy Sargisson claims that feminist utopias are, in particular, critical of approaches which emphasize perfection and the idea that utopias constitute blueprints for the perfect polity (Sargisson, 1996). Rather, they are spaces for speculation, subversion and critique, social dreaming, intellectual expansion of possible futures, and expression of a desire for different (and better) ways of being. Sargisson further points out, that it is often common to find in contemporary feminist utopian literature and theory, descriptions of several worlds, sometimes contrasting – none perfect. These worlds then play speculative, meditative or critical roles instead of instructions about how to create a perfect world. In this light, Elise Boulding's vision of 'gentle' and Riane Eisler's vision of 'partnership' societies are exemplary. Both are critical of present gender relations and attempt to envision better (not best) worlds in the future. Both focus on non-violence, gender cooperation and the pivotal role of social movements in creating a new future for humanity – both believe we can imagine and create peaceful societies.

When thinking about gender relationships in the future we have to be aware that the gender might be seen differently than it is today. Feminists are aware of this fact, especially as they are the ones who started to destabilize categories like 'women' and 'men', categories which have for millennia been seen as fixed, natural, and in no way to be made problematic.

The futures of gender

Most futurists agree that the future is not predetermined, at least in the sense that there is always some place left for human agency. For the first time in human history it is possible to imagine different futures for gender, gender being more socially constructed and less grounded in what nature 'intended'. While some mythological figures have been described in previous times as transgressive of gender bi-polarities and gender fluid, for the first time (thanks to modern medical science) it is possible to create such images in reality. Here I will represent three main scenarios for future gender relationships and identities.

Unisex androgyny

Unisex androgyny should be imagined as a psychological condition or characteristic where men would increasingly adopt traditional women's virtues (nurturing, caring, empathy, compassion, intuition, relationship orientation) while women would increasingly adopt virtues traditionally seen as masculine (protection, exploration, ability to plan and organize on a grand scale, goal orientation). Aburdene and Naisbett believe that 'successful human beings have to possess a combination of masculine and feminine traits' (Aburdene, 1992: 262). They also argue that as a group, women have better absorbed positive masculine traits, mostly because those were valued for centuries by male-dominated societies. Scenarios in which women and men would become physically closer to each other (as in the case of hermaphroditism, where the individual has primary and secondary sexual characteristics of both genders) are highly unlikely, although some claim that in the future it will be more difficult to establish which is the 'natural' gender for some people. Development of medical science could enable such mutations that we would be able to change gender as we wish, and alternate procreative functions as they are today. Women would not need men (sperm banks) and men would not need women (artificial wombs); reproduction would not need either women or men (reproduction of babies in factories). If seen as a way for eliminating sexual stereotyping of human virtues, androgyny would be very close to some feminist ideals. Since gender is one of the oldest and most established divisions between humans, movement towards androgyny might be one of the potentially most liberating and revolutionary. But some feminists, for example Gloria Steinem, reject the concept of androgyny as proposing conformist and unisex visions which are the opposite of the individuality and uniqueness embodied in their understanding of feminism.

On the other hand, an ideal society would be one in which all differences would have freedom of expression. If the next centuries bring into reality reproduction external to the human body, the main reason for maintaining different social functions and roles for women and men would disappear and probably contribute to the formation of androgynous societies. Androgynous societies might be also formed as a by-product of removing socially prescribed qualities for each gender and we might see future societies consisting of humans, rather than of men and women.

Female–male polarity

This is the traditional model, where differences between genders are exaggerated and potentiated. Gender is constructed as fixed and there is little escape from socially constructed gender roles. In feminist writings this model appears in two main ways. First, the utopian model of one-gender societies where males would not be able to oppress female members and where separation of women and men would lead to creation of space in which women are better able to express themselves and develop their unique potentials. These societies are either imagined as heterosexual (some males are allowed to live in all women countries, or they meet at some type of 'fairs' in order to reproduce) or exclusively lesbian.

Second, dystopian images in which women's characteristics are exaggerated to satisfy men's desire for objectification of women: bigger breasts, bottoms, lips and eyelashes, while thin and lean in other places, including brains. These images are, thanks to plastic surgery, increasingly becoming part of our reality and might be even more common in the future. On the other hand, men are imagined as ultimate and omnipotent future warriors, images which appear very often in popular science fiction. These images assume unchanged and unchallenged patriarchal relations between genders.

Female/male bi-polarity might happen as a result of a male backlash or if some religious and political fundamentalist sexist doctrines win (eg Taliban in Afghanistan or right-wing organizations in western countries). This would take us back in time prior to the discovery of 'gender' as a socially constructed category and prior to the appearance of feminism. Although its residues are going to follow us into the future, this model is, in general, most likely to remain a product of pre-modern and modern times.

Multiple-gender diversities

For postmodernists, essence as 'women' and 'men' does not exist as such any more. There are hardly any criteria left which would suffice to describe two different and opposite genders. Criteria like appearance can be challenged by transdressers and transvestites. Sexual orientation has always been problematic as a criterion, since homosexuality among humans has (probably) always been present. The natural characteristic of the sexes can be transformed and changed, women becoming men and vice versa. Woman (or man) as a social category is also problematic since any universalist statement about woman (man) can be questioned from the position of epistemological (and group) minorities and different perspectives. At the end of the twentieth century the general trend is rather towards this type of recognized multiplicity than towards forced uniformity. This scenario is most likely for the future since there is no longer a simple answer to the question 'Who is woman (man)?' The position which describes gender as ultimately a biological category is now considered naive naturalism and essentialism. The development of medical science has further destabilized essentialist views of gender. If we accept that 'women' and 'men' are mostly socially constructed categories it is obvious that we cannot have only one construction and that those constructions will change throughout time. The creation of a society in which every difference is able to find ways of expression is in the heart of most liberals and feminists. A society in which we could have multiple gender diversity would definitely create the most space for individual freedom and non-conformists. Ultimately, this will be another way of destabilizing the importance of gender in defining personal roles and functions within society. This appears to be the most likely of all three scenarios to appear in the twenty-first century western world.

At the doorstep of a new era

So what can we learn from feminist futures? At the doorstep of not just the twenty-first century, but also of a new era, many believe that our current ways of thinking and doing are becoming more and more obsolete and that they will not be able to carry us and our children into a better future. Feminists have tried to envision alternatives which will help change existing power structures and create more balanced cultures. They have criticized traditional knowledge as it is our understanding of reality which guides our actions and plans for the future. Feminists have also stressed that current trends are not bringing a better future for women – or for men. Man's instrumental rationality and superior 'expertise', apart from helping develop some technologies and social institutions which have improved people's lives, have also left us lamenting over the current world of power struggles, polarities, mass destruction and selfishness. If we want to survive, we need a sustainable and ecologically balanced future, probably based on decentralized, local and communal societies in which differences will not be the basis for oppression and where women's work and knowledge will be respected.

In order to achieve that we have to change radically our ways of living, acting and thinking (Boulding, 1988). Changing not only what is taught in schools but how we imagine and situate 'education' is just one of many things needed to be done in our march towards better futures for our children and for all.

References

Aburdene, P and Naisbitt, J (1992) *Megatrends for Women*, New York: Villard Books.
Bartkowski, F (1989) *Feminist Utopias*, Lincoln, NEB. and London: University of Nebraska Press.
Boulding, E (1976) *The Underside of History: A View of Women through Time*, Boulder: Westview Press.

Boulding, E (1988) *Building a Global Civic Culture: Education for an Interdependent World*, New York: Teachers College Press.

Dator, J (1994) 'Women in Future Studies and Women's Visions of the Future – One Man's Tentative View', in *The Manoa Journal of Fried and Half-Fried Ideas*, Honolulu: Hawaii Research Center for Futures Studies.

Eisler, R (1987) *The Chalice and the Blade: Our History, Our Future*, San Francisco: HarperCollins Publishers.

Eisler, R (1997) 'Cultural Shifts and Technological Phase Changes: The Patterns of History, The Subtext of Gender, and the Choices for Our Future', in Galtung, J and Inayatullah, S *The Macrohistory and Macrohistorians*, New York: Praeger.

Halbert, D (1994) 'Feminist Fabulation: Challenging the Boundaries of Fact and Fiction', in *The Manoa Journal of Fried and Half-Fried Ideas*, Honolulu: Hawaii Research Center for Futures Studies.

Kurian, G and Molitor G (1996) *Encyclopedia of the Future*, New York: Simon & Schuster Macmillan.

Milojevic, I (1996) 'Towards a Knowledge Base for Feminist Futures Research', in Slaughter, R *The Knowledge Base of Futures Studies*, vol 3, Hawthorn, Australia: DDM Media Group.

Nandy, A (1987) *Tyranny, Utopias and Traditions*, New Delhi: Oxford University Press.

Nielsen, J M (1990) *Feminist Research Methods*, Boulder: Westview Press.

Sargisson, L (1996) *Contemporary Feminist Utopianism*, London: Routledge.

Thiele, B (1986) 'Vanishing Acts in Social and Political Thought: Tricks of the Trade', in Pateman, C and Gross, E *Feminist Challenges: Social and Political Theory*, Sydney: Allen & Unwin.

Section II:
The practice of futures education

8. Futures in early childhood education
Jane Page

Summary

A central concern motivating early childhood professionals is their shared commitment to the fundamental objective of laying foundations of life-long learning for the children in their care. Early childhood professionals play a vital role in imparting the skills, attitudes and aspirations which are central to young children's development. The relevance of futures studies to early childhood educational frameworks has hitherto not been studied systematically by either futurists or early childhood professionals. In the main, the discourse has addressed issues in isolation and lacked reference to the relative values and shared concerns of both disciplines. This chapter will demonstrate the many principles that are shared by futures studies and early childhood education and will argue that the implementation of a futures-focused curriculum provides the means of extending and rearticulating existing developmental objectives from the vantage points of new perspectives.

Introduction

Early childhood education constitutes a fundamentally appropriate forum for the exploration of futures issues. Its positioning at the commencement of formal education provides it with the critical role of introducing children to concepts and principles which will remain with them through their education and into their later lives. Early childhood professionals are thus faced with the challenge of laying the philosophical foundations necessary for the acquisition of skills, abilities and attitudes that will enable the young children in their care to negotiate successfully the education system as a whole and the broader contexts in which they will function as adults.

There can also be no doubting the potential effectiveness of pre-school education as the medium for the transmission of the broad cultural and social concerns with which futures studies seek to engage. Around half a million children attend Australian pre-school programmes for example (Castles, 1993). The pattern of increasing full-time parent employment ensures that this number can only increase. It has recently been estimated, for example, that many Australian children spend up to 12,500 hours in childcare before entering school (National Childcare Accreditation Council, 1993). Early childhood professionals thus need to give consideration to their often considerable influence upon children and their corresponding responsibility to best meet the future needs of the young children in their care. In order to achieve this, they need to address how they can provide children with the skills and outlooks necessary to devise positive frameworks of understanding for the future and to cope as adults in an increasingly complex and dynamic society.

Long-term objectives in early childhood education

It might, in the first instance, be argued that it would be unrealistic to apply the long-term perspective of futures education to the essentially short-term objectives of early childhood. But this argument would seriously underestimate both the principles of early childhood education and the significance of the early childhood curriculum. Early childhood professionals share with the proponents of futures studies an understanding of education as the means for enhancing long-term development (Woodhead, 1985; Lee, 1990; Sroufe, 1990; Wasik, 1990; Zigler and Muenchow, 1992; Schweinhart, 1993). The formulation of long- and short-term learning objectives in the early childhood curriculum is thus fundamentally directed towards fostering future development.

By addressing curriculum concerns and content in terms of the long-term needs and skills of children, early childhood professionals seek to lay the foundations for life-long learning. The work of the High/Scope Educational Research Foundation during the 1960s corroborates this by demonstrating the extent to which a sensitively planned pre-school programme can have a long-term influence on young children's development (Halliwell, 1990). Longitudinal studies have established that the children attending Head Start programmes were better equipped with long-term developmental skills than children from comparable backgrounds (Woodhead, 1985).

The Head Start programme shared with the principles of futures education the aspiration to look beyond the relatively narrow developmental concerns of traditional curricula. As with futures education, the Head Start programme sought to engage meaningfully with the broader social issues which negatively effect growth and development (Woodhead, 1985). Part of the programme's success in achieving these aims lay in its emphasis upon another key principle of futures education, that of encouraging students to renew their connections with the wider social contexts with which they engage. Woodhead has noted of the project that:

> the positive experience of pre-school triggered a virtuous cycle of changes not only in the children, but in their relationship to their family and school, and in turn to their wider social context in which they were gaining competence (Woodhead, 1985).

This is, or should be, a major emphasis in early childhood education since early childhood centres often constitute the first social institutions with which young children come into contact. In contradistinction to the rhetoric of much educational research and policy making, the High/Scope programme seriously addressed its stated aim to foster lifelong learning. It thus stands as an important model for the application of the long-term goals of futures studies in early childhood education.

Futures studies and early childhood education: shared understandings

Early childhood education shares a number of key principles with futures studies. As with futures studies, early childhood educational theorists stress the multi-dimensionality of growth and development. Theorists have long emphasised the extent to which early childhood development occurs as a result of the interaction of a complex range of psychological, physical, sociological and other factors. In order to understand the full richness of the integrated model of development, early childhood theorists have joined with the proponents of futures studies in adopting an inter-disciplinary approach which blends the insights of education with those of psychology, philosophy, sociology, critical theory and political science (National Association for the Education of Young Children, 1991).

Piaget and Vygotsky have acknowledged the importance of the dynamic interaction of past, present and future learnings in child growth and development (Piaget, 1951; Vygotsky, 1978). This understanding emphasises the importance of individuals revisiting past learnings in order to make sense of the present and to project their new understandings into the future. These theorists view children's thinking as constantly evolving as thought processes are continuously reassessed and modified in the light of new information. Their concentration on the flexibility of thought processes accords with the stress in futures studies upon flexibility as a fundamental means of dealing with diversity and change. Bronfenbrenner's ecological model recognises the connections between these evolving growth patterns and the wider social contexts with which children come into contact (Bronfenbrenner, 1979). His comments on the reciprocal links between the significant environments in

children's lives and the manner in which children form part of an interconnected network of social forces also accords with the social and cultural
orientation of futures studies.

These theories provide the conceptual underpinnings to many of the concerns dealt with in the formulation of early childhood curricula. The different
theoretical perspectives involved in the study of early childhood developmental theory means, nonetheless, that the early childhood professional is
faced with the challenge of bringing together certain key concepts in order to
achieve a view of development which is holistic yet integrative and internally
consistent (Mialarat, 1976). Futures studies offers a cogent and flexible framework with which to respond to this challenge.

Futurists, early childhood theorists and futures education

A number of futurists and early childhood theorists have recognised the
relevance of futures studies for early childhood. Futurists frequently highlight
the fact that children will create the world of the future, with some arguing
from this the need for a greater attention to futures studies in early childhood
education (Masini, 1986; Shane and Shane, 1974). Troutman and Palombo have
argued from this that the developmental emphasis of the early childhood
educational curriculum renders it a highly appropriate context for the application of futures concerns (Troutman and Palombo, 1983). A number of futurists
have also stressed the importance of early childhood education as a forum
for laying the foundations for future growth and lifelong learning (Benjamin,
1989; Pierce, 1980; Masini, 1981; Allen and Plante, 1980; Ford, 1980). Ford has
noted, in this context, the need to co-ordinate a futures-focused curriculum
at the early childhood level of education with similar initiatives at later levels
of education. If this were achieved, she argues, futures studies could form an
effective counter-agent to the fragmentation of learning which frequently
occurs in more conventional educational curricula (Ford, 1980).

Several futurists have highlighted the degree to which young children
already possess some of the attitudes which futures studies seeks to encourage.
Nicholson and Masini have noted the liveliness and unpredictability of young
children, as well as their ability to question, create, co-operate and intuit
(Nicholson, 1979; Masini, n.d.). Lorenzo has stressed children's powers of
imagination and creativity and their interest in fantasy. He observes that these
qualities allow children to explore possibilities and options for the future
which adults frequently neglect. He also points out that children's quick-
wittedness and natural inclination to treat the world as a laboratory provide
them with a real insight into humanity's potential to create alternative worlds
(Lorenzo, 1989).

These are all qualities which adults should seek to rediscover and which
young children begin to lose all too soon as they enter primary and secondary

education. To illustrate this, Lorenzo cites an American comparison of the drawings of pre-school, primary and high school children. According to this study, pre-school children perceived the future in more positive and humorous terms than the older children whose depictions of the future demonstrated a 'progressive lack of expressiveness and excitement' (Lorenzo, 1989). Similar conclusions were reached by Gisele Tromsdorff, whose study found that children in first grade evaluated the future less positively than younger children and that their powers of anticipation were less developed than those of younger children (Tromsdorff, 1993). More recently, a pilot study undertaken in Australia to examine how four and five year old children conceive time and the future, has stressed the degree to which young children possess positive attitudes towards the future and a sense of personal connectedness with the outside world (Page, 1995).

Whether this is typical of four and five-year old children's views of the future remains to be determined. More research is required to readdress a significant imbalance which exists in our understanding of the development of young children's thinking on time and the future. Early childhood professionals would be in a much better position to plan for the long-term needs of children and to incorporate into their frameworks an awareness of young children's attitudes to the future if they were able to clarify this fundamental research question more conclusively.

Several authors have focused on the futures-oriented skills, attitudes and wider learnings that young children need to acquire during the early years of education. The skills most commonly stressed in this regard are adaptability, imagination and fantasy (Pierce, 1980; Shane and Shane, 1974; Toda, 1993). Other skills and outlooks which have been noted include altruism, sensitivity towards others, conflict resolution and decision making (Pierce, 1980). Harold and June Shane have emphasised the importance of introducing children to the nature of change and choice for future alternatives. Their study stresses the importance of encouraging children to develop a strong self image which can be projected into the future (Shane and Shane, 1974).

Early childhood theorists generally address future-related issues from a slightly different perspective. Lacking the methodological orientation of futures studies, they have tended to focus more commonly on the identification of skills which a futures-focused educational programme should address. A number have highlighted the need to impart in children the necessary skills and knowledge for the future (Keliher, 1963), with some noting the need for these skills to be relevant to the dynamic nature of contemporary society (Short, 1991; Caldwell, 1988; Watts, 1987). When moving to specifics, early childhood theorists tend to reiterate many of the skills identified by futurists. Ebbeck and others have noted that, in order to cope with dynamism and change, children need to develop resilience, empathy and adaptability, an interest in creativity and in other cultures, and skills in communication, problem-solving and lateral thinking (Ebbeck, 1983; Caldwell, 1988; Watts,

1987; Clyde, 1984; Hilderbrand, 1991). Almy has noted that early childhood professionals will also need to possess these skills and attitudes if they intend to encourage their development in young children (Almy, 'The Early Childhood Educator at Work', 1975, *cit.* Saracho and Spodek, 1993). The ability of early childhood professionals to consider their feelings towards the future and attitudes towards their roles in shaping the future is a fundamental consideration in the effective translation of these skills into early childhood curriculum frameworks.

A smaller number of commentators have related the concerns of futures studies to the wider issues of curriculum construction and the role of early childhood education in contemporary society. Clyde has recognised the relevance of futures studies to the task of creating early childhood curricula which are fully accountable to the changing needs of the educator's clientele (Clyde, 1984).Watts, Power and Balson have, in like manner, emphasised that futures-related issues can assist early childhood professionals to develop curricula which remain educationally relevant to the changing demands of contemporary society and which do not fall into the trap of replicating outmoded social and cultural stereotypes (Power, 1993; Watts, 1987; Balson, 1981).

Few commentators have sought to engage with the broad social and cultural issues dealt with in futures studies. Halliwell has noted the need for early childhood professionals to understand and address the wider social contexts in which they work (Halliwell, 1990). She notes the limitations inherent in the common tendency among educators to concentrate too narrowly on the child's immediate environment (Halliwell, 1992). Her comments are shared by Morris who has also stressed the responsibility of early childhood professionals to adopt a global dimension to their educational outlook (Morris, 1991). Finally, Keliher has noted the importance of adopting creative learning strategies if such objectives are to be realised in early childhood curricula (Keliher, 1986).

Despite these initiatives, it should nonetheless be recognised that very few early childhood theorists have addressed the implications involved in utilising futures studies in curriculum construction. This constitutes a significant limitation in the study of futures and early childhood education. It is a relatively easy task to articulate general ideals for learning. It is much more difficult to identify the specific objectives and strategies necessary for achieving these aims in operative curricula. This approach has also been lacking in the work of futurists, mainly because the outlook of their discipline is not so commonly directed towards the practical implementation of educational curricula.

This task is made more difficult in early childhood education by the fact that futures studies has not yet directed its attention to the field. Futures studies was initially directed towards tertiary and secondary education and thereafter to an examination of its relevance to primary education. It has not, as a whole, taken on the task of addressing early childhood education. Further-more, futures studies is not, at present, being taught systematically at the level of pre-service training. Early childhood professionals remain largely unaware of the relevance of futures studies to curriculum formulation. The lack of research and writing in this area has tended to exacerbate the problem, resulting in the production of very little accessible information on the topic. A programme of research, teacher training, in-service and publications will need to be developed in order to offer support to early childhood professionals in this respect.

These challenges should not be perceived as insurmountable obstacles to the development of futures-focused curricula in early childhood (Page, 1992, 1993). We have already seen the many principles which are shared by futures studies and curriculum theory and practice in early childhood education. These parallels become even clearer when we examine more closely the principles and practices involved in the construction of early childhood curricula.

Futures studies and curriculum formulation

The fundamental purpose of curriculum construction is to define the para-meters in which future development will be fostered. As such, it should constitute the main focus of any attempt to achieve a futures orientation in education. It is through the curriculum that knowledge and attitudes are imparted, skills are refined and time and direction are offered to children in a manner which encourages them to engage actively with the issues and concepts addressed by the educator. The early childhood curriculum is particularly well suited to incorporate a futures studies framework since early childhood professionals are not required to teach a set syllabus, as are their colleagues in primary and secondary education. They thus have the flexibility to construct curricula which remain responsive to the complexity of child growth and development with a greater sense of freedom than the prescribed curricula of primary and secondary education.

Curriculum construction in early childhood education is, moreover, an inherently futures-oriented process. It combines the practical with the theoret-ical in a manner which is directly commensurate with futures issues. The formulation of the early childhood curriculum involves the translation of theoretical tenets into a series of practical applications. Early childhood professionals translate their broad philosophy into a set of values which are refined into both general and specific objectives. This process is then refined further into the practical implementation of individual learning experiences within the time and space of the programme session.

This process, it should be stressed, is not primarily aimed towards the achievement of easily definable outcomes such as are promoted by the behaviourist school of developmental theory. As Clark has pointed out, the behavioural model limits itself through its definition of behavioural objectives as a series of quantifiable terminal behaviours. This suggests a passivity on the part of the learner and involves the assumption that knowledge is finite and can be somehow measured as a series of factual building blocks (Clark, 1988). The early childhood professional, rather, aims to construct the curriculum as a series of dynamic and open-ended objectives which are continuously modified to suit the changing needs and interests of the child. Early childhood professionals are accordingly concerned with the total child, rather than with dissecting development and growth into easily observable components. This holistic orientation towards curriculum construction requires them to take into consideration the inter-relations between the many differing aspects of child growth, be they physical, emotional, psychological, intellectual or social.

The principle of active learning is also commensurate with the objectives of futures studies. Curriculum planning has always incorporated an emphasis upon providing time, space and direction for the manipulation of learning materials. This approach accords with the stress in futures studies on assisting individuals to feel in control of the environment by understanding their place within it.

The concepts of change and adaptation are also central to the objectives of the early childhood curriculum. Early childhood professionals focus on the developing thought processes, skills and abilities of individual children. They modify the curriculum constantly in order to render it responsive to the changing developmental needs of each child, thus recognising appropriately the importance of individualised learning, which has long been a central premise of early childhood curriculum construction. By adopting this approach to education, early childhood professionals signal their commitment to valuing the need for children to set their own agendas for change, an objective which they share with the proponents of futures studies.

The process of planning for the individual in the curriculum brings the early childhood professional into further contact with a number of the principles of futures studies. Over the course of the year, the early childhood professional observes the different ways in which each child engages with the environment in order to gain meaning from it. These observations provide important insights into the position of each child in the broader pattern of developmental norms. They form the basis of an individually tailored programme of experiences which is designed to reinforce and extend the child's skills and understandings. Early childhood curricula are thus founded on a detailed awareness and recognition of the dynamism and complexity of child growth. Early childhood professionals, in this respect, share with the proponents of futures studies the aspiration to move beyond the traditional, unitary model of teaching. They recognise the extent to which each early childhood curriculum is comprised of a number of inter-connected, yet inherently flexible, educational programmes which operate concurrently.

The ability of early childhood professionals to be responsive to the complexity and diversity of child growth is, in part, attributable to the flexibility of their methods of evaluating the children's development. The constant modification of the curriculum to best meet the objectives set for each child's development grows out of a continuous process of observation and evaluation of children's activities. This information is based on profiles compiled on each child attending the programme. The system of child profiles frees the educator from the restrictions imposed on many primary and secondary school teachers. Rather than having to fit the child to a pre-set programme, the early childhood professional is able to match the programme to the differing needs of each child. The information contained in the child profile further reflects this diversity. It may take the form of anecdotal pieces of information, running records of a child's interaction, samples of language and/or art work, thus recognising within the very methods of curriculum construction, the kaleidoscopic nature of child growth and learning.

This approach to education provides the educator and the children with a sense of shared ownership of the curriculum. By incorporating within the learning environment a number of diverse, yet inter-connecting learning experiences, the educator encourages the children to develop a sense of independence and freedom to exercise choice and to explore alternative learning experiences. The responsiveness of the curriculum to differing needs and interests enables children to begin to perceive that their goals are accessible and that their ideas can be realised. At a vital stage of their early development, children are to be given an understanding of the extent to which their ideas can be put into action and the outcomes to their ideas can be explored, the benefits of which have been stressed in the work of Ray Lorenzo and L'Età Verde (Lorenzo, 1986; L'Età Verde, 1978).

An orientation of this kind significantly empowers children in the process of learning. Children now recognise their control over a curriculum which has become personally meaningful to them in a manner which is in complete accordance with the previously stated principles of futures education. Through the collaborative process, the child gains a sense of being valued and recognised as an autonomous and active participant and decision maker within the early childhood environment. Children who come into contact with this form of curriculum will learn not to fear change but, rather, to feel in control of the processes of change and adaptation. This dynamic understanding of the concepts of change and adaptation, once again, shares common values with the objectives of futures studies.

Of equal importance is the extent to which this multi-faceted, participatory model of education encourages children to recognise the broader social dimension to each individualised learning experience. This model encourages children to recognise the manner in which the projection and realisation of ideas within a learning environment involves them in sharing and negotiating those ideas with others. The curriculum functions, in this respect, as a combination of individually and socially oriented learnings. The relative value of each factor in this combination will vary constantly according to the differing needs and developmental levels of each individual involved. It is also contingent upon the input of the adult educator who, as Vygotsky and Bruner have stressed, provides a social meaning and purpose to the learnings undertaken by the children (Fleer, 1992).

The links forged between children in the learning environment thus convert the early childhood curriculum into a microcosm of the broader social contexts with which the children will engage throughout their lives. The children's interaction with the social environment of the early childhood centre acts both to validate their understanding of the world and also to provide them with the opportunity to reflect this broader social experience back into the personalised agenda for development which is equally to be nurtured and extended by the educator. The sensitively maintained balance between the personal and social contexts of the early childhood curriculum, once again, aligns early childhood education with the central objective of futures education, providing a forum for individuals to recognise their links with the outside world of culture, society and the environment.

An awareness of this aspect of the curriculum also requires that the educator establish connections between the learning environment and the many other environments with which the child engages. The role of parents and care givers in the child's education, for example, should constitute a further important consideration in curriculum design. Parents and care givers are the child's first educators and, as such, should be drawn upon as significant sources of information about their children. Conversely, early childhood professionals can offer parents and care givers important perspectives on their child's development.

By sharing information, early childhood professionals and parents can collaborate in order to ensure that the curriculum best accommodates the differing needs of each child. As Keliher has noted, part of the importance of the development of positive parent–educator relationships lies in the manner in which it provides a means of demonstrating to children the connections between the different aspects of their lives (Keliher, 1986). This approach has the additional benefit of enabling parents and educators to act as resources for each other so that links and continuities can be built between the child's experiences in the early childhood programme and in the home environment. It further allows the educator to build into the curriculum a fuller consideration of those family, ethnic and community considerations which equally influence a child's development. In so doing, the educator recognises the importance of the principles of empathy for others and appreciation of social and cultural diversity which are commonly stressed in futures studies.

Practical applications of futures issues

The principles of futures studies can thus be interpreted as commensurate with the existing objectives of early childhood curriculum processes. Futures studies should be seen as providing the means of extending and rearticulating existing developmental perspectives from the vantage point of new perspectives. The challenge nonetheless remains how best to realise these principles in a manner that is sensitive to the developmental needs of the children concerned. The early childhood professional should be continually mindful of the need to frame each exploration of a futures-oriented issue in a manner which is conceptually and developmentally appropriate to the children attending the programme.

This is particularly true of such abstract futures-related concepts as the interconnectedness of the past, present and future. An initiative of the College of Education Lab. School of the University of Hawaii, can be cited as an example of how this idea can be translated into a developmentally appropriate experience for four-year olds. Each day at this centre the children take turns to contribute to a year-long calendar by entering onto paper (individually, in pairs or in small groups), what they consider to be the significant aspects of the day. The paper on which they write and draw forms part of an extended roll which is unrolled at regular intervals throughout the year in order for the children to walk through and discuss what they have identified as the past, present and future. This activity allows the children to explore time in a manner which emphasises its direct connection with them. Time is not abstract, since the events and concepts placed on the time scale are those which the children themselves have identified and depicted on their communally owned time-roll. Time is given a sense of stability and definition, since the recorded events remain on the paper as historical records. Yet time equally remains a fluid and ongoing continuum extending infinitely into the boundlessness implied in the act of unravelling.

An initiative of this kind could be developed as the basis for an exploration of other futures-related concepts. Change and continuity, for example, could be discussed in the context of seasonal change and experiments such as the observed growth cycles of animals or plants. The exploration of futures could also be drawn out in terms of possible or preferable outcomes of experiments or other significant events occurring in the learning environment. The direct relevance of the future in the present could be emphasised by these and other means in a manner which is immediate and readily accessible to the children rather than too abstract or remote.

Susan Fountain argues a developmental approach can be achieved by defining those elements of children's life experiences which are immediate and relevant to them but which also relate to the broader objectives of the programme (Fountain, 1990). She illustrates this point in the context of global education, noting that the instance of young children calling each other names which are sometimes gender- or race-related could provide the educator with an opportunity to explore with the children the concept of prejudice. The occurrence of children excluding others from play for arbitrary reasons could also form the occasion for an exploration of the concept of discrimination. In like manner, the common occurrence of children arguing over materials could provide an opportunity for discussing the issue of resource distribution. Fights among children could be used as a forum for the discussion of the issues of peace and conflict. The discovery among children that more can be accomplished by sharing and working together could be used as a means of demonstrating the principle of interdependence. The negotiation between children in order to arrive at an agreed solution to a dispute, could be used as a means of introducing the concept of co-operation and the importance of being conscious of other perspectives. Protest among children that rules are unfair could lead to a discussion of human rights. The use of consumable materials in a sometimes environmentally thoughtless manner could generate discussion on environmental awareness (Fountain, 1990).

In this manner, Fountain illustrates how the macro dimension of global issues can be explored through the micro dimension of the children's own experiences. Such an emphasis gives rise to the importance of recognising that futures issues cannot be discussed with pre-school children within the same conceptual frameworks as adults, but rather must acknowledge and capitalise on the outlooks and perspectives of the children themselves. In so doing educators retain a child-centred approach to their work. A futures-focused curriculum in early childhood thus has the potential to engage meaningfully with these issues and in so doing to open the curriculum out to the children in order to make it more accessible to them without sacrificing the integrity of the educational programme.

Another recent example of a futures-oriented, problem-solving activity took the form of a litter experiment undertaken with a group of children who sought to develop means with which to monitor and control the amount of litter which entered their kindergarten. The initiative incorporated into the programme the outlooks and concerns of the children who were also encouraged to perceive the extent to which they were able to exert an active influence over their educational environment (Page, 1991). Manning has sought to extend this focus. Building on Lorenzo's initiatives, she has suggested ways in which early childhood professionals might explore the possibilities for change that exist within other familiar local environments. Her initiatives involved the examination by four and five-year old children of their local playgrounds and the identification of which aspects they enjoyed and which they wished to change (Manning, 1990). At the completion of their project, their designs were taken to their Mayor who invited them to choose equipment for their local park. Thus, the children involved in this project were given a sense that their ideas were recognised and realised by an adult outside their immediate educational environment. Initiatives of this kind demonstrate to children early in life that they can exert a positive influence on the environment for the benefit of others as well themselves. In so doing, they have the potential to strengthen children's self concepts and underlying sense of motivation and purpose. In this respect, Manning also noted that the project itself offered the children a wider range of learnings which included an increased sense of spatial awareness, an examination of gender roles in relation to the playground equipment, social awareness and responsibility and decision-making skills (Manning, 1990). In this manner a futures-focused, early childhood curriculum has the potential to integrate and extend existing concerns with a renewed sense of purpose and direction.

To date, a futures-focused emphasis in early childhood programmes has only been achieved through the isolated initiatives of individual practitioners and theorists. What is clearly lacking in the research literature is a more systematic examination of how a futures-focused curriculum in early childhood could be defined and translated into practical learning experiences in a manner that embraces the principles and practices outlined in this chapter. The initial stages of this process were developed in a recent pilot study which identified possible objectives of a futures-focused, early childhood programme and outlined their translation into practical learning experiences (Page, 1995). The study reiterated many of the principles outlined in this chapter, together with a stress on objectives related to laying the foundations of thinking skills and abilities for the future such as the children developing forward looking perspectives, skills of independent thinking and problem solving, exploring conceptual possibilities and making intentional decisions, putting their ideas into practice, engaging in fantasy and role play, imaging preferred and desired states, exploring a variety of modes of communication and exploring the concepts of change and continuity.

Further objectives were defined as a means of laying the foundations for developing attitudes for the future, such as the children identifying with the environment, developing an awareness and tolerance of other individuals and cultures, identifying common needs and shared interests with different cultures and individuals, developing a respect for diversity, appreciating other points of view, co-operating and resolving conflicts peaceably, developing a sensitivity towards other children's needs and feelings and developing an understanding of others regardless of gender (Page, 1995). Such objectives, it should be stressed would always need to be resolved against the changing interests, needs and life experiences of the individual children and families involved in the programme. A futures-focused curriculum of this kind could then be interpreted as complementing and extending upon the existing objectives of early childhood education in a manner that is sensitive and responsive to the immediate and long term developmental needs of the young children.

Conclusion

We have seen that a futures-focused curriculum should not involve anything radically new or not in keeping with the educator's fundamental objective to remain responsive to the developmental needs of the children. The early childhood curriculum has the potential, in this respect, to act as a nexus between the practical and the theoretical dimensions of futures issues. Both the curriculum and futures studies can provide a reference point for each other so that the range of exploration remains neither too remote nor too limited in scope. While individuals have been successful in generating initiatives in the field, a fuller examination of how these outlooks and perspectives can be fully integrated into early childhood curriculum frameworks remains one of the critical tasks to which the early childhood field should now focus its attention.

References

Allen, D W, Plante, J (1980) 'Looking at the Future of Education' in Jennings, L and Cornish, S (eds) *Education and the Future*, Bethesda: World Future Society.

Balson, M (1981) 'Preparing Personnel to Work in the Early Childhood Field in the '80s', *Australian Journal of Early Childhood*, 6(2), 24–8.

Benjamin, S (1989) 'An Ideascape for Education: What Futurists Recommend', *Educational Leadership*, 7(1), 8–14.

Bronfenbrenner, U (1979) *The Ecology of Human Development: Experiments by Nature and Design*, Cambridge: Harvard University Press.

Caldwell, B M (1988) 'Early Childhood Education in the 21st Century', *Child Care Information Exchange*, 64, 13–15.

Castles, I (1993) *Australian Statistics Yearbook*, Canberra: Australian Bureau of Statistics.

Clark, T (1988) 'Believing is Seeing – Not the Reverse', *The Quest*, Autumn, 49–56.

Clyde, M (1984) 'Pre-Schools for the Next Century', *Links*, 4, 4–8.

Ebbeck, M (1983) 'The Pre-School Curriculum: Its Relevance for Children and Their Future Needs', *Australian Journal of Early Childhood*, 8(3), 9–12.

Fleer, M (1992) 'From Piaget to Vygotsky: Moving Into a New Era of Early Childhood Education', in Lambert, B (ed.) *Changing Faces: The Childhood Profession in Australia*, Watson: Australian Early Childhood Association.

Ford, S (1980) *Redress the Education System*, Washington: U.S. Department of Education, National Institute of Education, Educational Resources Information Center.

Fountain, S (1990) *Learning Together: Global Education 4-7*, Leckhampton: Stanley Thornes Ltd and World Wide Fund for Nature.

Halliwell, G (1990) 'Infusing Critical Pedagogy into Early Childhood Teacher Education? A Response to Battersby', *Unicorn*, 16(1), 47–51.

Halliwell, G (1992) 'Practical Curriculum Theory: Describing, Informing and Improving Early Childhood Education', in Lambert, B (ed.) *Changing Faces: The Early Childhood Profession in Australia*, Watson: Australian Early Childhood Association.

Hildebrand, V (1991) 'Young Children's Care and Education: Creative Teaching and Management', *Early Childhood Development and Care*, 71, 63–72.

Keliher, A V (1963) 'Believing and Doing', *Childhood Education*, 40(2), 62–5.

Keliher, A V (1986) 'Back to Basics or Forward to Fundamentals?', *Young Children*, 41(6), 42–4.

Lee, V E, (1990) 'Are Head Start Effects Sustained? A Longitudinal Follow-Up Comparison of Disadvantaged Children Attending Head Start, No Preschool, and Other Preschool Programs', *Child Development*, 61(1), 495–507.

L'Età Verde (1978) *Come gli studenti vendono i problemi mondiali*, Rome: Edizioni L'Età Verde.

Lorenzo, R (1986) *Some Ideas and Goals for Environmental Education*, Milan: Associazione Italiana World Wildlife Fund, Settore Educazione.

Lorenzo, R (1989) *Let's Shape the Future*, Milan: Associazione Italiana World Wildlife Fund, Settore Educazione.

Manning, J (1990) 'Infants are Powerful Too!', *World Studies Journal*, 8(1), 34–8.

Masini, E B (1981) 'Images of the Future by Children', research manuscript, Rome.

Masini, E B (1986) 'Early Education for the 21st Century', *Bernard Van Leer Foundation Newsletter*, May, 7.

Masini, E B (n.d.) 'Les Enfants et leurs images du futur', *Temps Libre*, 6, n.d., 71–84.

Mialarat, G (1976) *World Survey of Pre-School Education*, Paris: Unesco.

Morris, J (1991) 'Investing in Children's Learning Through the Curriculum', *Early Childhood Development and Care*, 73, 87–93.

National Association for the Education of Young Children (1991) 'Guidelines for Appropriate Curriculum Content and Assessment in Programs Serving Children Ages 3 Through 8: A Position Statement of the National Association for the Education of Young Children and the National Association of Early Childhood Specialists in State Departments of Education', *Young Children*, March, 21–38.

National Childcare Accreditation Council (1993) *Quality Improvement and Accreditation System Handbook*, Sydney : National Childcare Accreditation Council.

Nicholson, S (1979) 'The Media in the Education of the Child', in Doxiadis, S (ed.) *The Child in the World of Tomorrow: A Window into the Future*, Oxford: Pergamon Press.

Noyce, P (1986) (ed.) *Futures in Education: The Report*, Melbourne: Commission for the Future and Hawthorn Institute's Centre for Curriculum.

Page, J (1991) 'Critical Futures Studies: Rendering the Early Childhood Curriculum Responsive to the Future Needs of Children', *Australian Journal of Early Childhood*, 16(4), 43–8.

Page, J (1992) 'Symbolising the Future: Developing a Futures Iconography', *Futures*, December, 1056–63.

Page, J (1993) 'Advocating the Future Rights of Our Children,' *Journal of Australian Early Childhood Association*, 11(3), 35–41.

Page, J (1995) 'Another World Like Here: Futures Studies and Early Childhood Education', M.Ed thesis, Department of Early Childhood Studies, Faculty of Education, University of Melbourne.

Piaget, J (1951) *Play, Dreams and Imitation in Childhood*, London: Routledge & Kegan Paul.

Pierce, C M (1980) 'The Pre-Schooler and the Future', in Jennings, L and Cornish, S (eds) *Education and the Future*, Bethesda: World Future Society.

Power, M B (1993) 'Early Childhood Education: Everyone's Challenge for the 21st Century' *Early Childhood Development and Care*, 86, 53–9.

Saracho O N and Spodek, B (1993) 'Professionalism and the Preparation of Early Childhood Education Practitioners', *Early Childhood Development and Care*, 89, 1–17.

Schweinhart, L J, (1993) *Significant Benefits: The High/Scope Perry Preschool Study Through Age 27*, Ypsilanti: The High/Scope Educational Research Foundation, Monograph 10.

Shane H G and Shane, J G (1974) 'Educating the Youngest for Tomorrow', in Toffler, A (ed.) *Learning For Tomorrow: The Role of the Future in Education*, New York: Random House.

Short, V M (1991) 'Childhood Education in a Changing World', *Childhood Education*, 68(1), 10–13.

Sroufe, A L, (1990) 'The Fate of Early Experience Following Developmental Change: Longitudinal Approaches to Individual Adaptation in Childhood', *Child Development*, 61(1), 1363–73.

Toda, M (1993) 'Future Time Perspective and Human Cognition: An Evolutional View', *International Journal of Psychology*, 18, 351–65.

Tromsdorff, G (1993) 'Future Orientation and Socialisation', *International Journal of Psychology*, 18, 381–486.

Troutman, B I and Palombo, R D (1983) 'Identifying Futures Trends in Curriculum Planning', *Educational Leadership*, 41(1), 49.

Vygotsky, L S (1978) ed. *Mind in Society: The Development of Higher Psychological Processes*, Cambridge: Harvard University Press.

Wasik, B H, (1990) 'A Longitudinal Study of Two Early Intervention Strategies: Project CARE', *Child Development*, 61(1), 1682–96.

Watts, B (1987) 'Changing Families – Changing Children's Services: Where are the Children Going? Are Kindergarten Teachers Ready To Go Too?', *Australian Journal of Early Childhood*, 12(3), 4–12.

Woodhead, M (1985) 'Pre-School Education Has Long-Term Effects: But Can They be Generalised?', *Oxford Review of Education*, 11(2), 133–55.

Zigler, E and Muenchow, S (1992) *Head Start: The Inside Story of America's Most Successful Educational Experiment*, New York: Basic Books.

9. Technology-based learning in US elementary schools

Sandra Ramos Miller

Summary

The conjoining of new pedagogical insights with computer-based technological innovations is producing a new strategic paradigm for US educators. That paradigm posits a need for greater child-centred teaching and more active, non-mimetic student learning. Today's sophisticated technology provides the technical wherewithal to accomplish these goals. As US educators move to implement this paradigm they are designing high-technology school infrastructures that support child-centred learning environments. They are redesigning curricula to focus instruction more directly on higher-level thinking processes and to integrate content disciplines in the investigation of of problems. They are also implementing professional development programmes that help teachers adopt practices which take full advantage of new pedagogical insights and contemporary technological capabilities. This chapter illustrates the progress being made towards this goal by describing three models of US schools: cutting edge, pioneering and transitional.

Introduction

As the twenty-first century techno-informational world approaches, new technologies will continue to alter the way we live, the way we do business and, most importantly for educators, the way we learn. Educators, business people, and scholars realize that tomorrow's citizens will need different kinds of knowledge and skills. These citizens of tomorrow are today's elementary students. In 10 to 15 years, when they enter a workplace filled with fast-changing technology, their ability to access knowledge, process information, think critically, make decisions, and interact with others, will be the keys to their success. Children themselves are fast becoming 'high-tech' as they acquire, almost unconsciously, new ways of learning, 'playing' with home computers and interactive games. Electronic play has honed their motor skills. They process huge amounts of nonsequential information and they embrace technological changes with equanimity. Emerging research suggests, further-more, that intensive electronic game play may actually redraw the brain's neural maps (Abbott, 1996).

As elementary schools change to accommodate those 'high-tech' students and capitalize on new technological capabilities, a new paradigm for element-ary education in the United States is unfolding. This new paradigm is being expressed in every aspect of schooling, from technological infrastructure and instructional practices to definitions of teacher/student roles and the nature and focus of curriculum content.

A new paradigm for schools

As schools move toward this new paradigm they will:

- utilize a technology infrastructure to improve the learning environment;
- implement professional development programs to help teachers adopt new instructional teaching practices that take full advantage of new pedagogical insights and technological capabilities;
- recognize students' new roles in the learning process, the need for active non-mimetic student learning, and personal responsibility;
- redesign curricula to focus more directly on higher-level thinking proc-esses and integration of content disciplines when investigating problems and developing project-learning activities.

As these characteristics become more widespread, elementary schools will shift from teacher-centered to student-centered. There will be, as a result, substantial changes in how children learn and what they are taught.

New instructional practices

What new paradigm schools are finding in the US is that the introduction of computer-based technology into the classroom is a catalyst for change as teachers face up to the fact that computers can transmit information more efficiently than they can. And that means even the best practices of traditional teaching are being challenged on two levels. First, if computers and modern telecommunication networks provide an information base way beyond the capabilities of even the most informed teacher or textbook, and technology provides all the information transfer needed in interesting, challenging, and fun ways, what do traditionalist teachers do? Second, children are coming to school with strong prior experiences and are predisposed to use technology. They perceive didactic lessons and textbook exercises as chores rather than exciting learning opportunities. In a world filled with technology, the trad-itionalist's old-fashioned practices are rapidly becoming dysfunctional.

As teachers question their own traditional techniques, as 'high-tech' students enter the classroom, and as professional development programs focus more directly on cognitive research to guide instructional practice, the elementary schools' learning environment is increasingly becoming *constructivist*, a cognitive theory that defines knowledge as temporary, developmental, and socially and culturally mediated, and thus non-objective (Brooks and Brooks, 1993).

The transformation to a constructivist framework challenges teachers to create environments in which they and their students are encouraged to think and explore. The depth of the transformation is illustrated succinctly in Table 9.1.

Few American schools have adopted constructivism as the dominant learning theory for all their instructional activities, but many have adopted constructivist learning for mathematics and science instruction. However, as the effectiveness of constructivist techniques becomes more evident, and as technology becomes more available, constructivist instructional practices will become more wide spread (Sandholtz, Ringstaff and Dwyer, 1997). As that change happens, and especially when further expansion of high-tech hardware and software accelerates change, new instructional practices will be introduced.

As America moves towards the twenty-first century, therefore, the need for changes in instructional practices is becoming more and more obvious to teachers. Many teachers now realize that the utilization of technology plus constructivist learning helps to create better instructional environments (Dwyer, 1994). As technologically rich educational environments expand, teachers can more easily move away from their traditional practices. The motivation for teachers to use technology is a belief that it will support superior forms of learning (Sandholtz, Ringstaff and Dywer, 1997). However, the effectiveness of instructional delivery will not, of course, be driven merely by technology.

Most educators agree that the introduction of technology is not an end in itself, but should support instructional goals related to increased student involvement with complex, meaningful tasks (Means, 1994). However, it remains true that as schools move into the twenty-first century, there will be more examples of teachers using technology to accelerate the transformation from teacher-centered to student-centered practices. As interactive software takes on many of their routine instructional tasks, the teacher's role will change from a textbook-dependent lecturer to that of a coach and learning facilitator. Teachers' interactions with their students will more often model effective ways to learn rather than merely talk about effective ways. In such settings, students will become active learners. After interacting with information from a variety of sources and, through dialog with classmates and teachers, they will create knowledge and develop richer conceptual schema, as Weir's (1989) research has clearly demonstrated.

Table 9.1 A look at school environments

Traditional classrooms	Constructivist classrooms
Curriculum is presented part to whole, with emphasis on basic skills.	Curriculum is presented whole to part with emphasis on big concepts.
Strict adherence to fixed curriculum is highly valued.	Pursuit of student questions is highly valued.
Curricular activities rely heavily on textbooks and workbooks.	Curricular activities rely heavily on primary sources of data and manipulative materials.
Students are 'blank slates' onto which information is etched by the teacher.	Students are viewed as thinkers with emerging theories about the world.
Teachers generally behave in a didactic manner disseminating information.	Teachers generally behave in an interactive manner, mediating the environment for students.
Teachers seek the correct answer to validate student learning.	Teachers seek the students' point of view in order to understand students' present conceptions for use in subsequent lessons.
Assessment of student learning is viewed as separate from teaching and occurs almost entirely through testing.	Assessment of student learning is interwoven with teaching and occurs through teacher observation of students at work and through student exhibitions and portfolios.
Students primarily work alone.	Students primarily work in groups.

Source: Jacqueline Grennon Brooks and Martin G. Brooks, *The Case for Constructivist Classrooms* (Alexandria, VA: Association for Supervision and Curriculum Development, 1993), vii

As the author has shown elsewhere (Miller, 1995), when technology is conjoined with insights from cognitive research, a dramatic effect on classroom practices is seen. Those effects will include these basic attributes:

- **Active learning** will be the predominant modality. Students will become more active in determining their own learning and will participate in activities which engage them personally and directly in the learning process

- **Process approach** learning which places the emphasis on 'learning how to learn' will predominate. Learning will move from the requirement of 'knowing' to an emphasis on 'searching'
- Education for **interpersonal communication** will include speaking and active listening skills and speaking another language than their own
- A structure for learners which permits more **individual attention** and small **group collaboration** will be the norm. Schools-within-schools, multi-age groups, personalized learning, and continuous progress are processes schools will use to achieve this new structure.

Essentially, schools will focus unambiguously on child-centered tasks and a meaning-centered curriculum.

Organizationally, schools will have extended blocks of time for in-depth work on projects and problem situations. The content disciplines will lose their separateness and become functional tools for students to view and analyze events and situations from multiple standpoints. Students will join in heterogeneous collaborative teams to investigate problems and work on projects. Through interaction with facilitative teachers, students will discover the relationship between their own findings and those of the conceptual frameworks of the content disciplines. Instruction will be interactive whether with team members, the teacher, or the technology. Assessment of student performance will be based on exhibition of knowledge and other performance-based techniques. Those assessment processes will undergird the school's assurance of continuous progress for its students (Means, 1994).

Obviously, such substantive changes in teacher behavior and the organization of schools will demand a corresponding change in the expectations and role of elementary students.

New student roles in the instructional process

Teachers who assume that learning is a mimetic activity, and thus adopt behaviorist teaching strategies, are not up to date with current research on how children learn. In constructivist, child-centered classrooms, roles will change as well. The teacher becomes a learner and the student becomes a teacher. Students will take more responsibility for their own learning. They will learn the skills of comprehension, reasoning, and experimentation through interaction with problems and projects posed by teachers. They will also generate problems to be pursued after thoughtful discussion with their classmates. Cross-disciplinary concepts will be integrated and used as analytic and interpretative tools applied to new situations and real-world events (Weir, 1989). Students will develop 'learning to learn' skills and attitudes, ie process

SANDRA MILLER

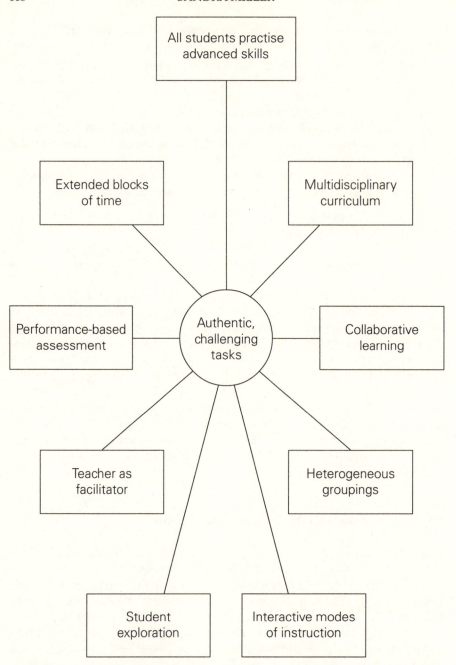

Figure 9.1 Authentic challenging tasks. (Source: Barbara Means, ed. *Technology and Education Reform: The Reality Behind the Promise*, San Francisco: (Jossey-Bass Publisher, 1994) 2).

skills such as metacognition, higher-order thinking, and creativity; attitudes such as learning to deal with uncertainty and ambiguity, flexibility in the face of new data, and skills for dealing comfortably with change.

Can students master those new roles and also cope with the inundation of new technology? Experts are confident they can. Elliot Soloway, who describes today's generation of youngsters as the 'Nintendo Generation', sees children moving comfortably into their new roles. 'In the classroom', he says, students will easily become 'knowledge navigators...where critical analysis skills and social skills are developed and where group discussion and interaction are paramount' (Soloway, 1991). The work of such scholars as Papert (1993) and Weir (1989) has also demonstrated that children easily accept technology as a useful tool and use it confidently. Students find technology central to their problem-solving and project development efforts (Weir, 1989). Students will both adapt to technological change, and embrace it as naturally as if they had been genetically endowed with technological insight.

As students' roles become more self-regulated, under the guidance of skilled, facilitative teachers, they will also engage in a more meaning-centered curriculum, one that should be more able to confront social and personal issues directly.

Redesigned curriculum content

The curriculum changes stemming from the impact of technology and newer theories of learning are becoming more evident across the United States. Curriculum developers are giving serious thought as to how to broaden the scope of contemporary curriculum. They want to incorporate more meaningful, universal themes and integrate important conceptual learning. More importantly they want curricula that will support child-centered instruction in a natural way. This means using computer-based technology as a major means for delivering instruction and making sense of information. No one can predict the exact nature of curriculum design in the future, of course. However, given the nature of rapid change and further technological innovation, it is reasonable to conclude that the future curriculum will provide a framework of generic topics that will allow local schools broad discretion to adapt to changing conditions.

In a recent study conducted by the author, an international panel of experts – futures-oriented educators, authors, social scientists, and futurists – was asked to identify what content or themes school children would be studying in the twenty-first century. They reasoned that new technologies and multimedia capabilities in homes, schools, communities, and work-places, would require a more comprehensive curriculum. The panel opined that such a curriculum would provide access to a wide variety of information, and would emphasize cross-cultural and global studies as global interdependence increases. The experts identified several focus areas for the new curriculum such as environmental concerns, critical thinking skills, and conflict resolution.

The panel's projections appear to be the direction in which elementary schools are heading. Of the many items so identified, seven curriculum universals received a strong consensus (Miller, 1995):

- environment: problems and solutions;
- diversity: challenges and opportunities;
- globalism: economic and cultural interdependence;
- work and careers in the high-tech world economy;
- inequality and ethics: issues and solutions;
- conflict resolution and mediation skill development;
- change: the individual, economy, and society.

The themes identified by the expert panel are reflected in the intellectual schema of other educators. For example, a task force report of America's most influential professional curriculum association, the Association for Supervision and Curriculum Development (ASCD) echoed and went beyond this panel's forecasts. ASCD posed these trends and issues as those American educators needed to consider when redesigning curricula for the future (Hays and Roberts, 1994). See Table 9.2 on pages 122–3.

Many schools have already responded to these trends, although comprehensive inclusion of topics based upon those trends and their systematic treatment in classrooms are still in the early stages of development. The interdisciplinary elementary curriculum called Education 2000 being developed in Eugene, Oregon, for example, captures many of the themes identified by the panel of experts and the trends identified by ASCD, as Table 9.3 (page 124) shows (Shoemaker, 1990).

Other communities and professional organizations are also developing new curriculum themes. Each attempts to focus on the trends that will affect the lives of children as the world moves into the twenty-first century. Much of the new curricula, especially in mathematics and science, reflect integrated disciplines that deal with authentic real-world situations. It is presumed that the new curriculum thrusts will promote children's personal and intellectual growth in a wide knowledge spectrum (Anderson *et al.*, 1994). The mission of curriculum developers is to help children develop the intellectual skills and attitudes they need to confront such issues intelligently and with a sense of empowerment. That is the real challenge for American educators and educators around the world.

Progress toward new paradigm schools in the United States appears inexorable. However, the rate of movement toward the new paradigm is not uniform. Indeed, America's elementary schools display wide disparities in technology utilization and infrastructure capability, and in their instructional practices, as discussed below.

Disparate school progress

Analysis of major US government reports suggests three qualitatively different conditions in American elementary schools. *Cutting-edge* schools are those already using a strong technological infrastructure to implement new paradigm curriculum and instructional practices. According to the US Government Accounting Office (GAO), however, 'cutting-edge' schools constitute only a handful of schools in the entire country (GAO, 1995). The same GAO analysis found that the majority of American schools are in transition from traditional to new paradigm practices. Even though they suffer severe fiscal constraints, these *transitional* schools are incorporating computer-based technology resolutely, with about 65 percent of schools now connected to the Internet compared with only 35 percent in 1994. Those schools are building new roles for students and teachers, as well as developing future-oriented curricula based on new paradigm concepts. Many of those transitional schools, the US Office of Technology Assessment suggests, are sufficiently advanced to be labeled trailblazers (OTA, 1995). *Trailblazing* schools, whilst not many in number, are those in the forefront, demonstrating that the drive to use sophisticated technology in the classroom can in itself be the catalyst for systemic change. Trailblazing schools, which have socio-economic attributes common to most American public schools today, are the model traditional schools wish to emulate as they move forward. A more detailed look at those three conditions, will illustrate the developmental range of America's elementary schools.

Cutting-edge schools

The affluent schools and those that have special relationships with corporate sponsors, have had the fiscal resources to develop cutting-edge, technology-rich environments for learning. They have reinvented themselves, using technology to alter teacher's instructional practices, reformulate the expectations they have of children, and redesign their curriculum. By developing a complex and sophisticated technological infrastructure, these cutting-edge schools, like the one described in the example that follows, are preparing students not only to be 'knowledge-workers', but also to be effective citizens and leaders in the twenty-first century.

Celebration School is a pre-eminent example of a cutting-edge school with a fully developed, up-to-date technological infrastructure (Tiedemann, 1966). It is found in Celebration, Florida, a new community developed by the Disney Corporation which also funded the school. The school started operation in 1996. Teachers and students are organized into multiage groups called 'neighborhoods'. Each neighborhood has a

Table 9.2   Trends reshaping our schools

GLOBALIZATION

1. Access to primary curriculum resources around the world will be available to all.
2. The number of languages taught will need to be expanded with special attention to Asian based languages.

INCREASING COMPLEXITY OF HEALTH ISSUES

1. The financial and human resources costs of responding to the needs of children with impairments will compete with the resources needed to maintain a quality curriculum that is current.
2. The current model of physical education will be re-designed to incorporate the concept of lifelong wellness.

ETHICS AND VALUES

1. Attention to moral and ethical issues in schools will be unavoidable and students will need to learn more sophisticated frameworks for decision-making.
2. The ability to 'customize' or predetermine characteristics and composition of future populations will necessitate attention to ethical literacy in schools.

GROWTH OF ALTERNATIVES

1. Schools will need to develop clearly definable curriculum standards and will be held accountable for the results achieved.
2. Communities will increasingly deal with issues of values and parents will expect the curriculum to closely reflect the values of the community.

AGE OF CONVENIENCE

1. As services which stress immediacy of gratification increase, the difficulty of convincing students of the long range benefit of education will increase.
2. School schedules will need to be re-examined in light of society's demand for convenience. Parents will expect schools to accommodate their own personal calendar and year-round school will grow in popularity.
3. As the need for retraining increases, adults will demand learning sites close to home.

CHANGING FAMILY

1. The program structure for curriculum will need to be broadened to serve birth to five. This will be critical in urban areas.

Table 9.2   Trends reshaping our schools (*continued*)

2. Schools will provide surrogate family structures for students by keeping them together in teams for extended periods.

DEMOGRAPHICS

1. Schools will be asked to make their facilities and programs available to meet continuing education needs of aging population.
2. Schools, especially those in suburbs, will need to alter their curriculum to be more culturally diverse especially in social studies and literature.

WORLD OF WORK

1. Schools will need to provide the opportunity for students to learn to work with people from other cultures.
2. Students will need skills that are transferable and flexible in their career development.

CHANGING NATURE OF GOVERNMENT

1. Parents will demand more consensus on curriculum, but consensus will be difficult to attain.
2. More informed voters will demand that the schools put renewed emphasis on citizenry.

INFORMATION TECHNOLOGY

1. Electronic data bases will replace the library as we know it and customized textbooks will become common.
2. Virtual reality will result in simulations of real life phenomena that schools could not afford to expose students to in real situations.
3. Science will be the first area to move virtual reality into learning.

Source: Leroy E. Hay and Arthur Roberts, 'Curriculum for the New Millennium,' speech at Association of Supervision and Curriculum Development Conference, 20 March 1994

learning space with approximately the square footage of five traditional classrooms. The spaces are designed to be used flexibly to accommodate students as they engage in a variety of tasks. There are self-contained areas that facilitate both large group instruction and small team-oriented learning. Other areas are designated for special projects such as science experiments or art projects.

Table 9.3 Education 2000's curriculum approach. Required major themes and concepts by curriculum strands

Strands	Communities	Change	Power	Interactions	Form	Systems
Human Societies	Global community Universality Diversity Environments Cultures Institutions Heritage Rules/laws Inhabitants Ethnicity	Cycles Adaptation Sociopolitical movements Cause and effect Migration	Authority Force Conflict Influence Use of power	Interdependence Competition Cooperation Survival Needs Wants Communication	Aesthetics Historical perspectives Design principles	Natural systems Created systems Organized systems Functional systems Institutions Families U.S. government Symbol systems Alphabetical systems Number systems Musical notation
The Earth and The Universe	Ecosystems Environment Inhabitants Balance Intervention	Cycles Adaptation Cause and effect	Energy Force	Interdependence Competition Survival Human intervention Balance	Matter Energy	Natural systems Ecosystems Created systems Organized systems Functional systems
The Individual	Participation Roles Citizenship Democratic ideas Rights Responsibilities	Growth Life cycle Wellness Dependence/independence HIV/AIDS Substance abuse Cause and effect	Conflict Leadership Influence Use of power	Interdependence Independence	Patterns Aesthetics Basic elements Media Style	Created systems Natural systems Body systems

Source: Betty Jean Eklund Shoemaker, *Education 2000: District 45 Integrated Curriculum and Planning Guide, K-5*, 2nd ed. (Eugene, OR: School District 45, Eugene Public Schools, 1990)

Such space utilization is not that unusual, but the school's technological infrastructure is. There is a computer for each student. Every neighborhood has 100 data ports so every student can connect to the local area network (LAN) at the same time when necessary. Students can read and leave messages on electronic bulletin boards, take part in on-going conversations via chat rooms, utilize video accessing ports for distance learning, telecommunicate and use other visual-media resources. All students and teachers have access to color printers, digital cameras, scanners, camcorders, and video editing equipment. Film and video – on laser discs, through cable television, and CD-ROM – are delivered on demand. Each teacher has a laptop computer with modem along with a hand-held note computer. The school's media center provides technological support for student research and facilitates connection to the information highway's limitless sources and consultations. A centralized media retrieval system, accessible to everyone, staff, students, parents, and the general community, is housed in the Teaching Academy at Stetson University (a small private university in Orlando, Florida). With its array of sophisticated technology, Celebration School is able to combine education's best practices: multiage environment, personal learning programs, flexible scheduling, and integrated curriculum design and delivery.

The school is operated by a differentiated professional staff. Four certificated teachers are assigned to each neighborhood of 100 students. The staff includes teachers and specialists – principal, counsellors, technology and media specialists, fine arts and foreign and language specialists – who work in collegial teams enabling them to focus their instruction and services as a professional collective. A special professional position called 'webmaster' services needs and handles technical issues. Master's candidates from the university work alongside the professional staff members as apprentice teachers, utilizing the best instructional practices. The entire learning community is involved in the educational process, including support personnel such as office staff, community experts, parent volunteers, and even certain students who assist other students in the learning process.

In every way, Celebration Schools' technology represents the cutting-edge in schools. It is an example of what happens when significant levels of technology are conjoined with exemplary practices to create a new educational environment. But even transitional schools have features that exemplify new paradigm concepts.

A transitional school

Throughout the United States forward-looking schools are modifying their current structure and programs in order to transform themselves for the future. Although these transitional schools' lack of financial support constrains them from developing a 'state of the art' technological infrastructure, they are moving forward by restructuring the areas their resources allow them to control.

C J Morris Elementary (CJM) is one example typical of those transitional schools. It is located in the suburbs of a major metropolitan area, one of nine elementary schools in a district of 14,000 students. Students at CJM come from all socio-economic levels. It is not a wealthy school and depends in a large measure on largesse of restricted federal and state funds, called 'categorical' to distinguish them from 'discretionary' funds, to support its innovative thrusts. And it is using those limited funds slowly to transition from a traditional, low-tech school to a state-of-the-art-school.

While not as extensive as Celebration, CJM has learned to use its space creatively. As an open space school with movable walls, it arranges its space to meet the changing requirements of the teachers' goals and students' diverse learning modalities. Classroom areas have the same square footage as traditional classrooms but are open to other classrooms as well as to one of two central areas. One of those areas, adjacent to the upper grade classrooms, is used by students and teachers for small and large group activities. The entire school of 550 students can meet in this area for special activities. A similar open area is adjacent to the lower grade classrooms and houses the combination library and instructional media center.

Technology plays an increasingly important role in instruction at CJM. The instructional media center has sixteen computer stations, three library stations, as well as thirty laptops. The library is automated and students can access information from it, their classrooms, or the library stations. Each teacher has a Macintosh with CD-ROM in his or her classroom area. All computers are attached to an ethernet network that connects the entire school's local area network (LAN) and provides access to the Internet. Several portable media stations give students and teachers access to VCRs, laser disc players, digital cameras, camcorders and overhead projection systems.

Many creative ways have been found to provide computer-based instruction even with limited resources. One federally funded program, for example, allows CJM to have some students attend special classes before school to learn to use the school's latest technology and then serve as tutors for their teachers and the other students. Another program gives students the opportunity for challenging work. Students are involved in school projects such as publishing the school's newspaper, assisting in the media center, working with younger students, and serving on special committees. Special programs give opportunities to learn life skills which will help to prepare students for future jobs. Specialist teachers also conduct before and after school programs utilizing the computer lab and multi-media stations to assist students in a variety of academic areas.

Instructional practices at CJM emphasize not only the staff's use of technology but also its commitment to child-centered and integrated learning. Because of that, facilitated instruction has become the primary mode of teaching and is evident in all curriculum areas, the basics as well as social studies and science. Multiage student grouping is found in the primary grades as well as a 'looping' program for upper grade children in which teachers move with their students from a lower to the next higher grade level. Technology is making it easier for teachers to practice a facilitative role in both settings since much of the routine and in-depth material to support inquiry and project learning can be found in software and through connection to outside sources.

Preparation of the staff for sophisticated inclusion of technology in instruction is on-going. The in-school professional development program focuses on better ways to implement technology and teachers are 'taught' using the same facilitative techniques they are expected to use in their own classrooms. Thus teachers get the double benefit of learning how to use technology more effectively while learning the nuances of facilitated instruction. In addition to in-school professional development activities, teachers and other staff members attend conferences and special classes conducted both by the central office and by nearby universities. CJM has agreements with several teacher preparation universities to let pre-service teachers or interns be placed at the school. They work with a master teacher and learn basic teaching and facilitation techniques. Daily practice is provided as master teachers involve apprentice teachers in using the new techniques. Pre-service and intern teachers are included in all professional development activities and often, being younger and part of the 'Nintendo generation' themselves, have new technology skills to share with senior staff and students.

Since CJM is located in California, its general curricula is governed to a large extent by the dictates of state curriculum frameworks. But the CJM staff has worked creatively within that framework to produce some unique approaches. Every area of the curriculum is influenced by the use of technology as a tool for completing projects as well as a means for eliciting a wide variety of information. Reading instruction is individualized with small groups focused on specific skills. Writing and reading are intertwined with an emphasis on language experience. Students are taught the writing process beginning in kindergarten using a technology-facilitated approach. Students utilize word processing programs on laptops, classroom and lab computers. Each child in the school writes several books during the year and presents at least one book at a special spring celebration. Science learning is guided by a single overarching concept with each grade level pursuing activities that build towards a broad understanding of that concept. In physical, life, and earth sciences teachers determine initial concepts for their students and then plan experiences to help students develop knowledge of that concept. There is much emphasis on 'hands-on' learning and science experiments in progress can often be seen throughout the school. In every aspect of the curriculum technology plays a central role.

Like other of America's fiscally-strapped transitional schools, CJM had only limited finances to create a new technological infrastructure, so it focused more on changing instructional practices, changing student roles in the learning process, and gradually redesigning the content of the curriculum.

However, there is a third type of public school that falls in-between technologically cutting edge schools and transitional schools. These schools were
given extraordinary technology support and have shown how technology
can act as a catalyst for changes in instructional practices, the roles of students
in the learning process, and the development of a new curriculum focus. These
schools have become the trailblazer public schools. Best known of the trailblazers are the Apple Classrooms of Tomorrow (ACOT) schools.

Trailblazing schools

In 1985 the ACOT project brought together a consortium of public schools,
universities, Apple Computer Corporation, and other research agencies to
explore whether or not a high infusion of technology into regular classroom
instruction would enhance the learning process and have an effect on teaching
and learning. In that sense, ACOT has been the longest running real test of
the influence of technology in the public schools. It was 'real' in the sense
that ordinary schools participated, those representing a cross-section of
American society. That means ethnic and gender characteristics were
accounted for; urban, rural, and suburban locations were included, and the
teaching staffs were professionally committed, mostly experienced, but nov-
ices when it came to technology.

   Apple Corporation played a significant role by providing computers to
students and teachers, both at school and at home. They also provided
printers, scanners, and other peripherals at schools to make the classrooms
high-tech. As technological resources improved, Apple cooperated by providing updates which allowed more students to use the latest technology. When
computer-based technology was miniaturized and lighter, for example, Apple
supplied portable computers. And when software became more powerful,
Apple provided new programs thus permitting even greater student independence to pursue assignments and projects.

   Interestingly, ACOT did not hold the teachers accountable for a particular
mode of instruction. Instead they encouraged diversity, new models of teaching, and receptivity to change. ACOT let each classroom find its own comfort
level with technology. That laissez-faire approach turned out, inadvertently,
to be a major vehicle for change. It gave significant support to the idea that
introducing sophisticated computer-based technology into classrooms is
in itself a catalyst for change in the instructional practices of teachers
and how curriculum are organized. In 1992 the ACOT project was strong
enough to receive support from the National Science Foundation (NSF). This
federal agency used the ACOT project as a model for helping teachers
everywhere integrate computer-based technology into their own schools, and
to learn about constructivist teaching approaches. Why had ACOT become
so influential? Because it pointed the way for achieving the new paradigm
for schools of the future.

ACOT researchers expected participating schools would have more individualization and self-paced learning, and a wider variety of multimedia projects. That occurred, but researchers got a lot more. Teachers at first translated their traditional text-dominated, teacher-directed, seat-work format into an electronic medium. Drill and practice, for example, was done on computers with drill software. But as teachers began to question their beliefs, as they began dialoging more with each other, and as they began experimenting with ideas that came from those discussion, they began to change. Soon teachers began to team and work across disciplines, and eventually had their students doing the same thing. As both teachers and students mastered the technology, their lessons became more complex and student projects more high-tech and student driven. Active learning became the norm. Soon teachers were modifying schedules to allow more natural time for projects to evolve and topics to be explored. As these things happened, ACOT teachers began to criticize the inadequacy of their traditional student assessment techniques and began exploring alternatives. That in turn led to the use of portfolios and authentic demonstrations of proficiency such as 'exhibitions'. These actual student products showed that students could integrate ideas and knowledge into a concrete outcome. After several years of the ACOT project, teachers had gradually adopted constructivist instructional practices as their major modality. Their roles changed from teacher-centered didactics to that of facilitator, coach, and guide, helping students see the relationship between their own ideas and theories to the wider structure of academic concepts and generalizations.

ACOT has proven to be the most influential of those projects testing ideas of the effects of technology on teaching. The dramatic results they found – that teachers could change school curriculum and instruction to accommodate the dynamic of computer-based technology and shift thereby into a constructivist, student-centered modality – are the real harbingers for elementary schools in the United States (Dwyer, 1994). That influence is demonstrated in the actions taken by many forward-looking schools that were not part of the ACOT experience but wish to emulate them.

Concluding remarks

Even though America's elementary schools are moving resolutely toward new paradigm conditions, there are still important realities that must be faced. The panel of experts mentioned above identified serious problems, some of which may severely affect elementary schools' smooth progress toward fulfilment of their mission. The United States is experiencing a growing gap in wealth between the rich and poor. In the panel's judgment, that inequality will be exacerbated if resources for schools continue to be unequal. The curriculum of affluent suburban and private schools now focuses on higher level thinking processes and stronger academic programs in science, mathematics and technology. That learning leads to high-wage professional, management, technical and similar symbolic analysts occupations. Yet, poor and underprivileged schools with less access to modern technology and curriculum are finding it more difficult to move people up the economic ladder. With the recent attention being given to education by the business community and federal and state governments, hopefully, such serious disparities may be addressed.

School infrastructure deficiencies also continue to pose challenges. Teachers in schools across the nation, at the same developmental stage as CJM in California, are finding that student access to computerized data bases, Internet information sources, and the currency of World Wide Web contacts, is critically dependent on the availability of up-to-date hardware, software, and connectivity to the world. As old buildings are retrofitted to bring in new fiber optic wiring and gain connectivity to telecommunication systems, a new world will open up for America's children. More money to purchase more computers will reduce further the 11-1 ratio now found in most schools (GAO, 1995). A hopeful sign that this may actually happen occurred recently as President Clinton announced release of some $200 million in grants to provide schools with computers and Internet training (*Los Angeles Times*, 1997).

Most American educators are positive, confident that such challenges will be met. In the near term, the direction in which elementary education's substantive instructional activities are moving is clearly exemplified by major developments in America's most forward looking schools. As elementary schools confront the complexity of future social, economic, and political challenges, they are developing curriculum that will give teachers the flexibility to introduce new content and problems, and devise new challenging projects that emulate real-world experiences. What elementary schools in the United States are finding is that the introduction of computer-based technology into classrooms is a catalyst for change. Today's elementary school professional staff knows it can only accomplish its new paradigm mission when they have developed well-grounded knowledge and practice. That has led many of them to demand further professional development, especially that which focuses on the integration of technology and the new pedagogy and leads to implementation of new instructional practices. Schools like C J Morris, the ACOT project schools, and Celebration are leading the way. It is time for the rest of the educational establishment to catch up with them.

References

Abbott, J S (1996), 'Zap! Splat! Smarts? Why Video Games May Actually Help Your Child Learn', *Business Week*, 23rd December, 64–71.

Anderson, R D, Anderson, B L, Varanka-Martin, M A, Romagnano, L, Bielenberg, J, Flory, M, Mieras, B and Whitworth, J (1994) *Issues of Curriculum Reform in Science, Mathematics and Higher Order Thinking Across the Disciplines*, Washington, DC: US Office of Education, Office of Educational Research and Improvement.

Brooks, J G and Brooks, M (1993) *The Case for Constructivist Classrooms*, Alexandria, VA: Association of Curriculum Development,vii.

Dwyer, D (1994) 'Apple Classrooms of Tomorrow', *Educational Leadership*, April, 4–10.

Hays, L and Roberts, A (1994) 'Curriculum for the New Millennium,' speech at Association of Supervision and Curriculum Development Conference.

Means, B (ed.) (1994) *Technology and Education Reform: The Reality Behind the Promise*, San Francisco: Jossey-Bass Publisher.

Los Angeles Times (1997) 'Clinton Begins Push for School Computers', section A23, February 2nd.

Miller, S (1995) *A Delphi Study of the Trends or Events that will Influence the Content of Curriculum and the Technological Delivery of Instruction in the Public Elementary School in the Year 2005*. Ann Arbor, Michigan: UMI.

Papert, S (1993) *The Children's Machine*, New York: Basic Books.

Sandholtz, J H, Ringstaff, C and Dwyer, D C (1997) *Teaching with Technology: Creating Student-Centered Classrooms*, New York: Teachers College Press.

Shoemaker, B J E (1990) *Education 2000: District 4J Integrated Curriculum and Planning Guide, K-5*, 2nd ed. Eugene, OR: School District 4J, Eugene Public Schools.

Soloway, E (1991) 'How the Nintendo Generation Learns', *Communications of the ACM*, 34: 23.

Tiedemann, D (1996) 'New Florida School Celebrates Education and Technology: An Interview with Paul Kraft, Media Specialist for Celebration School', *Techtrends*, October, 14–18.

Weir, S (1989) 'The Computer in Schools: Machine as Humanizer', *Harvard Educational Review*, 55: 62–71.

Further reading

General Accounting Office (1995) *School Facilities: America's Schools not Designed or Equipped for the 21st Century*, GAO/HEHS-95-5.

Office of Technology Assessment (1995) *Teachers and Technology: Making the Connection*, OTA-EHR-616, Washington, DC: US Government Printing Office.

USA Today (1996) 'Surfing Kids Share Their Cyberspace Views', section 4D, October 24th.

10. Young people's hopes and fears for the future

Frank Hutchinson

Summary

This chapter explores salient questions relating to young people's hopes and fears for the future at secondary level. It not only critically reviews research evidence on young people's images of the future but considers some important educational and cultural implications. Business-as-usual approaches are questioned and a case is put for negotiating futures in education that better respond to young people's hopes and fears. Particular attention is given to the need for educational approaches that support an explicit futures dimension in the curriculum, encourage critical and socially imaginative literacies, and challenge fatalistic fallacies about 'trend as destiny'.

Why study young people's images of the future

A crucial aspect of a forward-thinking approach to education is the value we attach to actively listening to young people's hopes and fears for the future:

> The images that young people have of the future will help to shape their aspirations as adult citizens in the next century. It is important, therefore, that appropriate attention be paid to their views and to the sort of education that is needed to prepare them more effectively for the future. This is a timely task for educators as we approach the new millennium – a time of transition which can be used to prompt deeper reflection on beginnings and endings, directions and purposes (Hicks, 1996: 143).

If we are to enhance the prospects of moving towards more peaceful cultures and more sustainable ways of living in the twenty-first century, it is important to share ideas, to learn from other cultural life ways and to listen to our children's voices on the future. In too many cases, children's hopes and fears are put at a severe discount, with a failure to address their concerns responsibly and in empowering ways. Their hopes and dreams may be marginalized and the need for an explicit futures dimension in the curriculum may remain forgotten. Relatedly, if our children's images of the future are discounted, this probably says quite a lot about ourselves, our schools, our societies and our expectations and aspirations not only for the younger generation but for unborn generations.

The pioneering work in critical futurism by Fred Polak (1961) highlighted the importance of images of the future in our own reflexive responses to our social worlds and to the worlds of our children's imagination about the future. Polak was particularly concerned at the impoverishment of social imagination among the young and with what might be done in a practical sense to transcend fatalism and short-sightedness. This latter theme is one that has been taken up strongly by a number of educators (Boulding, 1988, 1996b; Beare and Slaughter, 1993; Hicks, 1994, 1997; Hutchinson 1993, 1996b, 1997a; Page, 1996; Rundall, 1996).

Young people's views of the future: are we actively listening?

Study of young people's views of the future has been a low priority area for a long time as evidenced by the comparative dearth of published research evidence other than of the anecdotal and often stereotypic variety in the popular media. Over the years, there has been a relative neglect of the views of younger generations about personal, local and global futures, except in the narrow or short time-frame sense of opinion polls for elections and diagnosis of the 'youth market' by advertising agencies. Even among more academic research, the quality has been distinctly uneven. With some of the latter, there has been a lack of critical awareness of issues of gender, ageism and western-centrism, as well as a tendency to decontextualize and psychologize young people's dilemmas about their social worlds and the future. There has been also a tendency to rely on simple, attitude-survey types of methodology.

The beginnings of systematic research on young people's anticipations of the future may be traced to the early 1950s. During that period Gillespie and Allport (1955) carried out a cross-cultural study of young people from several different countries. Surveyed in the early years of the Cold War, most of the youth respondents were found to be pessimistic as to the possibility of a third world war being averted during their lifetimes.

However, with a few notable exceptions such as Elise Boulding's study in the 1970s of New Hampshire school children (Boulding & Boulding, 1995), it has not been until recent times that studies have occurred with an explicit interest in educational implications, and open to new ideas from areas of cross-disciplinary enquiry, such as peace research, gender studies, environmental studies and futures studies. Some of this newer research on young people's perceptions of the future has been inspired by more critical methodological approaches to researching the views of adults about the future. Important examples of the latter are the World Images 2000 Project (Ornauer *et al.*, 1976) and the Ontario 2000 project (Livingstone, 1976).

The more innovative of the latest studies of child and youth futures point to possible new ways forward. These studies highlight the need to explore the notion of futures and associated concepts such as 'broadened social literacies', 'resources of hope' and 'young people's empowerment', rather than focussing narrowly on student attitudes via their concerns for the future. Epistemologically, there is a shift from an interest in 'predictive or forecasting values' to 'proactive or applied foresight values'.

Exemplifying the 'predictive values' style of research are time-lag studies, such as those by Kleiber *et al.* (1993), that replicate the pioneering work of Gillespie and Allport (1955) and seek to identify trends in young people's views of the future. Illustrating the newer style of research are studies such as Hutchinson (1993, 1996b); Hicks and Holden (1995) and Gidley (1997). With the latter, the interest is not so much in identifying whether there are trends of increased pessimism or a rising 'sense of meaningless' among young people but in challenging assumptions that trends are destiny:

> Images of the future in the Western world often hinge narrowly around scientific and technological developments, sometimes seen as beneficial but more often as dystopian. It is as if science and technology have a life of their own which the ordinary citizen feels she can neither understand nor control. In the face of such fears it is increasingly important to focus on people's images of preferred futures. If they can be elaborated and envisioned more clearly then perhaps they can provide the basis for creating a more just and sustainable future (Hicks and Holden, 1995: 51).

To illuminate this proposition further, it is worthwhile briefly describing some relevant research projects. Whilst influenced by Ornauer *et al.* (1976) in the design of a questionnaire instrument, the 'Futures Consciousness and the School' Project received more significant inspiration from the work of Galtung (1988) on using dialogue techniques in research and Boulding (1988) and Ziegler (1989) on 'imaging futures' workshops. The research involved 650 Australian secondary students. It entailed a stratified sample of government and Catholic schools from rural and urban areas, and had a representative mix in terms of gender and socio-economic background. A one in four systematic sample of students from the original sample were invited to participate in small-group dialogue sessions and futures workshops. The full text of the questionnaire is contained in Hutchinson (1993: 320–29). An outline of the procedures for the small group dialogues and futures workshops is given in Hutchinson (1993: 331–38; 1996b: 214–20).

The study identified a number of major themes among young people's concerns for the world and for the future. These included a depersonalised and uncaring world; a violent world; and a world divided between 'haves' and 'have nots'; a mechanised world of largely oppressive technological change; an environmentally unsustainable world; and a politically corrupt and deceitful world.

In addition, the study was very much interested in exploring young people's preferable futures. A number of significant themes emerged from the small group dialogues and futures workshop activities. First, a strong strand of technocratic dreaming was found in which techno-fix solutions to many life crises tend to be accepted very uncritically. Such a way of imaging the future was usually stronger among boys than girls. Second, there was social imaging related to a demilitarization and 'greening' of science and technology to meet genuine human needs. Girls were found to be more responsive in this respect than boys. Third, there were images concerned with intergenerational equity, as well as with a perceived imperative for greater acceptance of our responsibilities for the needs of future generations. Fourth, there was an important strand concerned about making peace with people and planet through reconceptualisations of both ethics and lifestyles. Finally, there was a strongly expressed need to learn about preferred futures in education. When invited to consider whether there was any point in visualizing an improved world for the twenty-first century, a majority of the student respondents were of the opinion that better opportunities in schools to imagine preferable futures are crucial for choice and engagement. A large majority of students indicated their support for learning proactive skills in schools, such as ecological literacy and conflict resolution (Hutchinson, 1996b, 1997b).

Although smaller in scope, a follow-up study by Gidley (1997) has confirmed many of Hutchinson's findings. Gidley's work, however, places particular emphasis on schools as sites of authentic possibility. Her preliminary findings suggest that young people who have been through a Steiner system of education are more likely to feel confident about contributing practically to shifting away from their feared futures toward their preferred futures. She also speculates on possible lessons for more conventional forms of schooling.

Another illustration may be given with the 'Visions of the Future' Project conducted by Hicks and Holden (1995). Based on a study of 400 UK children aged 7 to 18, this innovative project both complements the findings of a number of earlier studies and moves beyond them. It brings out very clearly variables associated with age and gender, and raises important questions about choice and engagement for teachers, teacher educators and schools.

Some of the project's findings may be summarized as follows, First, age is a significant variable in terms of optimism and pessimism. Among the children surveyed, it was found that older children were more likely to be pessimistic in their assumptions about global futures than younger children. Second, in relation to feared futures a number of salient issues stand out. In the case of UK children these related to violence and war in the twenty-first century, with concerns about the environment also ranking highly. Third, while girls are generally less likely to be optimistic about the future than boys, they are also less likely to embrace uncritically technocratic dreaming or glamorous high-tech solutions to things. Finally, the project discovered that whilst some young people feel confident to act on a personal level to help create a better future, for many the social or political literacy skills are lacking. At the same time, it was found that many young people acknowledged such a need and would like more information, discussion and advice within schools in ways of making hope practical.

Some critical issues raised by the research

What are some of the major issues raised by the research findings? Are there important educational and cultural implications? It is not proposed to consider such questions exhaustively but to highlight a number of points for further consideration and research, including possible action research initiatives both in formal and non-formal educational settings.

Young people's images as 'a mirror on society'

The first major issue is a societal or even civilizational one that invites deeper reflection on beginnings and endings, directions and purposes. Why is it that so many young people in late industrial, western societies anticipate predominantly negative global futures? (Eckersley, 1996b). Relatedly if our images (and those of our children) about the future are important for what we do, or do not do, in the present, what does this suggest for our schools and other social institutions? In the words of a US election campaign song a few years ago, do we simply need to substitute positive visions of the future for negative ones and 'Be happy, don't worry'? Or, in relation to our schools at least, do we need to move beyond both business-as-usual thinking, that operates on a crisis management rather than foresight model, and the allure of therapeutic futurism that markets morale-boosting psychological antidotes for pessimism among young people? (Slaughter, 1995; Tough, 1995; Hutchinson, 1996b).

The salience of violent imagery

A second major issue that emerges from the research goes deeper than the conventional division between optimistic and pessimistic views of the future amongst the young. It asks not only why there is a tendency for pessimism to increase as a child gets older but also what may be happening to our children's futures-imaging capacities and skills in democratic participation. Why, for example, do many young people and more especially boys from an early age begin to develop fairly concrete images of war and violence but comparatively flimsy images of what a peaceful and environmentally sustainable future might be like? (Lacey *et al.*, 1986; Hall, 1993; Hakvoort and Oppenheimer, 1993; Hagglund, 1996; Elkins and Sanson, 1996; Pettman, 1996; Strogonow and Sanson, 1996).

While deserving more research, including questions concerned with political socialisation, gendered violence and cultural constructions of masculinity, are there important cultural and educational implications here? Is there a need for greater image literacy of social alternatives to violence? Is there a need for our schools to take a more proactive approach through both the formal and informal curriculum? (Boulding, 1988, 1996a; Bjerstedt, 1994; Bretherton *et al.*, 1994; Harris, 1996; Hutchinson, 1996a, 1996b). Elkins and Sanson (1996: 59–60) argue for example:

> The current findings suggest that children's highly negative future outlook needs to be placed on the agenda of educational policy and family interaction. It is important to encourage adults to listen to and acknowledge their children's fears, since this may be the first step toward mitigating the intensity of concern. Children's views of the future are dominated by images of war and violence. While they hope for peace, this is largely conceptualised as an absence of war or as a 'warm and fuzzy' feeling. The lack of a clear and elaborated image of what a peaceful world might be like is potentially a major barrier to achieving such a world. Opportunities to express concerns with family, teachers and community leaders would afford young people the chance to vent their concerns and to learn from and with adults how to confront their concerns and act responsibly towards creating a more positive world.

The salience of technocentrism

A third major issue relates to the salience of technocentrism in the imagery of many young people about both feared and preferred futures. Technocratic dreaming exercises a powerful pull on the social imagination of many of our youth. Even in the case of more grimly predictive technological visions of the world of the new millennium, it is not uncommon to find science and technology described in ambiguous terms as liberator and oppressor, destroyer and saviour.

Here, for example, is what Gordon had to say about technological evolution and human society twenty years into the new millennium. For this sixteen year-old, who attends a government high school in an inner suburb of a major Australian city, science and technology of war will bring destruction but salvation is promised by more benign science and technology:

> In the year 2020, there are lots of computerized things. Everywhere you go computers will do the hard work... The Earth may have had a nuclear war and be badly polluted – so the surviving people live together in cities. They may have huge bubbles over the cities to protect the people... Outside of the bubbles would be a desolate Earth with lots of pollution but inside [the bubbles] every-thing would be a nearly perfect environment to live... [Beyond our present planetary home] there may also be people living on Mars or the moon (Quoted in Hutchinson, 1996b: 82).

As previously mentioned, boys, rather than girls, are more likely to be uncritical believers in the credo of technocratic deliverance. A major recent study of over 800 young people commissioned by the Australian Science and Technology Council (1996) lends weight to this observation (see Table 10.1). What does such evidence say about conventional classroom offerings in science and technology? What does it say about media portrayal of such issues? What does it say about possible, probable and preferable social futures being narrowed to assumptions of technocentrism and the future, especially among boys?

Table 10.1 Technocratic dreaming by gender

	Male respondents	Female respondents
Environmental problems will be solved by science and technology without the need to change the lifestyle of Australians	50%	40%
Science and technology offer the best hope for meeting future challenges	74%	64%
Sample size: 802 Age group: 15–24		

Source: adapted from ASTEC (1996, p. 44).

What does it imply about the need for more gender inclusive forms of science and technology education in preparing our children for the early decades of the twenty-first century? What does it say about the need for more critical forms of scientific and technological literacy? (Orr, 1992; Fien, 1993; Lewis, 1993; Eckersley, 1996a; Harper and Holdsworth, 1996; Hutchinson 1996b).

In pursuit of a psychological prophylactic

Closely related to the assumptions underlying technological deliverance are those concerned with the expert knowledge systems of Western medicine, psychiatry and psychology. Such systems tend to psychologize and medicalize what young people are saying about the future and to raise hopes of medical miracles for restoring individual health and normality. In the case of the younger generation, one influential diagnosis has been to identify an 'epidemic of depression' among US children. Contextually, this is seen as tied to the need to restore faith in the American dream: 'until recent times, America was a nation of optimists. The first half of the nineteenth century was the great age of social reform, whose cornerstone was the optimistic belief that humans could change and improve...' (Seligman, 1995: 49).

Major assaults on this faith are identified with the years of political protest and disillusionment in the United States during the Vietnam War:

> Pessimism escalated in the 1960s from just a fashion of seaboard intellectuals to become the required posture of educated Americans.... In those days, to say at a social gathering that we do not live in 'terrible times', or that technological progress can clean up the mess it creates, or that nuclear holocaust was not inevitable was to mark yourself as shallow – an ignoramus, a Pollyanna... (Seligman, 1995: 51).

Yet, is it as simple as this either in terms of history or implied needs for the future? To dispute catastrophist thinking, especially among children is socially and educationally responsible but is this the same as 'prettifying' reality? Is the conceptual division that links pessimism with negative thoughts and optimism with positive thoughts an oversimplification? Is the crucial point not so much whether our children are optimistic or pessimistic but the quality of their responses and the quality of our responses? Is a more enabling conceptual division for futures in education one that considers motivational states and action competencies related to hopelessness, passive hope and active hope? (See Table 10.2).

'Learned optimism' is prescribed by Seligman (1995) as the therapeutic remedy for the problems of 'the pessimistic child'. It is claimed to offer 'psychological inoculation' against a child being infected with pessimistic

Table 10.2   Hope, literacy and a dialogue on futures

Anticipations about the twenty-first century	Related motivational states
Hopelessness	Low self-esteem; feelings of worthlessness; impoverished creative imagination about social alternatives; flight; violence turned against self or others
Passive hope	Bland optimism; technological cargo-cultism; reductionist literacies for accommodation to 'future shock'.
Active hope	Foresight; pro-social skills; appropriate assertiveness; enriched social imagination; optimal literacies for facilitating integration of the personal, the political and the planetary.

Source: Hutchinson (1996 b, p.208).

beliefs, but are pessimistic beliefs necessarily negative? Can optimistic beliefs also be negative if they merely substitute for hopelessness a sense of passive hope? Even if backed by the mastery of cognitive skills prescribed by Seligman for fighting childhood depression, can 'feel good' optimistic images of the future lead to complacency and passivity? Can potentially disturbing existential questions be defused through such a therapeutic approach becoming 'a phenomenon of control – an internally referential system in itself'? (Giddens, 1991: 202). Do we need to go beyond 'learned optimism' if hope is to be made practical and empowering for many young people in our schools? Worrying trends in adolescent male homicide and suicide rates in the US, for example, will not be adequately responded to by worrying less but by quality responses. Whether in the US or elsewhere, the promise of 'learned optimism' for the young in meeting life's crises is an exaggerated one. It assumes a level playing field. In pursuing the goal of a psychological prophylactic, attention can be easily diverted from highly damaging scores made against educational budgets and social infrastructure, including child and youth support services. According to a recent international study of eighteen late industrial societies the safety nets for children are weakest in the US (UNICEF 1996: 45).

Fatalistic fallacies

The tenor of much media reportage of issues concerned with young people's images of the future has been sensationalist. Whilst such representations may serve to alert a wider readership, do they also risk perpetuating fatalistic fallacies? Are accounts such as 'children of the apocalypse', 'children as casualties of change' and 'youth with the world on their shoulders', likely to perpetuate stereotyping? In our parenting and our teaching, is it important to take a more dynamic, interactive view of structure and human agency than hard determinist myths imply? Do we need to move beyond the languages of both fate and victimology?

There is a major interpretative strand that sees our children through a hard determinist lens as victims of fate, biology, 'future shock', technology or economic structure. At best, according to these readings of reality and potential reality, all that teachers and schools can do is to help their students adjust to 'the future'. Otherwise, they are said to be likely to suffer 'the dizzying disorientation brought on by the premature arrival of the future' (Toffler, 1970: 13).

Consistent with such assumptions, the essential pedagogical task is likely to be seen as skilling our children in adjustment to 'future shock' so as to lessen the risks of them becoming traumatized victims of technological change. In such educational discourses, what is likely to be promoted as most crucial for schools in preparing their students for the future is the addition of a fourth 'R' to the three traditional 'Rs'. The new basics are defined in these discourses as including the R of ROM, i.e. computer literacy, but often in a remarkably unreflexive and uncritical form. If young people are to be empowered rather than disempowered, is there a need to include in any new basics more critical forms of multimedia or new information technology literacy? In listening to young people's hopes and fears for the future, do we need to move beyond simple 'coping mechanism' strategies that leave essentially intact the fallacies of technocentrism and technological fatalism?

The challenge of making hope practical

An associated major issue relates to the challenge of making hope practical rather than fatalism convincing (Bjerstedt, 1994). While for many young people, the future looks uninviting or even a mindscape of barrenness and bleakness, this is likely to be more so among marginalised youth. Here, for example, are the summary comments from a study of the views of street-frequenting youth of non-English speaking backgrounds from lower income areas of Sydney.

> According to the majority of young people in our study, the scenario for the future is grim.... There will be more street kids. There will be more drug addiction among young people and more drug dealing.... There will be more crime.... There will be lots of trouble between groups of young people and with the police, and many will end up in jail. Tensions will increase because of racism.... There will be less money for young people, so more of them will be on the dole. It will be hard times, and much harder to get a better life.... (Pe-Pua, 1996: 112).

While such expectations among marginalized youth are crucially related to broader questions of social policy, deprivation and poverty, arguably educational organisations, both formal and non-formal, can play a constructive role. Whether from more or less affluent backgrounds, the research evidence suggests that many young people in late industrial societies support opportunities for developing skills in social imagination for preferable futures but, especially among more socially disadvantaged groups, there is a lack of awareness of possible bridging strategies for moving away from feared futures toward better outcomes. In such circumstances, a critical question emerges of how to foster learning environments likely to enhance outcomes that actually benefit young people and empower them to change their situations (Boulding, 1995; Hutchinson, 1996b; Slaughter, 1995; Wildman, Gidley and Irwin, 1996).

In whose interests?

A further major issue relates to whose interests are being served by the study of young people's perceptions of the future. Is, for example, much of the research to date an illustration of a 'moral panic' by the older generation in which its concerns are projected on the younger generation rather than the younger generation being enabled to give authentic voice to its views? How valid is such a criticism?

The cautionary point about a possible moral panic affecting research findings should not be dismissed lightly. However, if accepted uncritically and over-generalized, it risks becoming the counsel of complacency or apathy and reinforcing a 'psychology of denial' about the severity of the problem. By default or design, it can easily deny the precautionary or foresight principle for our schools and other educational organisations.

More important are questions of whose interests are served by particular forms of research on young people's anticipations of the future. Especially in the case of studies commissioned by advertising companies, such as *Teenmood* (Foote *et al.*, 1996), there is less interest in hearing what young people are actually saying about the future and more with mining their concerns, insecurities and hopes so as to enhance marketing opportunities. There is a commodification of young people's fears and hopes through integrated marketing of television and toys for younger children and the design of product lines for older children and 'the elusive youth market'.

It is important that commodification does not carry the day unopposed either in our schools or at the societal level. Schools have a significant role to play in developing forms of critical consumer literacy that will enable children to reassert themselves in creatively responding to the processes of commodification. One study of youth futures in 24 countries by a transnational advertising company warned its corporate clients that there is a need to pitch advertisements for the youth market with a greater attention to humour, irreverence and high-production values, as this marketing segment is becoming 'extremely...advertising savvy' (Foote *et al.*, 1996).

Another example may be cited about the cultural politics of researching youth anticipations of the future. During the 1980s there were a number of surveys of youth opinions about the risks of nuclear war (Lacey *et al.*, 1986; Mack and Snow, 1986). In the Cold War climate such evidence was put forward not to argue the case for peace education and conflict resolution literacy in schools but to scapegoat teachers as 'vipers in the classroom'. The latter may be seen as a twist on the moral-panic theory but with the particular claim that schools and teachers were subverting young people's confidence in the future. Instead of telling 'the good news' about the effectiveness of nuclear deterrence in preventing a war between the US and the Soviet Union, teachers were allegedly 'morally culpable' in filling their students' minds with gloomy prognostications about nuclear Armageddon.

Education as if young people's views mattered

The complexity of the cultural politics involved in research on young people's views of the future is also illustrated in the claims of a crisis in literacy standards. 'Excellence' is a keyword in many contemporary educational discourses but what does it mean? It is usually defined in terms of 'eminence', 'superior merit' or being 'remarkably good', but by whose standards? Who decides? Who judges? Does it have a forward-thinking dimension? Or are standards assumed to be somehow timeless and the product of a past golden age in Western civilisation?

Arguably the claimed crises of falling literacy standards and the anxious pursuit of excellence in the school systems of late industrial societies have little to do with developing high quality responses to our children's dreams and fears about the future. They may have a lot more to do with the push of the past and of Western-centric and patriarchal ideas of what constitute progress. In better preparing our children for a changing world, we need to resist the temptations of the apparent securities of a 'back-to-basics' curriculum and of monocultural forms of literacy.

To imagine a past 'golden-age' of moral absolutes, good discipline and educational excellence, in which young people knew their place in parent-child and teacher-pupil relationships, imbibed the wisdoms of their elders and were 'seen and not heard', is arguably just as inadequate as assuming that there is only one route into the future and that it is via technocentrism and 'future shock' adjustment in our schools and other social institutions. In both visions, there is an impoverishment of educational imagination. In both visions, there are myths that deny the possibility that adults can learn much of value from listening to what children's hopes and fears for the future are. Do we want to risk perpetuating short-sighted patterns of age-segregation, dependency and helplessness? Or do we want to work for more empowering learning environments and experiences as if our children's views of the future really mattered?

The institutional constraints are considerable but there are site-specific opportunities for ourselves as teachers, teacher educators and parents to actively listen to young people's voices on the future and to do something together with our children that helps to make hope practical. An essential challenge is to admit our children to co-participation in social thinking, dreaming and planning.

> ...Given the age-segregated nature of [our] children's world, the further along they move in age, schooling, work experience, and socialisation to adulthood, the more likely they are to reject their own wisdom and accept adult 'wisdom' as the price of entry into adulthood. Conventional adult wisdom at present confirms a rather violent, inequitable and increasingly polluted world. Admitting children to co-participation in social thinking, dreaming and planning while they are still free to draw on their own experiential knowledge of the world will help make the adult social order more malleable, and more open to new and more humane developments... (Boulding, 1995: 153).

References

Australian Science and Technological Council (ASTEC) (1996) *Having Our Say about the Future: Young People's Dreams and Expectations for Australia and the Role of Science and Technology*, Canberra: Australian Government Publishing Service.

Beare, H and Slaughter, R (1993) *Education for the Twenty-first Century*, London: Routledge.

Bjerstedt, A (ed.) (1994) *Education Beyond Fatalism and Hate*, Malmö, Sweden: School of Education, Lund University.

Boulding, E (1988) *Building a Global Civic Culture: Education for an Interdependent World*, New York: Teachers' College Press, Columbia University.

Boulding E, (1996a) *Our Children, Our Partners: A Vision for Social Action in the 21st Century*, Kelvin Grove, Australia: Religious Society of Friends.

Boulding E, (1996b) 'Toward a Culture of Peace in the Twenty-First Century', *Social Alternatives*, 15 (3), 38–40.

Boulding, E. and Boulding, K. (1995) *The Future: Images and Processes*, London: Sage.

Bretherton, D, Maree, L & Allard, A (1994) 'Conflict Resolution in Children', in: Bjerstedt, A (ed.) *Education for Peace*, Malmö, Sweden: School of Education, Lund University.

Eckersley, R (1996a) 'Science and Technology: Threat or Saviour? A futures Perspective on Science and Technology Attitudes', paper presented at the 4th International Conference on the Public Communication of Science and Technology, Melbourne, Australia, 11 November.

Eckersley, R (1996b) 'Young Australians' Views of the Future: Dreams and Expectations', *Youth Studies Australia*, 15(3), 11–17.

Elkins, K and Sanson, A (1996) 'Children's Views of the Future: Concerns Expressed in Letters and Questionnaires in the Post Cold War Period', in: Hagglund, S, Hakvoort, I and Oppenheimer, L (eds) *Research on Children and Peace: International Perspectives*, Goteborg, Sweden: Goteborg University.

Fien, J (1993) *Education for the Environment* Geelong: Deakin University Press.

Foote, Cone and Belding (1996) *Teenmood*, Chicago and associated international offices: Foote, Cone and Belding Advertising (CD ROM format).

Galtung, J (1988) *Essays in Methodology*, vol. 3, Copenhagen: Christian Ejlers.

Giddens, A (1991) *Modernity and Self-Identity: Self and Society in the Late Modern Age*, Cambridge: Polity Press.

Gidley, J (1997) 'Imagination and Will in Youth Visions of Their Futures', MA, Southern Cross University, Lismore, Australia.

Gillespie, J and Allport, G (1955) *Youth's Outlook on the Future: A Cross-National Study*, New York: Double Day & Co.

Hägglund, S (1996) 'Developing Concepts of Peace and War: Aspects of Gender and Culture', *Peabody Journal of Education*, 71 (3), 29–41.

Hakvoort, I and Oppenheimer, L (1993) 'Children and Adolescents' Conceptions of Peace, War, and Strategies to Attain Peace', *Journal of Peace Research*, 30 (1) 65–77.

Hall, R (1993) 'How Children Think and Feel About War and Peace', *Journal of Peace Research*, 30 (2), 181–96.

Harper, B and Holdsworth, R (1996) 'Environmental Consciousness', *Research Report*, 12, Youth Research Centre, University of Melbourne: Melbourne.

Harris, I (ed.) (1996) 'Peace Education in a Postmodern World', *Peabody Journal of Education*, 71 (3), 1–190.

Hicks, D and Bord, A (1994) 'Visions of the Future: Student Responses to Ecological Living', *Westminster Studies in Education*, 17, 45–55.

Hicks, D (1996) 'Young Peoples' Hopes and Fears for the Future', in: Slaughter, R (ed.) *The Knowledge Base of Futures Studies*, vol 2. Melbourne: Futures Study Centre.

Hicks, D (1996) 'Retrieving the Dream: How Students Envision Their Preferable Futures', *Futures*, 28 (7), 741–749.

Hicks, D and Holden, C (1995) *Visions of the Future: Why We Need to Teach for Tomorrow*, Stoke-on-Trent: Trentham Books.

Hutchinson, F (1993) 'Futures Consciousness and the School', PhD, Armidale, Australia: University of New England.

Hutchinson, F (1996a) 'Building Alternatives to Violence: Are There Needs and Opportunities for Teachers and Teacher Educators to be Practical Futurists?' *Peace, Environment and Education*, 7 (20), 3–18.

Hutchinson, F (1996b) *Educating Beyond Violent Futures*, London: Routledge.

Hutchinson, F (1997a) 'Education for Future Generations: Challenges and Opportunities for Peace and Environmental Educators', *Future Generations Journal* (forthcoming).

Hutchinson, F (1997b) 'Our Children's Futures: Are There Lessons for Environmental Educators?' *Environmental Education Research*, 3(2), 189–201.

Kleiber, D, Major, W and Manaster, G (1993) 'Youth's Outlook on the Future IV: A Third Past-Present Comparison', *Youth and Society*, 24(4), 349–62.

Lacey, R, Heffernan, C and Hutchinson, F (1986) *Educating for Peace*, Canberra: Commonwealth Schools Commission.

Lewis, S (1993) 'Lessons to Learn: Gender and Science Education', in: Kelly, F (ed.) *On the Edge of Discovery: Australian Women in Science*, Melbourne: The Text Publishing Company.

Mack, J and Snow, R (1986) 'Psychological Effects on Children and Adults', in: White, R (ed.) *Psychology and the Prevention of Nuclear War*, New York: New York University Press.

Ornauer, H, Wiberg, H, Sicinski, A and Galtung, J (eds) (1976) *Images of the World in the Year 2000*, Monton: The Hague.

Orr, D (1992) *Ecological Literacy: Education and the Transition to a Postmodern World*, Albany: State University of New York Press.

Page, J (1996) 'Education Systems as Agents of Change', in: Slaughter, R (ed.) *New Thinking for a New Millennium*, London: Routledge.

Pe-Pua, R (1996) *'We're just like other kids!': Street-Frequenting Youth of Non-English Speaking Background*, Melbourne: Australian Government Publishing Service, in assoc. with the Bureau of Immigration, Multicultural and Population Research.

Pettman, J (1996) *Worlding Women: A Feminist International Politics*, London: Routledge.

Polak, F (1961) *The Image of the Future*, E. Boulding (trans), 2 vols, Leyden, The Netherlands: AW Sitthoff.

Rundall, K (1996) 'Malaysian Project for Global Visions: Linking the World of Tomorrow', *Futures Bulletin*, 22 (3), 14.

Seligman, M (1995) *The Optimistic Child*, Sydney: Random House.

Slaughter, R (1995) *The Foresight Principle: Cultural Recovery in the 21st Century*, London: Adamantine Press.

Strogonow, L and Sanson, A (1996) 'Children's Conceptions of War, Peace and Strategies to Attain Peace in Local and Global Contexts', paper presented to 16th General Conference of the International Peace Research Association, University of Queensland, Brisbane, July 8–16.

Toffler, A (1970) *Future Shock*, New York: Bantam.

Tough, A (1995) *Crucial Questions about the Future*, London: Adamantine Press.

UNICEF (1996) *The Progress of Nations*, New York: UNICEF.

Wildman, M, Gidley, J and Irwin, R (1996) 'Futures Visioning Workshops as Empowerment with Marginalised Youth', Research Project, Lismore, Australia: Faculty of Education, Work and Training, Southern Cross University.

Ziegler, W (1989) *Envisioning the Future: A Mindbook of Exercises for Futures Inventors*, Denver: Futures-Invention Associates.

Further reading

Livingstone (1976) 'Intellectual and Popular Images of the Educational Future in an Advanced Industrial Society', *Canadian Journal of Education* 1(2), 13–29.

11. Teachers and postgraduate futures education

Allyson Holbrook

Summary

This chapter describes two postgraduate courses which focus on futures at the Faculty of Education at the University of Newcastle in Australia. The students enrolled, almost exclusively teachers, exhibit a very positive futures orientation. This finding is based on futures orientation data routinely collected from students between 1992 and 1995. These data also support the notion that individuals work within different time frames for different purposes. The main message is that futurists, teachers, and educational researchers pay too little attention to the combined cognitive aspects, and cultural construction of future time. We make too many assumptions and this may be a critical factor impacting on research findings in the area of 'future orientation' and life-planning.

Introduction

What do we know about the futures orientation of teachers and lecturers? It is an important question, given that they are in a position to facilitate the futures awareness of their students and also have a role to play in guiding the direction and growth of educational institutions. At the University of Newcastle, futures subjects have been offered to postgraduate coursework students in the Faculty of Education for close to a decade. The two subjects have been described in detail elsewhere (Holbrook 1992), so they will be fleshed out only a little here. The main thrust of the chapter is about the 'futures orientation' of the students who take one of those subjects, namely their predisposition to think about the future and what they choose to think about when they do. Hence the discussion will have general relevance for any individual or group attempting to instruct in, or use the literature emanating from, the field of futures education, as well as those simply interested in how educationists perceive the future.

Education would seem to be a future oriented institution because its focus is the intellectual and social preparation of the young for their adult roles but, as Slaughter (1993: 305–306) has pointed out, education is inherently backward looking. Certainly scores of academics have argued that our educational institutions are reactive not proactive with the school curriculum reflecting the society it serves. Yet while our society is not particularly forward looking, it is capable of rapid change. It follows that there is a frightening mismatch between the potential we have for change and the intellectual and cultural devices we have to deal with it. To be part of a truly futures enterprise those engaged in the education industry need to be active in fostering (and experiencing) the desire to envision future options, and to promote necessary change as well as maintain essential aspects of social and environmental continuity. If educators have a futures orientation, and are conscious of it, the more likely it is they will be able to recognise and develop such an orientation in others. Hence a key responsibility for those engaged in the futures field is to ensure that there is effective futures instruction for current teachers including appropriate, accessible texts informed by research on futures thinking and futures teaching.

Sadly, teachers are rarely exposed to futures research even though they have become more and more conscious of, and involved in, educational research. For more than a decade in Australia, as elsewhere in the Western world, educational research has changed very significantly (Bessant and Holbrook, 1995: 236ff). There is now a strong emphasis on qualitative research, forms of practitioner research, and on a more inventive, more reflexive, approach to what should be researched and how. Many new texts have been written about research methods in education but not one that explains, lists or even acknowledges futures or research methods pertinent to gathering and analysing futures data, eg the Delphi technique or scenario generation. Most teachers would not be aware that there is a futures field with its own methods, practitioners and conferences, nor do they get much encouragement in this from the tertiary sector.

In universities in Australia futures studies are generally perceived as an extra, an eccentricity, a 'frill' to be dispensed with when finances are tight. Ironically educational institutions will call in a consultant, sometimes a well known futurist, to lead the staff when there is a need for strategic planning, but rarely encourage staff to pursue futures studies or futures research. When new educational policy documents emerge they are usually analysed from every perspective but a futures one, yet most such documents purport to be futures oriented!

It is common to hear the work of futurists denigrated by the academy. The basis for such criticism is often ignorance, which tends to take one of two forms. First is a genuine lack of knowledge about the field and to be fair, futurists acknowledge that the variety and scope of futures pursuits mean their field is hard to delineate (Garrett, 1993). The second is incomprehension resulting in dismissiveness. There are those who have narrow views on what constitutes knowledge. Because the future is uncertain it seems to most people to be unknowable, even unthinkable, and certainly not a serious subject of study, despite the fact that as a society our anticipation informs our actions along with our knowledge of what happened in the past and what is happening now. While planning and goal setting are generally seen to be extremely important and worthy activities, very long term planning still tends to be resisted, along with the notion that we can really influence the future. The phenomenon of incomprehension, resistance and rejection is as thought provoking as it is worrying in the western educational context.

The ways in which we think about the future (futures thinking) has not been a high priority for educational psychologists, which is not surprising given the systems they serve. Studies are scarce except in the area of decision making as it is related to life skills, adolescent self-esteem and life chances. Yet, even in that area, how one develops a predisposition to futures thinking has been greatly neglected. How we deal with the combination of temporal extension and envisioning possibilities of events yet to come needs solid research. From a cognitive standpoint, is futures thinking similar to historical thinking, or is comprehension of the abstraction 'past time' very different to comprehension of the abstraction 'futures time'? As educators we actually know quite a lot about how children learn to comprehend abstractions such as time, yet adults can experience considerable difficulty thinking very far ahead. Rogers and Tough (1996: 492) refer to the resistance of adult students to futures thinking, and just how challenging stepping out of one's 'usual temporal orientation' can be. Some studies that have explored the temporal orientation of professional groups, managers for example, have noted inability to set long-term goals, even when the individuals considered themselves predisposed to engage in systematic, futures oriented thinking (Lewis, 1992).

Much of what we know about time is socially conditioned, hence we draw on many assumptions about time and unfortunately these assumptions, unexplored and unquestioned, mostly guide what research there is into temporality and futures orientation. What we need are some really insightful questions about cultural constructions of time (Inayatullah, 1993). Historians and anthropologists faced, as are educators, with new research methods and new ways of seeing the world and its past, are having to rediscover how they think about time so they can meaningfully interpret, for example, oral tradition, memory and myth (Hughes and Trautmann 1995). But this still leaves us with the fact that many educators have never been prompted to think about the cognitive or cultural constructions of time.

Several years ago when the author was teaching history methods to trainee teachers with degrees in history one of her topics was 'time'. Every year the students, many of whom were married with children of their own, were reluctant to believe that very young children had little conception of time. They could quote me examples of historical time sense in the young, that is until they put this surface knowledge to the test, and found that the young did indeed have difficulty dealing with such an abstract concept in an intellectually 'deep' rather than 'surface' way. What is more, self-examination indicated their own explanations, while 'informed', were very narrow. Theirs was primarily a linear pragmatic and functional stance on time.

Similarly, trained teachers will give examples of how 'futures oriented' their young pupils are. They note with satisfaction that their pupils can talk and write about the environment, space journeys, dinosaurs, robots and the year 2000. All of which seem to indicate a futures orientation and the ability to deal with the concept of future time. Psychologists gathering temporal orientation data count such images without pausing to stop and think where such images emanate from. Are they appropriated, eg from advertising or film, or conceived in imagination? If appropriated are the images re-configured imaginatively? When asked to nominate a distant future time do people do so in much the same way as they nominate a lottery number or do they really attempt to image the world at that time? What time frame(s) do they normally function within?

Another set of questions relate to the responsibility of those who do research on young people's visions of the future to question their own assumptions. Why, for example, do psychologists implicitly accept that the young do not project beyond their thirtieth birthday and feel more optimistic about their own future, but paradoxically feel very pessimistic about the future of others? If we asked better informed questions would we get such perplexing, and not very helpful, results? So far recent forays into interview methods and away from cognitive psychology in the study of futures orientation and planning have not seemed to overcome the basic uncritical assumptions many western academics hold about time. In addition we still do not know if children with 'futures oriented' parents have a different time sense to other children. Practically nothing is known about how teachers deal with temporality in the classroom. How often do they ask their students 'But what if...?'. In short when someone talks about the future, what are their actual temporal reference points, how meaningful are the words, how elastic the ideas, how deep is the knowledge?

How can futures educators be effective if so little is known about the particular influences and processes involved in futures thinking? To make the best of our own efforts we have to undertake forms of practitioner research every time we become involved in futures instruction. From these humble beginnings hypotheses can be developed and tested, so that we will eventually have a better understanding of what we are dealing with. When the author teaches her own courses she finds it necessary to engage in some early exercises with her students for that very purpose. The results are most encouraging. It is this information which forms the basis of much of the subsequent discussion.

Futures for postgraduates

Postgraduates at the University of Newcastle are able to take two subjects relating to futures. These are Application of Futures Studies in Education and Futures Planning and Policy in Australian Education. Class sizes are generally small, ranging from 5 to 20. In the first subject students are introduced to the futures field and futures concepts. Specific methods are introduced in tandem with futures issues relevant to education. Students and lecturer work together to identify the issues and then students are introduced to the tools and methods futurists use to explore such issues, and to generate ideas about the future. Students learn to run brainstorming and nominal group technique sessions and how to employ focus group interviews, Delphi and other forms of survey to collect futures data. They learn how forecasts are made, how to evaluate them critically, and are introduced to specific methods to forecast and analyse futures data, ranging from simple trend line regression to cross-impact analysis and scenario generation. The generation of images of the future, and the utility of speculative fiction are also the subject of examination. How methods are combined and their strengths and weaknesses are also examined. The underlying theme reinforced in each lecture is the wide applic-ation of such methods in everyday contexts in education. In assignment work students apply what they have learned to 'research' topics of their own choice. Many teachers opt to explore futures thinking in their own classrooms. Often this means they design a series of lessons on a futures theme and observe how students respond to futures ideas and tools.

The second subject introduces students to critical futurism. Emphasis is given to the importance of exploring education within the framework of an extended present (ie the notion of a 200-year present which embraces both past and future) and to asking critical questions of so-called futures oriented documents. Students are expected to collect and evaluate such documents within the area of greatest concern to them, for example, if they are nurse educators, this may be the futures of nurse training. The list is endless: primary mathematics, school sport, the educational role of the Internet, gendered education, to name only a few. Within their nominated area students seek data that establish trends or signals change and they attempt to identify continuities, conventions and traditions. They bring this knowledge to bear on the critical futures evaluation of key Australian policy blueprints, and the possible impact of the recommendations they contain on their particular area of concern. They operationalise their understandings and awareness by gener-ating alternative scenarios (Holbrook 1992: 32ff). Students often become angrily aware of how much disjointed, temporally restricted, and futures-absent policy making there is. They are encouraged by the lecturer to use their scenarios in staff development contexts, submission writing and instit-utional or curriculum planning.

Since 1991 in the applications subject the author administers a brief futures thinking exercise right at the start of lectures. The original intention was to simply get a grip on the student's predisposition toward futures, but the responses were so interesting and picked up on so many aspects of futures orientation in a short space of time that the instrument was improved and given every year thereafter. Fifty-seven students confidentially completed the task in class between 1992 and 1995. The task consists of a very short series of questions about previous exposure to futures studies, their sex and age group, followed by four timed ten minute exercises.

Questionnaire responses indicate that the vast majority of students doing 'futures methods' have not previously engaged in any form of futures study. While this has not changed over a decade, the students' reasons for doing the futures subjects have changed. Since about 1991 there has been devolution of responsibility in the state school system, hence the escalation of 'account-ability'. Free tertiary education is in transition back to full fee-paying and all state-funded sectors of education are subject to financial stringencies. Not surprisingly these factors are influencing the choice of university subjects. In education faculties there are some subjects that are more desirable than others because they have been given priority by educational bureaucrats, among them educational administration and financial management, special eduction and computers in education. The vast majority of Masters in Educational Studies students choose the priority areas. This has put the squeeze on 'found-ation' subjects such as history and philosophy of education, and on areas deemed 'marginal' such as futures. To keep the numbers viable in the futures subjects the author chose to offer them additionally at an outlying campus and as part of the summer program. In both cases the students had restricted subject choices.

Between 1992 and 1995, over half of the students enrolled in futures subjects chose them because they were intrinsically interested in them. Of these a small proportion were attracted because there is a futures component in one of the subjects they were teaching. Others were attracted by the off-beat nature of the subject, the fact that they can read and do an assignment on science fiction, or because they wanted 'relief' from the strand of subjects necessary for promotion. Of the remainder one or two thought futures sounded like an easy option, but most chose the subjects on pragmatic grounds – related to location and timetable. This is borne out by the routine confidential student subject evaluation forms collected at the end of the semester. Needless to say some students have to be convinced of the utility and validity of futures as a field of study!

The introductory exercise

The introductory exercise in futures thinking provides an assessment of how far students tend to project into the future (temporal extension). It also asks them to construct images of their own and global futures and determines how positive or negative they are about those futures. Hence it covers some key elements of futures orientation. As a measure of such things it has proved a very robust instrument. Only the findings will be dealt with here but more about the measures, including statistical tables can be found in Holbrook and Bourke (forthcoming).

The exercise is very simple and takes about forty minutes to complete. First the students plot their life in all its ups and downs, highs and lows, as a graph with no specific scale. To do this you provide them with the barest of graph templates. A vertical line with a horizontal one emanating from its midpoint and the instruction that what is above the line represents positive experiences and below, negative ones. Students designate the end point. They then repeat the exercise as a social plot (ie of Australian society) on another graph, and nominate the start and end point (eg 1953 and 2001). The next exercise requires them to complete an open ended sentence, 'In…I will be…' They are asked to write as 'expansively' as possible and they nominate their own date. Most fill two thirds of a page with writing. The final task is the same except 'The world' is substituted for 'I'. Once again most complete two thirds of a page. Ten minutes is allocated for each of the four tasks. The exercise is given during the first two-hour lecture of the futures method subject after introductions have been made and a lecture outline has been handed out. The lecturer explains that no-one else but they and the lecturer will see the sheets. Students are told that the task is an orientation to several key concepts that will be discussed in the first group of lectures (ie the role and scope of futures studies, temporal orientation, imaging and imagining the future and alternative futures).

From observation, and based on the amount of data generated in a relatively short time, they attack the exercise with considerable enthusiasm. Before they do I point out that there are no right answers and that this is an exercise they will be able to repeat in classroom and workshop contexts in their own workplace and in the next lecture I explain how. My enthusiasm for the task may rub off on them, but many see it as great fun, intriguing, and different from normal 'academic' tasks. The exercise seems to be intrinsically interesting and some make the point of telling me it is the first time they have written imaginatively for years! There can be no doubt from the content that some write cathartically outlining aspirations and fears for self and family. A small number use the words 'wish' and 'hope'. Only one person wrote entirely outside of experience. Her bubble cities (dealt with when she wrote of personal and world futures) were other-worldly. By contrast one wrote in great detail about a particular birthday dinner in the future, naming the wines (obviously already purchased) and the dishes. Clearly these present the extremes of imaginative and what I came to call 'functional' imaging. Both dealt with the nominated points in depth and with fluency, that is bearing in mind the restricted time allowed for the task.

The short time allocated to each section of the exercise results in a sort of individual brainstorming. It casts up developed images as well as undeveloped ones, including constructs of individual imagination and popular myth. If a person has dwelt on the future they already have some worked and rounded ideas which translate into quite dense and connected images, for example, often describing how a state of affairs came to be or what something will be like in considerable detail – as if they had already seen it happen. This is especially so in the personal futures section. A few explain in great detail where or how they will teach in the future, elaborating on one or a few connected items:

> By the year 2002 I will be principal of a high school…which caters for students with performing arts talents. The school will be a comprehensive school which involves the community in…teaching, performance and use of facilities. The school will operate on flexihours to meet demands of students and have a curriculum which involves academic and performance with a vocational orientation in related areas of performing arts…

And so it goes on explaining more about how the school operates. In contrast some simply provide lists, eg 'there will be overpopulation, famine, acceleration of war…' Some are wish lists – I hope to be retired, happy, have grandchildren, and so on:

> By the year 2000 I will have completed this degree and one or two others – perhaps a law degree. I will have two or three children and will be enjoying watching them grow up and develop, and I hope helping them and being a good friend to them. I will live in a place I like on the north coast of New South Wales with a few acres and not far from the ocean. I will continue to be interested in water sports…I doubt I will be working in the same career I am currently in…

What can be undertaken is an assessment of positives and negatives in their thinking, their temporal extension, density of future imaging and a comparison of the way they see their own as opposed to national/global futures.

With respect to temporal extension the students have to think about five points in time, one representing a projection of their life, one nominating the time at which they wish to start thinking about Australian society, and one projecting to a point in the future for that society (engaging the notion of an extended present). When they move to the written exercise they are asked to nominate a future point in their own life, and also nominate a point for discussion about the future of the world. Is there any consistency in the dates they nominate? Is there a difference between the three contexts, self, Australian society, global future?

How positive and how negative the students feel about personal, Australian and global futures is determined from the graphs and from the text. For purposes of description and further analysis the images can be categorised, counted and evaluated for style (connectedness, fluency), approach (imaginative through to functional) and density or depth (from well developed through to bare bones of ideas). In the case of the vignettes the students wrote about the future each item was scored by the author as positive, negative or neutral. If they didn't venture a position, for example, if they wrote 'population will grow' this was seen as neutral (if there were no contradictory contextual clues), but if they wrote population would 'explode' or 'grow worse' both were classed as negative, especially if this judgement was borne out by the thrust of the surrounding text. Neutral comments were scored as zero, positive ones as +1 and negative as –1.

Futures predispositions

The group consisted of an equal number of males and females and the great majority were over 36 years of age. With a couple of exceptions, no statistically significant differences in responses related to either age or sex, so it is possible to speak of the results in terms of the group as a whole. The most interesting result is that the group saw the future in positive terms, whether they plotted it on a graph or wrote about it, and whether or not they were referring to personal or social and global futures. Moreover they were significantly more positive about personal futures throughout. This does not, however, mean that there were not some very pessimistic responses:

> In 2005 the world will be a difficult place. Population will have continued to explode; natural beauty ripped asunder in that endeavour to utilise that last piece of resource. Crowds of people will wander aimlessly around because man has been so clever to replace himself with machines and computers...

But there were some positively idyllic ones as well:

> In 2050 the world will be smaller – fewer governments. [The] Baby Boomers will be leaving behind a developed geriatric system.... Education of a formal nature will occur in smaller groups, not based on a chronological system. I have a sense of the time of the Golden Age of Greece – philosophers, art, medicine, astronomy...

When plotting the highs and lows of their life the average life span was 61 years although the minimum was 34 and the maximum was age 100. In nominating a year to start the plot representing Australian society the average starting date was 1882 with a range from zero to 1990 (extreme year values were dropped when calculating the mean projected dates). Social projection finished on average at year 2031 (range 1950 to 3000). These data indicate most respondents were operating within an 'extended present' encompassing a reasonably distant past and future. Males tended to project further ahead with respect to social futures than females, and females tended to graph more ups and downs (in terms of peaks and depressions) in their personal plotting exercise.

On average the year nominated for the personal future sentence completion exercise was 2007 (the range was 1993 to 2050). The average year for the world futures exercise was 2086 (range 2000 to 3000). When plotting the social future of their own society the students were generally less extended in their projection than when they were asked to nominate a date as a starting point to write about world futures. This may be a function of the method provided to respond to the task but, given the general strength of consistency in response across tasks, this information seems be signalling the operation of futures thinking in different time frames.

What future images were presented? For example war and aggression featured quite strongly in world futures, but the tendency was to imagine a world in which aggression was reducing rather than escalating. Based on emergent themes in the texts nine major categories were identified by the author. They are futures of: family and other relationships, family welfare, own welfare, community and nation, international affairs, world problems, technology. Another quite separate category is 'aliens', although only a few posited that earth would have contact with aliens. Space travel, along with medical advances, advances and innovations in computers and Artificial Intelligence, including those relating to aggression, were sub-categories that fell within the grouping technology. When the students mentioned international affairs it was in either the area of politics or economics, all other references to the world fell into the categories of world problems and technology. World problems included the gap between rich and poor nations, natural resources, health, population, war and aggression. In the community and national context housing and cities, personal security, education, government, and resources were some sub-groups. When referring to their own welfare popular categories were retirement, self education, career, travel, finances, leisure, lifestyle (embracing possessions), and feelings about self. In the relationships category mentions of children and a relationship with spouse or significant other and growth of family size (including children's children) are the sub-groups. Family welfare incorporates comments on the careers and health of family members.

Family relationships and welfare were, not surprisingly, more mentioned in relation to personal than world futures. Mentions of technological change featured quite prominently in relation to world futures, but there was also a tendency for mention to occur in personal futures. Given the vast majority were teachers engaged in further education themselves it is not surprising to note they very often mentioned the future of their own studies or referred to education in personal, national and global contexts.

Given that only ten minutes were allocated to each writing task, it follows that students had to orient themselves toward thinking about the future rapidly. An analysis of the style of response provides some indication of the complexity and depth of their thinking, and flags whether or not they have previously given thought to futures in the different contexts nominated by the author. When students wrote about their personal futures some 20 percent wrote in such a way that the points were interwoven, exhibiting strong connection with one another, providing a convincing and plausible picture. In 38 percent of cases some of the text exhibited these traits (ie a part of the vignette was sketchy and disjointed) and for 42 percent the items were quite unconnected. On the whole the vignettes tended toward an extension or variation on everyday themes (for example they talked about what would happen when they retired). Did students flesh out their ideas in much depth? Actually one third of students did. As for the number of different items covered, about half presented up to five different items and almost as many presented 6–10 items.

When students wrote about world futures less than two thirds presented items in a connected or partially connected style. Close to half were 'imaginative' and well over half of the student texts exhibited depth, ie, the ideas were well or reasonably well formed. About 50 percent covered between 6 and 10 items, and close to one fifth 11 or more items. Those who wrote in a very developed way in the personal area also did so in the world area, whether or not they wrote about a few or about very many items.

Some reflections on futures orientation

The literature, the author's teaching experience and her – as yet very limited – research on the temporal orientation of teachers, all point to the fact that futures orientation involves working simultaneously in various time frames. The time dimensions involved vary from individual to individual. For the present these can be called 'functional time', 'life time' and 'mythic time'. The outer limits of the functional time frame are bounded by reasonable certainty where long term does not exceed a few years. It is the pragmatic time frame pertinent to daily and yearly planning. The boundaries of life time are determined by the personal, adult expectation of life span, where long term can be a months, years or many decades away. Mythic time can span into the very distant future. It is characterised by that psychological determination that all is uncertain and that one is entering the realm of fantasy.

It can prove very effective for a futures educator to alert students to these time frames, their own temporal predispositions and those of others. These time frames are most obvious in the context of planning and projection when the individual needs to specify a time frame – hence engage in purposeful, conscious temporal extension. Yet it is not helpful or useful, as a futurist, to ask a child or an adult to think X years ahead, say to 2001. For some, 2001 is impossible to conceive as anything but a number not much different to 2500. Others will have already envisioned several things happening to them by that time and will probably have some well formed expectations about social futures pertinent to that date as well. For the former group, no matter what age, 2001 falls well within a mythic time frame whereas the latter are working within a life time or even a functional time frame. Hence as futurists we may be able to extend the boundaries of one or more of these time frames, but it certainly makes sense to find out and then work with how each individual in a class or a think-tank, or a community planning group functions with respect to framing time. For example when someone thinks of personal futures they may only think in functional time, yet when thinking of social futures extend into life time, but not mythic time. Those whose functional or life time frame is quite extended may show particular commitment to, or aptitude for, long range imaging and planning.

The idea of multiple functioning time frames may cast quite a new light on the results of temporal extension studies and even posit an explanation for the positive/negative futures disparity between personal future imaging and social imaging.

The pace of change in society may be already having an impact on the time frames we work within. We could well be on the brink of a significant cultural shift in our predisposition toward futures imaging. The teachers in Newcastle attending futures classes show a diversity of time frame use and, encouragingly, a tendency to positive self and social futures imaging. Bearing in mind that not all the teachers who enrol in futures subjects do so from a strong motivation to learn about futures, they nonetheless exhibit an extraordinarily promising futures orientation. Promising enough to cause me to take a different perspective on futures orientation than those who suggest that 'the West's repertoire of positive future images would seem to be at an all time low and this vicious circle somehow needs to be broken' (Hicks, 1995: 11).

References

Bessant, B, and Holbrook, A (1995) *Reflections on Educational Research in Australia. A History of the Australian Association for Research in Education*, Coldstream Vic., AARE.

Garrett, M (1993) 'A Way Through the Maze: What Futurists Do and How They Do It', *Futures*, 25(3): 254–74.

Hicks, D (1995) 'A Lesson for the Future: Young People's Hopes and Fears for Tomorrow', *Futures*, 28(1): 1–13.

Holbrook, A (1992) 'Teachers With Vision and Visions of Teaching: The Role of Futures Studies and Research in Post-Graduate Teacher Education', *Futures Research Quarterly*, 8(4): 27–48.

Holbrook, A and Bourke, G (forthcoming) 'Accentuating the Positive: The Futures Views of Some Teachers in NSW, Australia'.

Hughes, D and Trautmann, T (eds) (1995) *Time: Histories and Ethnologies*, Michigan: The University of Michigan Press.

Inayatullah, S (1993) 'From "Who am I?" to "When am I?": Framing the Shape and Time of the Future', *Futures*, 25(3): 235–53.

Lewis, E (1992) 'Futures Orientation in County Government: Testing a Model of Strategic Management', *Futures Research Quarterly*, 8(1): 77–95.

Rogers, M and Tough, A (1996) 'Facing the Future is Not for Wimps', *Futures*, 28(5): 491–6.

Slaughter, R (1993) 'Futures Concepts', *Futures*, 25(3): 289–314.

12. Futures studies at the University of Houston-Clear Lake

Peter C. Bishop

Summary

The graduate program Studies of the Future at the University of Houston-Clear Lake was founded in 1975. Far from starting a trend, US colleges may actually have fewer futures courses today although interest around the world may be growing. In the meantime, the UHCL futures program has developed an approach to prepare its graduates for professional practice. It employs many of the emerging innovations in education: combining school with work, suiting the curriculum to student schedules, and teaching to a prescribed set of outcomes. It has also distilled a futures perspective suitable for general education at many colleges and universities.

Origins and history

The University of Houston-Clear Lake's graduate program in studies of the future (as one of only two such programs in the United States) was hardly the start of a trend. In fact, the program was started quite by accident. In 1973, the State of Texas received an economic windfall from taxes on the suddenly higher price of oil. They used the funds to expand the state's higher education institutions. In the process, they expanded the University of Houston – a large urban campus – to a system of four campuses, including new suburban, inner-city and rural campuses. UH-Clear Lake was the suburban campus in this new system.

Situated next to the NASA Johnson Space Center in southeast Houston, UH-Clear Lake was in an ideal location for a professionally and technologically oriented regional university. The new university, however, was established with a number of provisions.

- It would be upper-division, beginning with the junior (14th) year of education because Houston already had a strong community college system that served the freshman and sophomore years.

- It would offer no doctoral programs since the main campus of the University of Houston was already offering a full range of doctorates.
- It would not offer any degree program that was already being offered at the main campus.

It was this last provision which allowed the creation of the futures program. Remembering that the main campus of the University of Houston was a full, comprehensive university, what was this new university to offer? One strategy was to rename traditional degree programs, so UH-Clear Lake has no English program, it has literature instead. History became historical studies, communication became media studies etc.

The other strategy was to create novel programs that did not appear in traditional universities. The original catalog was a wonderland of programs. Most of those programs did not survive. UH-Clear Lake now offers a fairly mainstream set of professional degrees in business, education, psychology, computer science, with some more academic majors in humanities, science and mathematics.

Futures studies was one, perhaps the only, non-traditional program to survive. Jib Fowles, author of *The Handbook of Futures Research*, and Chris Dede, well-known educational futurist from the University of Massachusetts, were hired to staff the program. Other faculty joined in, and the program flourished during the heady days of the late 1970s.

The original mission of the program was intellectual: a discussion and critique of the forces shaping the future. Growth versus no-growth was a popular debate. The educational futurists sponsored a large World Future Society meeting on the future of education. Students, most of whom were in high school during the riotous sixties, eagerly joined in. It wasn't Woodstock, but it was the closest thing that 1977 had to offer!

That mission began to fade after four or five years as students became more career conscious. The second question, after 'What is futures studies?', was 'What can I do with the degree?' and then 'How much money do futurists make?' Careerism hit higher education with a vengeance. Even futures studies felt the shock waves. In 1978, Oliver Markley came from SRI International to introduce a more professional mission to the program. The faculty developed a new, standard curriculum, and the program settled into its current mission of launching professional futurists or 'futurizing' the approach of those with established careers.

The core of futures education

One of the striking features of the futures program is how much graduates attribute their success to it. They speak about openness and creativity, concepts which are difficult to pin down. No doubt a futures education represented a profound shift for them in how they thought about and related to the world.

That shift has even caused some concern over the years because it can stir up fears and issues which are frightening and difficult to deal with. Those who come with little awareness of the world or the future and seriously engage the content of the program, enter a temporary depressive state during the first few months. Although the program has no specific data, more than one student has reported how overwhelming the sheer enormity of the change and its problems can be. They feel impelled to do something; someone should do something about the risk, the suffering, the insanity of what they see. Yet they feel powerless as one person to do much. While we tout the ability of one person to change the world, realistically, few of us have the position, the skill or the resources to affect the big problems in a significant way.

Fortunately, students do not stay in that state for long. They begin to sort through the masses of information, to understand the macro forces, to make meaning of the enormity for themselves. What is more important, they realize that, although they cannot solve the large problems directly, they can do something in their own sphere. That realization provides energy and meaning to their work and their lives. Not every student experiences these ups and downs, but the best ones usually do – or have done so at some time.

So just what is this experience of acquiring a futures perspective? Graduates claim it is important if not essential to their lives and their work. Students pass through a period of turbulence and discomfort as they confront the future. What is going on here? At the individual level, it is like the experience of leaving home. In our early years, home is not part of the world, it is the world. It contains a complete set of assumptions, beliefs, rules and practices to guide our life; these are obvious, so obvious that they are invisible and never known at the conscious level. Children leave home for school where they find a different set of assumptions, beliefs, rules and practices. They meet people with different homes and realize over time that their home is also different. It is not how the world is, but how their world is, others being different. College students experience this difference more deeply and talk about it more, sometimes endlessly. The sophomore is the 'wise fool' who has just discovered 'truth' at the hands of his philosophy professor, who explains how 'wrong' his parents have been for so long. Confronting people from different cultures, different social classes, different countries, realizing that they are not like the kids in the old neighborhood can be a shattering experience. Adults who travel outside their culture for the first time experience the same disorienting feeling of being on someone else's turf.

The same happens to those who travel in the future. The past is real (in western culture at least), but the future is not. It is an unreal place of fantasy and hopes, of danger and risk. Not thinking about it seriously, most people ignore the possibility of radical change. It's like death or catastrophe; it happens to someone else. Futures studies requires that we contemplate ourselves in a world that is as different from the present as China is from the United States. People have a right to be upset the first time! 'That's my world that they're talking about changing!' But just as European explorers expanded intercultural contact and paved the way for the appreciation of all cultures, so futures studies may open our minds to non-stereotypical images of the future and pave the way for the appreciation of alternative plausible futures. If that is true, futures studies may be another great episode in the intellectual history of the West.

Sigmund Freud characterized history as the process of unseating human-kind from its comfortable place in the universe. Scientists evicted humankind from one comfortable home after another – at the center of the universe (Copernicus), at the pinnacle of creation (Darwin), at the core of our rational selves (Freud). Now feminism, multiculturalism, and post-modernism remove men, Europeans and ideologues respectively from their favored perches. Where does one stand any more? Is there no refuge from alienation and change?

The present is the last bastion of security. The present is special, it is a favored place. All history has led to this moment, the past is prologue, and we are the final chapter, the climax. The universe is about us, today, in all our glory...but here come these futurists! They don't believe that the present is special in any absolute sense. It is just one moment in the flow of history. The river moves on from here to other lives, other generations, other eras. Future generations will look down on us just like we look down on the past – unfairly stereotyping, somewhat pitying, and mostly forgetting. They won't know what it was like to live in these times.

If history stops with the present, then the present is a special, favored place. If it goes on, we are just a chapter, like the other chapters, in a never ending story. When the future is real, as real as the past, then we lose our special place in history. Our time can still be special to us, since it is our time; but it won't be special on an absolute scale. We are making history. That's good. But someday we will be history. That's not so good.

Futures education is at root the realization that we are part of the flow of history, from the past, through the present and into the future. Once we accept that, it's not so bad. After all, we have recovered from being 'the third rock' from an ordinary sun in an ordinary galaxy. It's still our earth. Even though we do not hold the lofty place that the ancients thought we did, our time is still special because it's ours. Getting to that point, however, requires letting go – letting go of the present, letting go of its assumptions, beliefs, rules and practices, letting go of home just like the first-grader has to let go of parents in order to get on with life. Our assumptions, beliefs, rules and practices are fine, but they are temporary. Future generations will have their own, and they will be fine, too. The present will not last forever. That awesome realiz-ation is the core futures education.

Graduates of a futures program are more capable than others in the present because they have incorporated that realization into their professional lives. They have no need to defend the trappings of the present, because they are temporary. They may stay, they may go. What are the possibilities? What's the best thing to do? How can we move forward? If change is inevitable, how can we use it for our purposes?

Program description

The program in Studies of the Future has graduated between 100 and 150 students in its 20-year history. It carries between 40 and 60 students at any one time, most of whom go to school part-time. Student characteristics and expectations follow no clear pattern, except that they are interested and/or concerned about the future and they are dissatisfied with the offerings of traditional degree programs. As with most students at UH-Clear Lake, futures students are older than the traditional 18–22 year olds. In fact, students with some work and life experience understand the impact of the futures perspective better. Students right out of undergraduate school do all right (ie they are good at going to school) but many of them miss the revolutionary nature of the futures perspective. Although the UH-Clear Lake program is only one of two such programs in the United States (the other being the University of Hawaii), most of the students still come from the Houston area. Nevertheless, a significant minority relocates for the year or two it takes to get the degree. Students have come from every region of the USA and from other countries as well (Canada, Mexico, Venezuela, Sweden, South Africa, China and Pakistan).

Students take a 36 semester hour curriculum consisting of 30 hours (10 semesters) of course work and 6 hours of a concluding Master's Option. The 30 hours of courses are divided evenly between required (Table 12.1) and elective courses. The elective courses are divided into those taken within the futures department (such as world futures, social change, strategic planning, visionary futures, facilitation skills, classic texts in futures studies) and those taken in other departments such as business, public administration, education or social science). The electives outside the futures program broaden students' background in a particular field and allow them to apply the futures perspective in that field. Futures students are welcome, even sought after by other programs. Their high-level skills and broad interests are an excellent mix with other majors whose expertise is confined to the narrower field. The program concludes with a Masters Option that comes in three types (see Table 12.2).

Graduates have been variously successful in achieving their career goals, depending on how well they mastered the futures perspective and acquired its skills and how well they networked and marketed themselves and their trade. The most illustrious of the graduates are principals of futures-consulting firms or independent consultants themselves. They have succeeded at journalism, public speaking, teaching or as key staff members in business and government organizations.

Table 12.1   Required courses

Introduction to futures studies	An introduction to the field, its concepts, methods, people and organizations
Qualitative research methods	Environmental scanning Scenario development Impact assessment Strategic planning and organization development
Quantitative research methods	Interviewing and survey research Descriptive statistics Measures of change Trend extrapolation Demographic projection Cross-impact analysis
Using systems approaches	Systems theory Causal modeling
Proseminar in futures studies	Summary of theories and methods Preparation for professional practice Integrative research project

Table 12.2   Master options

Thesis	A permanent contribution to the theory or methodology of the futures field (eg a published article)
Project	Futures work useful to a specific client at a specific time (eg a forecast or plan)
Internship	Work with a professional futurist or someone who practices long-term forecasting and planning (eg a futures consulting firm)

Most students, however, do not aspire to full-time careers as professional futurists. Rather they come from established careers in business, education, government or the military and return to those careers with the capacity to incorporate the future into their on-going work. It is harder to track their progress, but those who report testify that the futures perspective made a big difference in their work and their careers.

New developments

WFS Professional Forum and the Institute for Futures Research

Futures studies is not learned exclusively or even largely in the classroom. It is a skill more than a body of knowledge and must be practised to become real. Jennifer Jarratt, an early graduate of the program and principal in Coates & Jarratt, joined the faculty for the 1987-88 academic year. She instituted the WFS Professional Forum, an annual student-directed event on a specific aspect of the future. Forum topics have been the future of the US Southwest, of work, of health care, of the City of the Houston, and most recently, images of the future from different cultural perspectives.

Under the leadership of Oliver Markley and Peter Bishop, the UH-Clear Lake futures program has also experimented with field practice to suit its varied population in these changing times. The program created the Institute for Futures Research to manage futures research and application projects involving faculty and students. The aim is to offer students the experience of working on futures projects before they graduate.

The intensive summer program

One of the serious obstacles to students attending the program from outside Houston is the need to relocate for one or two years. While a fully supported distance education program in futures studies would be ideal (and a dream at this point), for the time being the program pursues more mundane approaches. In that vein, the program created an intensive summer program whereby students get a futures degree by spending six weeks in two success-ive summers in Houston. They do the rest of their work (preparing for the summers, doing term projects, taking two courses and completing the master's option) in their local area. Although an unusual way to package a graduate degree, the experience of the first cohort demonstrated that the quality of the students and the intensity of the interaction during the summer sessions produce a concentration and quality of work that is difficult to achieve in the more 'leisurely' standard semesters.

New work roles

The program is also pursuing a number of other experiments in order to better serve its clientele. Dr Wendy Schultz, a graduate and long-time researcher at the University of Hawaii, joined the program as a visiting professor. Other faculty are experimenting with part-time appointments in order to integrate futures work and futures education more closely. The program recently hosted a Futures Search Conference involving faculty, students, administrators, alumni and business representatives. Initiatives to emerge from that confer-ence were:

- involving more university faculty in the futures program;
- integrating alumni into the life of the program;
- launching a more vigorous marketing campaign;
- strengthening the work of the Institute for Futures Research;
- increasing the program's presence on the Web.

Thus the future is continually unfolding.

The outcome of a futures curriculum

The futures program at UH-Clear Lake is also participating in a university-wide movement to make the outcomes of education more explicit. Behavioral objectives have been around for a long time and professors often ridiculed them as trivial. 'What we teach is much too important to be reduced to a set of objectives!' Well, some behavioral objectives are trivial, but that does not change the fact that keeping a goal in mind usually increases the quality of the effort towards that goal and the chances of it occurring. After all, don't we recommend that our clients work toward a set of explicit and measurable goals? Should we not take that advice ourselves?

In that vein, the futures faculty is discussing its outcomes with students, alumni, professional futurists and other faculty. Slowly they are coming to an understanding of what they are attempting to accomplish with an education in futures studies. The current list of outcomes is shown in Table 12.3. It is by no means a final list, but one that illustrates the general types of knowledge and skills required of a professional futurist. A task group with the capstone Proseminar is working on the next version of these outcomes, to be implemented with the next summer class in 1997.

Futures studies in higher education, however, has a higher purpose, one beyond the mission to prepare professional futurists. The future should be as common in the curriculum as the past is. How many professors, departments and courses do we have in studies of the past? Thousands. How many in studies of the future? A handful. Which is more important, the past or the future? Neither, each is important in a different way. But should we not then study them both as part of every educational curriculum? If not to prepare professional futurists, then what does futures studies offer the college student?

Knowledge of trends and issues shaping the future

The STEEP (Social, Technological, Economic, Ecological, Political) categories can serve as a taxonomy for the forces shaping the future. Students should know those forces and their implications at many levels – for themselves, their communities, their nation and the world, at least.

Table 12.3 Learning outcomes for studies of the future

Profession

- Enumerate the concepts, people and schools of thought in futures studies
  Describe the differences between futures studies and other perspectives
  on the future
  Choose and describe an appropriate futures method for a given futures
  objective

Pattern recognition

- Describe general conditions and trends in the nation and the world that
  affect the future (or explain the basic changes going on in demography,
  economics, technology, politics, the environment and socio-cultural systems)
- Find relevant statistics and reviews which document those changes, using
  spreadsheet and presentation graphics
- Describe how the future might be different if those conditions and trends
  continue
- Gather key information relevant to the future of a given topic from people,
  published and internet sources

Critical thinking

- Identify the main idea (inference), evidence and assumptions in an argument
- Develop an alternative inference to an argument using alternative evidence
  and alternative assumptions
- Develop a forecast based on evidence and assumptions, including quantitative evidence

Creativity

- Identify the multi-level implications of trends and proposed changes
- Paint alternative, detailed images of the future in scenario format

Systems thinking

- Describe the roles of feedback, level and context in the behavior of a system
- Identify the behavior of a system as a time series of one or more variables
  in that system
- Explain how the system behavior is produced by the operation of its comp-
  onents
- Use systems thinking to create multiple scenarios of the future

Table 12.3 Learning outcomes for studies of the future (*continued*)

Change

- Work toward a personal vision of the future
- Help others articulate their vision for the future
- Plan and implement a change in an individual, group and organizational system

Communication

- Share information and ideas in written and oral form
- Contribute to and facilitate skillful discussion about the future, including listening and dialogue
- Use communication tools, including word processors, presentation graphics, e-mail and other internet tools

Business skills

- Write a proposal and carry out a project to satisfy an identified client's need
- Make a demonstrated contribution to a joint project
- Behave according to the highest standards of integrity and ethics

A systems view of change

This includes the role of feedback and non-linear causality, the importance of context and outside influences, and the emergence of surprising consequences at higher system levels. The systems perspective has been around for five decades now. While many subscribe to it, few understand it and fewer use it. Breaking the bounds of linear-causality, reductionist thinking, the presumed isolation of systems from outside forces and the neglect of unintended cons-equences is high on the agenda for society's ability to navigate the challenges of the future and emerge with itself in one piece. The stakes of global prosperity or catastrophe have never been higher. We had better get it right this time, or we won't have future generations to worry about.

The role of assumptions in forming judgments about the world

Better known as critical thinking, one of the unique products of futures studies is to question most fundamental assumptions with a straight face. 'Why not directly link mind to computer communication?' we ask. While that may be far-fetched, futurists are ready to accept different assumptions more than any other discipline, except perhaps for the more critical branches of the human-ities. In fact, uncovering the plausible alternatives of the future requires reversing many deeply held assumptions about the past and the present.

Every other discipline is based on its assumptions that become inviolable rules for thinking about the future. One of the fundamental assumptions in futures studies is not to accept any assumption as inviolable, even those which concern the future of its own disciplines.

The role of choice and influence in shaping the future

Choosing a preferred future and working towards that future is a necessary component of an effective life. Fatalism opposes the futures perspective with its belief either that the future is predetermined or that effort by an individual or a group to influence it will make no appreciable difference. Futures studies provides the hope, not only for individual success, but for group and organizational achievement as well. If a group pursues a preferred future with vigor and good sense, the chance of that preferred future occurring increases. Getting the group to act that way requires skill, but that skill will never be successful if the image of its success is never conceived.

Responsibility for the future

Responsibility is the trickiest and most controversial outcome. Some applied futurists might even dispute its being on the list. 'Our job is to help our students and clients achieve their goals, not impose our own goals upon them.' The more normative futurists will take just the opposite position. 'If futurists fail to make moral choices and act on those choices, why should anyone else do so? Who then will be responsible for the future?' The dispute strikes at the very core of the discipline. Making moral choices is part of what a college education is about, and futures studies should direct those choices to that all important realm where the choices matter – the future.

Futures studies has the opportunity to support the traditional college curriculum by emphasizing the systemic and contingent nature of the world around the student and the need, indeed the obligation, to do something about that. A future curriculum with those goals cannot help but be successful in a college curriculum, academic resistance notwithstanding.

Epilogue

The Studies of the Future program hosted a Dean of Education for a few months sabbatical in the early 1980s. We had a conference at the end in which he said, 'You have done a clever thing with this program. You have wrapped the liberal arts in a professional package.' We took that as a high compliment.

Futures studies is indeed informed common sense. It's not brain surgery or rocket science. It's a simple shift in perspective from stereotyped images of the future to a richer range of alternative futures; from futures which are predetermined to futures that we have a hand in creating; from ignoring the complexity and uncertainty associated with the future to using that complexity to paint interesting and compelling pictures of change. But simple is not always easy. That is where futures education comes in.

Tearing away our death-grip on the present, admitting to the possibility of fundamental change, allowing ourselves to use that change for our own advantage are all marks of the futures perspective. Getting to that perspective involves the liberal arts – observing, listening, reading, analyzing, synthesizing, deciding, speaking, discussing, writing and ultimately acting. To make a profession out of these ancient skills seems redundant or absurd. Nevertheless, the world needs thoughtful people practicing these skills more than ever. Handing the future over to specialists ('the best and the brightest') whose narrow field of view precludes their understanding the systemic and holistic nature of change is the highest form of risk in a rapidly changing world. The future perspective, the perspective that views the shoreline, the rocks, the channel, the sky and the sea all at once, is the perspective of the lookout, the navigator, guiding the ship through the rough waters of the present. Educators need to prepare people with perspective and vision by incorporating futures thinking into their lessons everyday.

13. Futures studies via the World Wide Web

Paul Wildman

Summary

This chapter seeks to outline some of the ideas, insights and strategies arising from developing a multimedia, on-line Web learning experience as a futures studies course designed for interactive learning. The development took 18 months and involved a core team of five members. The content area of futures studies at masters' level and delivery via the World Wide Web, is in line with a key strategic direction at Southern Cross University, Australia, moving from a 'classroom teaching' to an 'elsewhere learning' organisation. Finally, principles of future learning experiences via course development for on-line WWW delivery are discussed.

Introduction

Networked learning is a new experience. It is a team process in its design, operation and evaluation and this chapter explores the network approach to co-generative learning. Valuable conclusions will be drawn about future developments in teaching future studies through the World Wide Web. Clearly, in any such process, the focus needs to be as much on the learning process and content, as it is on technology.

Initially the development of the unit was preceded by several faculty meetings where the content author, Sohail Inayatullah, from the World Futures Studies Federation (then based at Queensland University of Technology) presented the case for futures studies. Some nine months later, the University Academic Board approved the development of the unit (ED730 – Futures Studies: Methods, Issues and Visions) to complement those in the program for the Master of Organisational Development and Training. A small authoring contract was made with the content expert who, over the next year, developed the unit to incorporate critique from the Southern Cross University (SCU) team as well as getting audio, video and still pictures for inclusion in the course.

Strategic areas in designing Web based courseware

This section identifies and reviews areas that proved to be strategically significant in the design of the course.

Authoring the curricula

The content author, chosen as an expert in the field, designed the unit within the standard three by fifty hour modules. In effect this was a tour of the futures field with Sohail Inayatullah as guide. The initial task was to provide a context for the course articles, e-mail discussion and assessment, through inclusion of the cultural and intellectual history of each contributor to the unit. In this instance, the author's first step in course development was to acknowledge his epistemic biases, thus framing both the future and the course, while also allowing it to be open.

The unit structure has three modules. The first gives an overview of the methods and theories of futures research. It articulates the knowledge base of futures studies, raising both ontological and epistemological questions. Essays are by writers such as Inayatullah (1990), Masini (1995), Schultz (1995), Slaughter (1993) and Tough (1991). They are intended to set out the content and basic methods of the field as well as various theoretical approaches. In particular, students explore the notion of temporality, the role of future generations, and the importance of both institutional and value-based change.

The second module deals with emerging issues that are likely to transform society: robotics, telecommunications, microvita, globalism, genetics, gender co-operation, metaphor and governance. This section is less philosophical and the essays chosen give a sense of what the future might be like. However, more than prediction, the essays force a rethink of the categories we use to understand the future. Authors include Dator (1990), Stevenson and Lennie (1995) and Rudreshananda (1989).

The third module looks at unconventional visions of the future. This section is more culturally diverse having, for example, essays on African, Buddhist, Islamic, Tantric and world systems futures. It begins with an essay by noted peace philosopher Johan Galtung (1988) and concludes with an essay by Ashis Nandy (1987) in which the costs of utopianism are explored.

Each module takes a different type of approach: the first is philosophical, the second content-focused, the third is visionary. Authors were selected as leaders in their field, for the thoroughness of their work and their ability to relate their personal stories. Each section includes textbook type questions which then feed into learner interaction using e-mail based, feedback sections after each reading and web-mounted, student assignments with the lecturer's critique. Rather than requiring feedback, which tends to elicit loyal responses, the goal of the unit is to give students a framework to investigate their own personal and institutional futures.

Managing the project

This role included overall project management and co-ordination. In particular, this meant keeping track of all the multimedia items. For instance, unlike
a conventional unit of three modules with hard copy readings (say five or
six per module) and a workbook per module (giving a total of 18 items to
manage). This unit had a photo and audio file with each of the eight articles
for each of the three modules (ie $3 \times 8 \times 3 = 72$). These also had to go through
a three stage process to digitise, proof read and mount them via Hypertext
Markup Language (HTML), so over 200 items had to be tracked at any one
time. Consequently very early on a tracking system using an Excel™ spreadsheet was put in place linked to weekly meetings and numerous chase-up
e-mails.

Managing the text

This task involved preparing the twenty-four text-based articles for the futures
studies master's course. Many of the articles appeared to be in relatively good
order, presented on floppy disks which, at first sight, seemed to require simple
transfer into Microsoft Word™ in order to make a hard copy for viewing and
editing by the lecturer responsible for mounting and delivering the course.

The first papers arrived as hard copy and had to be scanned into the
computer. This necessitated using Omnipage 5.0™ for the scanning because
of its superior Optical Character Recognition (OCR) capabilities. However,
this did not always solve the problem of 'L's turning into '1's and 'e's turning
into 'c's during transfer. Some text would simply turn into total gobbledygook
with the resultant hieroglyphics being totally unreadable. Therefore many
sessions necessitated transcription from the draft direct to the new Word™
documents. We then transferred all of this onto a removable hard disc platter
for transfer to HTML.

Like the papers, many of the photographs came in as 'happy snaps' which
had to be scanned in and then worked up to publishable state using Microtek
Scanning™ and Adobe Photoshop™. Some photographs had been sent with
notes written all over the pictures which had to be cleaned up on the digital
image. The files were saved as TIFF™ (Transfer of Information For File) images
and later resized and converted to GIFs using a simple GIF™ (Graphic Interface Format) converter to enable them to be mounted on the Web.

To summarise, the preparation of such a diverse array of documents, photographs and tapes to the Web was simply a full turn of the multimedia wheel
reminding us of the pre-computerised days in media production when layout
was tailor made for each product. Past experience in audio production also
meant a fairly painless transfer of audio 'grabs' into Sound Edit Pro™.

An innovative web-based unit such as this requires a well-designed web
presence. It is not enough just to convert paper-based documents to an electronic medium and expect it to be effective. While not being entirely divorced

from the underlying paper structure, this unit has experimented with several new methods of presenting information to a digital audience. Feedback is an important aspect of this unit, so each article has an option which allows the reader to tell others what they thought of it. Because users must authorise themselves via user name and password to the Web browser before entering the unit (using the WWW security mechanisms), it has been possible to prevent students from viewing other students' feedback before providing their own. Once a student has given feedback on an article, he or she is then free to read that of other students. Each of the three modules also has an associated bulletin board, ie electronic mailing list through which students and teachers can communicate with each other. This mailing list is archived on the Web and can be viewed by date, thread, author or subject.

Finally, in order to facilitate the input of students who are using this material, a simple web interface to the '.htpasswd file' was developed which allows authorised users to add, modify or remove user names/passwords within this file. Authorised users can also add or remove other users, thereby making the system self-contained and maintainable by people with minimal UNIX knowledge or experience.

Instructional design

Instructional design in the development of the futures unit has been a matter of considering how to best utilise web technologies for teaching and learning. Initial discussions regarding the strengths and weaknesses of electronic course delivery, focused on the scope for asynchronous interactivity offered by computer-mediated communication (Rice, 1995). It was agreed that the potential was there for an innovative and unique course not only because of the *avant garde* nature of the subject area, but also due to the delivery methods being considered. Thus the facilitation of learning through electronic dialogue, on-line data gathering and collaboration between teachers and student peers, provided exciting goals for the teaching of this unit. Additional use of technologies such as full-length audio tapes, telephone tutorials and teleconferencing were also considered and could be incorporated in future reviews of teaching strategies. In particular, the work of Mason and Kaye (1989) provided a great deal of encouragement for the use of Computer-Mediated Communication (CMC).

This helped to inform the team not only of the benefits of this kind of delivery, but also gave us ideas about what has worked for others and pitfalls to be avoided, such as the intensive demands on memory to download large graphic, audio and video components of the materials, and e-assignments looking like a long e-mail (Ng, 1994). Discussions regarding the spirit and style of assessment (Rowntree, 1977) were pursued collaboratively by team members, with the final choices being determined by the SCU based coach, the author of this chapter.

The team proceeded through the questions of technical standards and the incorporation of variety in presentation and assessment (Morgan, 1993), at the same time as the work was being done to convert all resources into digital form for upload onto the Web. Questions on the quality of these resources recurred, as decisions were made to select suitable graphics and audio components for inclusion in the Web learning product.

Since the flexibility of web delivery is not only a result of the level of dialogue possible between lecturer and student, but also the level of interconnections possible between students, effective use of hypertext links and hyperarchiving is an important feature of the course (Cheek, Cook and Rudge, 1995). Dialogue, peer review and student interactivity with subject experts are also focal points for teaching and learning in this mode of study.

The e-mail and hypertext archive facilities also serve to promote both interaction (between people) and interactivity (between individuals and electronic resources). By its nature, the Web is a democratic environment with the extent and pace of interaction and interactivity being determined by individuals (Rice, 1995). To some degree the development of students' writing skills can be enhanced by providing a structured format which necessitates contribution to electronic discussion throughout the course. Practice in writing is thus gained by measured steps in a collaborative and inspirational context.

The major weaknesses identified in the use of the Web for course delivery centred around the technical difficulties and equity issues for students establishing connectivity. A further concern was the question of whether the university server would be reliable enough to handle increasing volumes of traffic as a result of its developing international presence on the Web.

Learning design and delivery

One of the hardest things here was to come to terms with the move from 'classroom teaching to elsewhere learning' under the World Wide Web. This meant letting go the idea of the lecturer controlling the learning process. As an example, the second assessment developed for this unit involves 100 percent peer review requiring the students to chart threads in e-mail discussions they have initiated without going 'outside' for references.

Assessment

Assessment emphasises interactivity in order to reflect the collegiate nature of networked learning. There are three assessments each of 2,500 words. The first is a standard piece on theory, the second an attempt at interactive peer assessment with each student distilling their e-mail contributions into a paper. No outside referencing is required or sought and the lecturer's opinion only given after the students have collectively arrived at a grade. For the third assessment students focus their work professionally into one of several categories of vocationally relevant futures. These include:

- types of futures studies;
- education;
- community development;
- environmental sustainability;
- peace research;
- human resource development futures;
- healthy futures;
- spirituality;
- gender;
- tourism;
- bio futures;
- ethics;
- Asia/Pacific futures.

If the student's professional interest is not represented by one of these categories, additional categories can be negotiated. References are recorded in the Professional Focus Folder, however, the text material is not. This means that students must also identify and access some information through web searches and conventional channels, ie a library.

The unit also offers students access to an editorial panel to review their paper (one of the three assessments) and help them prepare it to conference presentation standard. As such, these can also be published in the Futures Studies Monograph series. Further student comments and chosen assignments have been mounted on the Web for reference by future students. In this way, to an extent, students co-generatively learn and author the curriculum for future students.

Elsewhere learning

The multimedia 'elsewhere learning' format of the World Wide Web was chosen as it can handle many interactive users simultaneously, ie many to many. It is time and place independent and interactive. This may be compared to distance education which is hard-copy mediated, one-to-many, and time-and-place independent. Finally, the traditional 'classroom teaching' approach of face-to-face lecturers is unmediated, with medium interactivity, many-to-many and time-and-place dependent. An overview of these issues is presented in Table 13.1.

Lessons learnt

In summary, the lessons learnt during development and first semester operation include:

Table 13.1   A comparison of three forms of educational delivery

Delivery form	Mediation	Type of interaction	Time and place	Level of interactivity
Face-to-face	direct	many-to-many	dependent	medium
Distance	paper based	one-to-many	independent	low
On-line	electronic	many-to-many	independent	high

- electronic courses are five to seven times more time consuming to develop and mount than conventional, distance-education material;
- there are more people involved in the development, ie a team as shown in the acknowledgement of this article;
- regular meetings of the development team proved crucial;
- scanning documents and subsequent proof reading can prove extremely time consuming.

Pedagogical insights and reflections

Many of us are familiar with the concept of replicating existing education environments through the use of alternate technologies. It is not uncommon then when discussing the use of technology to hear people say that we need to make it as much like the 'real' situation as possible. Some firmly believe this is essential for success; others take a different point of view.

The authors of this Futures Studies unit proposed that utilising the new technology is about using its characteristics to create new and exciting learning environments as opposed to replicating existing educational environments. It may well be that traditional, face-to-face education will not best serve the learning needs of our society as it continues to develop into the information age. For instance face-to-face education may well be becoming only one option of the education spectrum, and be organised for particular educational purposes, such as the direct transfer of information, workshops, or to foster social interaction between students. We need to explore the possibilities and not limit ourselves to the electronic imitation of existing models.

The use of technology may extend interaction, provide a variety of delivery options, improve student access and encourage learning, but it is imperative that it is transparent, easy to use and well managed. The internet, for example, offers an opportunity to deliver courses globally. It also raises quality assurance issues. How is quality maintained if there is little content validation process or instructional design input? (Wildman and Inayatullah, 1996). How can institutions undertake their copyright responsibilities if staff can release materials direct to the net without a vetting process? What of the instructional quality of the material? Technology, while a powerful tool, has the propensity (if poorly managed) to erode the standards being achieved in education, in particular distance-education today.

Orality versus literacy

Over 90 percent of the world's cultures are oral and usually use symbolic systems of meaning, eg myth, dance etc. (Ong, 1982). Early versions of internet that were text- and ASCII-based offered little opportunity to embrace, celebrate and maintain this diversity and non-textual cultures faced an uncertain future. Inclusion of multimedia capacity in web platforms such as Netscape and Mosaic offer an opportunity, albeit a small and technologically complex one, to include symbolic logic, not only literal logic. This illustrates the tension between noetic and poetic realms of meaning (Campbell, 1988; Phenix, 1964).

In today's society with its predominant western, positivist-scientific and technological imperatives there is an enormous danger that culturally diverse discourses will be lost to the dominant discourse of western, rational textuality. This also calls to mind the post-modern critique that today power is manifest as we language the world. So one may well ask whose language, whose world and how is this languaging occurring?

Copyright versus text authenticity

In many ways copyright and maintaining the authenticity of the author's contribution have diverged as copyright has become even more pedantic and detailed, while the technological opportunities with the World Wide Web have multiplied exponentially. Much of the compliance superstructure of copyright law and the Universities Copyright Agreement, is focused on print and remains fundamentally unequal to the challenges of the new multimedia technology.

Challenges abound in making a reading available for students. First it has to be digitised by being scanned in and then marked up in HTML. Journal credits are given, yet layout, page breaks and placing of graphics vary from the original, ie the context of presentation changes yet it is still possible to maintain the authenticity of the author's intention as far as it is evident from the article.

Maintaining content authenticity

Multimedia-based interactive learning, changes forever:

- the meaning of learning from 'classroom teaching' to 'elsewhere learning';
- the meaning of teaching from 'sage on stage' to 'learning coach';
- the roles of student and lecturer who are now co-authors as they use interactive communication modes;

- the power relationship between lecturer and student as assessments and feedback are made available to all, including student feedback.

The role of the lecturer, now a learning coach, can easily get lost in the arcania of academia and HTML, ie getting the latest blink on a variable-coloured screen. The course has to say something beyond the on-screen flashing 'blink' buttons. In many ways the roles of lecturer/student/class have become institutionalised even as 'sacred' as if learning is a fixed way of maintaining stability in a changing society. In this regard academics have a special responsibility to represent the text fairly in context and critically direct it through interaction with the learners to an ethical outcome. This takes earnest endeavour, application to task, strategic questioning, provocation, critical thinking, professional praxis and personal attention to students needs and capacities.

Maintaining student presence and an 'open' text

In producing a hypertext, we, as first authors – for in hypertext, readers are also overtly authors – found ourselves confronting a number of dilemmas. The main dilemma was that in producing what we hoped would be 'open', flexible and relatively unstructured learning and teaching materials we, in fact, had to be extremely structured in approach to the development of the hypertext. We confronted, for instance, the need to provide for management of individualised reading pathways, vertically, horizontally or diagonally through the text, by writing screen-sized paragraphs, individually titled. However the very act of creating a title for a specific piece of text meant that in some ways we were creating closure in that the title and associated 'hot links' direct the reader in certain ways.

Similarly, to cater for intra-textual leaps in the hypertext the author optioned jumps across topics to be located where ideas intersect. This technique may prevent total 'free floating' inside hypertext. Thus in the very desire to open text for reader self-direction, we found ourselves creating more and more techniques for closure. We were in danger of re-establishing, and re-naturalising, authorial control with the presence of the reader again reduced to the position we had constructed within the hypertext.

Changing the locus of authenticity

As the technology available through the World Wide Web becomes more multimedia oriented the student may well come to see the point of using the technology to mark up, do web searches, load graphics etc. In this sense the 'locus of authenticity' moves from the text to the technology for accessing the text, ie from the message to the medium.

Access and equity in cyberia

Interestingly, bulletin boards and hyperarchives may well lead to accusations of inequity. In the external world equity is often defined as treating everyone the same. If one group of students get external materials they shouldn't also get workshops unless all of the students are able to attend. With e-mail some students tend to be more active than others but as the lecturer is monitoring e-mail activity he is involved in communicating with students on a one to one basis. Further the lecturer may outline specific activities for the student and so leave himself open to claims of inequity. Finally students can directly assess other students' opinions or, in some instances, past work, which once again raises equity issues.

On a wider scale, with most computers being owned by middle income earners and above, access becomes an issue for the increasing number of people outside 'normal' society ie. the homeless, long term unemployed etc.

Couch potatoes versus imagination

The average Australian spends up to 30 hours a week watching TV and several further hours in front of other screens. This time is largely passive, ie little visualisation is required, unlike reading text where imagination is necessary to evoke the sights of the text. An argument can therefore be made that participating in modern communications technology actually limits the use of the active imagination. It is therefore important that in using hypertext sophisticated multimedia should not take imagination/mythic agency from participants. The viewer should be actively incorporated rather than seen as passive receptor.

Songlines in the morphogenic web

Some concern has been expressed at the metaphor of 'Information Highway' since this suggests it may have the same problems as physical highways, eg changing from two to six lanes as demand requires without considering alternatives. Here information is seen as many still see highways, ie as a social 'good'. This view comes from the way in which science reifies information as 'objective'. So if information is good more information is better. For us the metaphor is not one of highway travel with its better cars and wider roads. Rather it is the ability to communicate meaning for what purpose? A more relevant myth/metaphor might be 'songlines of meaning' in our morphogenic fields.

Cybersweat and creativity

As new markup languages come on stream, ie HTML to VRML to Java, lecturers may face rapid skill-obsolescence. Putting 80 percent sweat into learning these new skills may only result in a 20 percent increase in creativity. It is not surprising, therefore, if the locus of authenticity is becoming the screen, ie. the 80 percent. Thus the major challenge for information technology is that the lecturer has yet another, even several, black boxes between himself and the student.

'Sage on stage' to 'mutual magic'

If used in the way discussed here, the Web offers great opportunity for net-worked and co-generative leaning. For instance, students contribute personal details to the geographic roll, to the on-line discussion with authors and others interested in futures issues via a hyperarchiving bulletin board, add their comments on readings and agree to have their assignment marked up includ-ing my comments thereon and peer assessment. Actual marks remain private, between the lecturer and student. In these ways we move from the sage 'teaching' the students to a 'learning coach' facilitating mutual learning, which at its best can be a sort of 'mutual magic'.

Just another unit

For at least a half of the first batch of students, ED730 was at best just another of the units they needed to do in order to get their Masters' awards. At worst it was a substantial imposition given the skill and cost requirements and competition from children for computer time. With the general lack of interest in futures issues in Australia such a view is at once understandable and disappointing. Clearly students represent a crucial 'edge' in changing the profile of futures studies.

Evaluation

Evaluation-feedback questionnaires were developed for course content, learn-ing facilitation and webbing, ie assessing students' use of the Web and its usability. Overall evaluations were positive with the key recommendations relating to the need for on-line technical assistance and easier assignment submission processes. Most students spent around ten hours per week on the course, two on-line and three off-line reading materials, preparing e-mails and working on assignments.

Next steps

Unit development based on student feedback and recent web browser initiat-ives will include the following for the next academic year:

- incorporation of an assignment lodging and assessment system, using set forms in Netscape 2.02 'Net forms' to enhance assignment submis-sion, assessment, peer comment and critique (version 3 is too memory intensive for many students' computers);
- direct hot-link reference to articles in on-line journals so that scanning, mounting etc of specific articles is not necessary;
- students' contributions to the course to date will remain in order to enhance the co-generative learning context;

- matching of ED730 with two independent study units and a two unit thesis gives five out of an eight unit masters, ie futures studies has now been developed into a masters specialisation option.

Conclusions

We live in an age when educational and information technologies are afforded so much status that the knowledge they convey can become seen as secondary to the technical feats being attempted to convey that knowledge. In such an age it is easy as educators to become seduced by technical wizardry without ever pausing to consider whether it is necessarily 'good', 'innovative', 'desirable', or for the betterment of the learning process. Yet such innovation must be more than merely packaging materials in new and visually exciting electronic ways. There must be sound pedagogical reasons for such innovation.

This chapter has provided a review of the development of a World Wide Web-based futures studies course and retains a positive and open mind about the potential of multimedia for a 'future university'. Such learning processes can allow Masters students to take the benefits of such interaction to their workplaces where they may become the 'mentors' of networked learning in their organisations.

Acknowledgements

Southern Cross University Futures Studies (ED370) unit development team: Rod Byrnes – HTML; Alan Ellis – multimedia; Jenny Gidley – project co-ordinator; Sohail Inayatullah – authoring; Danny Mortison – text management; Meg O'Reilly – instructional design; Paul Wildman – learning design and delivery; the various students of the unit.

References

Campbell, J (1988) *The Power of Myth,* New York: Doubleday.
Cheek, J, Cook, J and Rudge, T (1995) 'Hypertext: Issues in Blending Tradition and Technology to Optimise the "Present" Reader', *Proceedings of the 1995 Annual Conference of the Higher Education and Research Development Society of Australia.*
Dator, J (1990) 'It's Only a Paper Moon', *Futures,* 22(10), 1084–1101.
Fletcher, G (1979) 'Key Concepts in the Futures Perspective', *World Future Society Bulletin,* (Jan–Feb), 25–32.
Galtung, J (1988) *Buddhism: A Quest for Unity and Peace,* Honolulu: Dae Won Sa Buddhist Temple of Hawaii.
Inayatullah, S (1990) 'Deconstructing and Reconstructing the Future: Predictive, Cultural and Critical Epistemologies', *Futures,* 22(2), 115–141.

Masini, E (1995) 'Why Think About the Future Today?' and 'Definitions and Character-istics', chapters 1 and 2 in *Why Futures Studies?*, London: Pluto Press.

Mason, R and Kaye, A (eds) (1989) *Mindweave*, Oxford: Pergamon Press.

Morgan, A (1993) *Improving Students' Learning*, London: Kogan Page.

Nandy, A (1987) 'Evaluating Utopias', in *Traditions, Tyranny and Utopias*, Delhi: Oxford University Press.

Ng, J (1994) *Distance Learning Using a Multimedia Network System*, Unpublished honours thesis, Perth: Curtin University of Technology.

Ong, W (1982) *Orality and Literacy: The Technologisation of the World*, London: Methuen.

Phenix, P (1964) *Realms of Meaning: A Philosophy of the Curriculum for General Education*, New York: McGraw-Hill.

Rice, M (1995) 'Constraints on the Use of Computer Mediated Communication to Facilitate Learning', *Proceedings of 1995 Access Through Open Learning Conference (ATOL)*, Lismore: Norsearch.

Rowntree, D (1977) *Assessing Students: How Shall We Know Them?* London: Harper & Row.

Rudreshananda, A (1989) 'The Microvita Revolution', in *Microvita: Cosmic Seeds of Life*, Mainz: AM Publications.

Schultz, W (1995) 'Defining Futures Fluency' in *Futures Fluency: Explorations in Leader-ship, Vision and Creativity*, chapter 5, Doctoral Dissertation, University of Hawaii.

Slaughter, R (1993) 'Futures Concepts', *Futures*, April, 289–314.

Stevenson , T and Lennie, J (1995) 'Emerging Designs for Working, Living and Learning', *Futures Research Quarterly*, 11(3), 5–36.

Tough, A (1991) 'The Future of Human Civilization' and 'What is Most Important of All?' chapters 1 and 2, in *Crucial Questions About the Future*, UPI: Lanham.

Wildman, P and Inayatullah, S (1996) 'Ways of Knowing and the Pedagogies of the Future', *Futures*, 28(8), 723–740.

14. An MA in Foresight and Futures Studies

Graham May

Summary

The Leeds Metropolitan University, UK Masters in Foresight and Futures Studies was developed by a University-wide team and first offered in 1996. The course was based on several years experience in futures education in a number of areas in the University. The philosophy and structure of the degree is outlined together with details of the core futures modules. Student evaluation from the first semester in 1996 and the ideas of the course team for further developments in futures education are outlined. The value of a broad academic base for futures is apparent from the experience of the staff and students involved in this development.

Introduction

Development of the MA Foresight and Futures Studies began in early 1996 with the first cohort of students being enrolled in September that year. The degree is the latest stage in the development of futures, at both Masters and undergraduate levels, which has been part of the curriculum at Leeds Metropolitan University since the late seventies. The early developments in the undergraduate town planning course, at the then Leeds Polytechnic, were described in a paper in *Futures* (May, 1984). Since then undergraduate modules in the social implications of information technology, the future for business, urban futures, construction industry futures and children and the future have been introduced in courses offered across the University. Masters modules or elements have been incorporated into the MA/PG Diploma in Town and Regional Planning, the Joint Distance Learning MA/PG Diploma in Town and Country Planning and the MBA in Education Management. The MBA attracted sponsorship from the Co-operative bank for two students to examine respectively the value of futures in school management and in the school curriculum. The latter has led to the development of a futures course for 11 year olds in a north of England secondary school.

In April 1995, senior management established the University Network Fund in order to encourage interaction between the University's five faculties. The

Futures Network, which brings colleagues from all faculties together, was established following this initiative. The Network held a number of meetings which acted as a focus for the exchange of ideas and established valuable working links between academic staff and Uni-Ventures, a University owned company concerned with business development. The funding enabled the Network to entertain recognised international experts in the futures field. The inaugural meeting was addressed by Terry Grim of IBM, a graduate of the Masters in Futures Studies of the University of Houston-Clear Lake and members also held discussions with Richard Slaughter, the Director of the Futures Studies Centre in Melbourne, Australia. The Masters degree was largely inspired by these meetings and developed directly from the close cross-faculty working relationships established through the Network.

The University's mission states that Leeds Metropolitan University is concerned with developing the capability of people to shape their future and to contribute to the development of their organisations and communities. The Masters in Foresight and Futures Studies directly supports this mission, its purpose being to enhance the ability to deal constructively with the future and to empower individuals to influence their own futures.

The philosophy of the masters

The Course Document which was prepared by the course team for validation by the University sets out its philosophy in these words:

> It has become increasingly clear that human decisions and actions play an important part in determining the future of both humanity and the world in which we live. At the close of the 20th century we are faced with a range of questions in economic, social, political and technological fields which could have major significance for the future. Many of these questions raise important ethical issues but they are also frequently surrounded by uncertainty as to the impact of alternative courses of action that could be taken. To make effective decisions we would need knowledge about the future that we cannot possess, yet we are often forced to make decisions which have long term implications in conditions of considerable uncertainty. Foresight and Futures Studies aims to critically examine the difficulties associated with making decisions with long-term future consequences in conditions of uncertainty and to provide methods through which these difficulties can be minimised.

> Among the questions facing humanity is the growing awareness of the impact of human activity over the last 200 years and our dependence on the fragile earth. We are faced with the possibility that our species could be working towards its own destruction. We cannot be certain, until it is too late, but the awareness of the possibility creates a novel circumstance. If, for example, as Orheim (1992) claims, 'We are the first generation that influences global climate, and the last generation to escape the consequences,' we have moved into a new era in which we are more than ever before responsible for what happens in the future.

To an extent, we have had this responsibility since humanity first planted crops, started making tools and began to use fire, but ours is the first generation to become aware of our impact and, consequently, to understand our responsibility. Previous generations have been able to live without this knowledge, to act in their present assuming that the future would look after itself. We do not have that privilege. Our technology, which if anything, is the cause of the problem, has also given us the ability to perceive it. Human technology has grown so powerful and human numbers have increased so remarkably that as the poet Paul Valery wrote, 'The future is not what it used to be' (Jupp and O'Neill, 1994). In such circumstances we need to develop our capability to assess critically our potential impact on the future.

Technology, which is itself a product of human ingenuity, is having increasing implications for society. Information Technology, for example, has been called a meta-technology because it has potential implications across a wide range of situations including employment, transport and the home. The nature of the impact, whether it will be beneficial or harmful and to whom, is subject to wide-ranging debate. The ethical issues raised by bio-technology particularly genetic engineering, are likely to increase as the possibilities of human intervention in natural processes grow. The potential of molecular manufacturing and other emerging technologies and the issues they raise have yet to be explored.

Social changes, particularly demographic changes in the size and location of world population and the ageing of western populations, pose major ethical and political issues. In the west, projections anticipate a smaller working age population supporting a growing number of pensioners who will require increasing expenditure on health care and social welfare. At the same time some commentators foresee major changes in employment which will raise important social concerns, (Rifkin, 1995) and question the ability of society to support large number of dependants.

The future, as we approach the end of the second millennium, seems ever more uncertain and even threatening. The mechanistic model of reality, on which industrial society was built, is increasingly challenged by advances in scientific knowledge. The developing ideas of, for example, chaos theory suggest that established methods of understanding reality and assumptions about influencing the future are more limited than once envisaged and that new approaches are required. The problems that confront us are frequently ill structured, 'We do not know what information is needed; we have few comprehensive models and no prescription for how to process the information we have. Even worse, there is no end to the problem' (Mendell, 1978). Such situations require an approach and an education that accepts complexity and uncertainty and provides the means to deal effectively with them. Foresight and futures studies offers such an approach accepting responsibility for the future and the importance of human action in influencing it.

This is no easy task and raises many philosophical and practical difficulties. The inherent uncertainty of the future means that we cannot know in advance what the impact of some of our actions will be, or how others will react to them.

While we can anticipate some of the future discoveries which will be made, we know little about the impact they will have on our lives.

Foresight and Futures Studies offer concepts and methods to work with the difficulties of an uncertain future and to help us deal constructively with a rapidly changing present. They can assist the development of the ability to influence the future rather than merely predict it. To make the future happen for us rather than happen to us. By focusing attention on the future, Foresight and Futures Studies is concerned with the direction that society is taking, rather than where it has come from. In doing so it offers a unique perspective and affords opportunities for the development of the understanding and skills necessary for dealing effectively with the future. The course aims to develop this understanding and these skills to assist a range of social actors in the private, public and voluntary sectors.'

(Leeds Metropolitan University, 1996)

Aims and objectives

This philosophy is followed through in the stated aims and objectives of the degree which are:

1. To develop critically informed futures perspectives and capabilities in foresight to enable students to become more effective actors in a rapidly changing environment.
2. To develop the ability to manage more effectively the opportunities and problems of a diverse and changing world through:
    - the critical understanding of change as a normal, rather than abnormal process;
    - the analysis of the relationship between present decisions and future consequences;
    - the critical assessment and construction of alternative futures;
    - the critical appraisal of current concerns for the future as seen from diverse perspectives;
    - an in-depth understanding of a particular area of concern for the future to an advanced level;
    - the development of a range of skills in foresight and futures research methods.

Course structure

In line with current University practice, the Masters course consists of ten modules at M level which are divided into core, elective and research modules (see Figure 14.1). Each module assumes a student workload of 150 hours and

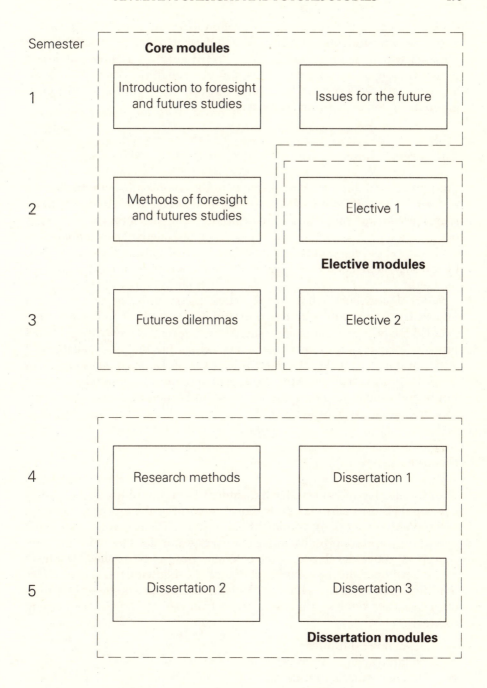

Figure 14.1   Course structure (Leeds Metropolitan University 1996).

carries 12 credits upon successful completion. The course is currently studied part-time with students required to attend three two-day study sessions per semester which are interspersed with directed learning. The normal period of registration is five semesters or 24 months though provision is made for an exit point with a postgraduate certificate after two semesters and a post-graduate diploma after three semesters.

The core modules

The four core modules are intended to define and consolidate the intellectual and academic philosophy of futures. The *introduction to foresight and futures studies* provides a firm grounding in the futures approach through: an analysis of the various strands of the field in practice and academe; an examination of the historical development of futures; discussion of some of the issues raised by foresight activity and an examination of the writings of major authors in the field.

Futures Issues offers a broad perspective of concerns that have potential importance for the future and an opportunity for students to begin a more detailed analysis of a particular issue. *Methods of foresight and futures studies* provides an overview of the range of methods and techniques available and an opportunity to develop abilities in selected areas. *Futures dilemmas* involves an in-depth examination of the theoretical and ethical issues raised by the future and human responsibility for it. An indication of the content of the core modules is given in Table 14.1.

Electives

The two elective modules offer the student the opportunity to explore or develop their own personal, professional or vocational interests in foresight within the framework of a defined field of study. The electives provide the opportunity to develop substantive knowledge and skills to which the foresight perspective developed in the core modules can be applied. The team which developed the degree initially offered the following menu of electives reflecting their expertise, although students are able to select electives from other Masters modules within the University or elect to undertake a learning contract.

- Technological futures
- Children and the future
- Strategic issues for business
- Design/creativity and the arts
- Alternative lifestyles and urban futures
- The future of health

Table 14.1   Details of the core modules

Core module 1: Introduction to foresight and futures studies

Why Futures? Studying and preparing for the future – approaches and issues. Foresight, Futures Research, Futures Studies, Futurology, Futurism, Future Generations, Futuribles, La Prospective. Different purposes of Futures – to predict, to foresee, to manage, to create.

Thinking about the Future: The future in everyday life, in business and government. The futures dimension. The interrelationship of past, present and future. Forms of futures – forecasting, studies, research, planning, policy making. The future and Futures, alternative futures. Attitudes to the future: determinism, choice, random. Metaphors of the future. Images of the future, optimism, pessimism, golden age to destruction. Human responsibility for the future and future generations. Possible, probable and preferable futures. Cultural perspectives on the future. The problem of prediction and 'knowledge' of the future. The current state of Futures Research.

The future in history, literature and the media. Past images of the future – Traditional, Renaissance, Industrial/Technological Progress, post-modernism. The decline of progress. Science fiction, its role in futures, stages in its development. Utopias and dystopias. Visionaries, successes and failures, doers, movers and shakers.

The origin and development of Futures Research in: the United States, France, 'The Eastern bloc' Japan and the UK. Major themes in the development of Futures. Futures in the military, in business, the environmental movement, social innovation. Futures in different countries and cultures. Major Futures thinkers, eg Wells, Kahn, Godet, Capra, Henderson, Meadows, Clarke, Boulding, Toffler, Masini, Marien, Bell, Handy, Slaughter.

Core module 2: Issues for the future

An examination of current concerns about the future and potential future developments: Topics will be selected which may be expected to include: Restructuring the economy, small firm/large firm interface; internationalisation, globalisation, the power of information, organisational change. Changing international relationships, a new world order? The future of Europe and other regional associations, The Third World, global inequality.

The global futures debate, limits to growth versus the resourceful earth, environmental issues, global warming, ozone depletion and pollution, resource shortages and conflicts, energy, water, population, sustainable development, the Gaia hypothesis.

Table 14.1   Details of the core modules *(continued)*

Technology, information technology, genetics and bio-technology, new materials and nanotechnology.

Social change, demographic trends, the growing world population, the ageing population of developed countries, migration; changing social patterns, religion, cultural and ethnic issues.

Work and employment: changing patterns of employment, sectorally, internationally. Scenarios for the future of work; entrepreneurship, intrapreneurship. Urban futures: cities in the developed and developing world, housing. Health: caring for an ageing population, natural and man-made epidemics.

Core module 3: Methods of foresight and futures studies

An overview of futures methods. Foreseeing, Managing and Creating the future. Examples of forecasting in differing contexts, the physical world, technology, economics, planning, population, social change. Advantages and disadvantages of different methods. Selecting appropriate methods.

Foreseeing: Prediction; Precognition; Prophecy; Astrology.

Extrapolation: Time Series/Trend Forecasting; S Curve; Envelope Curve, Precursor Analysis.

Analytical Forecasting: Quantitative and Computer-based forecasting models. Hands-on experience with a range of forecasting packages. Interpretation of results. Development of computer models. Advantages and shortcomings of computer based models. Cycles; Systems Dynamics.

Speculation: Science Fiction and Speculative Writing.

Judgemental Forecasting: The theory and practice of judgemental methods. Evaluation and selection of judgemental methods. Delphi; Cross-Impact Analysis; Content Analysis.

Managing: Scenarios; Scenario development, a detailed examination of the approaches to scenario construction and experience in their development. Issues Management; Environmental Scanning; Impact Assessment; Cost Benefit Analysis; Risk Assessment; Role Play; Simulation.

Creating: Policy Making; Planning; Strategy Formation; Problem Solving; Decision Making; Imaging; Brainstorming/Brainwriting; Group Support Systems.

Innovation: The role of creativity and innovation in shaping the future. The importance of vision. Developing creativity and innovative abilities. Futures Workshops; Visioning; Incasting; Backcasting; Relevance Tree; Creative Imagery; Action; Politics.

Table 14.1   Details of the core modules *(continued)*

Core module 4: Futures dilemmas

Concepts of ethics, absolute and culturally relative, of times past, present and yet to come. The nature of rational change, response to change and accommodation to change. Fatalism, choice, the concept of alternatives, uncertainty, risk, reward, faith and other factors which have powerful ethical components.

Theoretical perspectives on the future, Systems theory. Chaos theory. Anti-Chaos, Catastrophe Theory, Complexity, Uncertainty, Future Pull and Past push.

Differing approaches to the future politically and socially. Cultural attitudes to the future, western male dominance of futures, non-western approaches, Black perspectives, feminist perspectives. Perspectives of those who control aspects of change and of those who can only accept them or not. Possible, probable and preferable futures for whom, World views and paradigms. Speculations on alternatives, including very radical alternatives such as hermaphroditic societies, the possibilities of parthenogenesis and exogenesis.

Ethical issues: the ethics of futures, the impact of new technologies, IT, bio-technology, nanotechnology, social change. The emergence of machine intelligence, issues around the enhancement of humans and/or animals mechanically or genetically.

Concepts of time, linear, cyclical, relative. Past, present and future. The value of history. The nature of the future, assumptions about the future. Influence pessimism and optimism. Self-altering predictions. Uncertainty in decision making. The limitations of futures research: futura and facta, ethnocentrism, historicism, colonizing the future. Assumptions about the future. The rationale for Futures Studies. The future of futures.

Change: The nature of change and its significance. Social, environmental, technological and other forms of change. Patterns of change, gradual, rapid, catastrophic. Changes of state and of nature. Causes of change. Theories of change. Consequences and reactions to change, present change, anticipating future change. Measuring change. Responding to change, resistance, reaction and proactive responses. Problems and opportunities. Ways of managing change.

Responsibility for future generations: the rationale for conservation, preservation, sustainability, waste management, resource husbandry, understanding the needs of future generations, practical difficulties, opening up options.

Source: Leeds Metropolitan University (1996)

At the start of the second semester in 1997 staff and students were involved in negotiation over the first elective modules. Student preference and staff availability at the time meant that the proposed menu, listed above, was not practical. After discussions between the student group and the course team it was agreed to organise a Group Learning Contract. Based on the principle of the learning contract in which an individual student contracts to undertake an agreed programme of study and the course team to provide the required support, the group element allowed the elective module to benefit from the continuing development of the collective study culture that had been evolved during the first semester.

Under the terms of the Group Learning Contract:

- Each student individually contracted to make a 20 minute presentation to the group and to make a final submission on their chosen topic.
- Each member of the group contracted to attend the presentations of other students and to take part in the ensuing discussion.
- Staff were allocated to mentor each student and be available for 1:1 discussions both at the scheduled two day sessions and between them. Students and mentoring staff were to negotiate the means of presentation to be used.
- Assessment for the module was agreed to be divided equally between the presentation which would occur during the module and therefore be part of the development of ideas and the submission at the completion of the module.

The topics eventually selected for individual study included:

- Social movements eg punk/anarchist movements in relation to mainstream society.
- Children.
- Community governance (NGOs, Local Government, charities).
- Organisational futures with particular emphasis on stress.
- Mental health using the stress vulnerability model.
- Quality at work.

Dissertation

The Dissertation is regarded as the culmination of the educational experience provided by the course in which students apply the understanding and skills developed in the core to a detailed study of an area of specific concern. This may draw on and develop work already undertaken during the electives or be related to issues of direct relevance to a student's own activities. Although traditional methods of presentation, in the form of a 15–20,000 word dissertation, are not discouraged, students will be encouraged to consider alternative forms and methods of presentation that may be more appropriate to their circumstances or topic.

Learning strategy

The course team has sought to encourage students to develop lifelong learning characteristics as appropriate to a dynamic and uncertain future. The students enrolled in 1996 have brought to the course a wealth of experience and skills to which the MA is adding a futures perspective and developing potentially new areas of expertise and application. This diversity of knowledge and experience has been valuable in group-work discussions and presentations throughout the course. This has emphasised the collegiate nature of post-graduate study and is assisting the development of a learning community engaged in working in and studying futures. One of the major benefits arising from the nature of the student body and the pattern of attendance has been the intensive mutual learning experience during the in-college sessions.

Assessment

Students are encouraged to use a wide variety of different presentational forms including graphic, verbal, video, electronic, written and the preparation of artefacts. In the first semester two of the most successful presentations took the form of a video examining the redefinition of literacy as we approach the twenty-first century, and an on-line presentation examining the future direction of a student's own company. This reflects the course team's philosophy which encourages students to relate their assessments to work and other experience and to link the assessments for individual modules to selected themes in preparation for the in depth study of the dissertation. See Table 14.2 for details of the assessments for the Core Modules.

Initial evaluation

At the time of writing only the first semester (1996–97) had been fully completed and, as is customary in the University, the MA students were asked to provide evaluation of the semester giving particular attention to two aspects of the course: i) the individual learning journal, kept as part of the Introduction to Foresight and Futures Studies module and ii) the first two modules: Introduction to Foresight and Futures Studies and Futures Issues.

Reflections on the learning journal were compiled during a student discussion and reported to the course team. This indicated that the journal had generally worked well, providing students with a discipline to record their

Table 14.2   Assessment of core modules

Introduction to foresight and futures studies

Students are be required to keep a self-assessed, reflective journal incorporating developments in their thinking during the module.

Issues for the future

A peer reviewed presentation of an issue of concern for the future.

Methods of foresight and futures studies

The assessment requires:

- The choice and use of a forecasting or futures method in an appropriate situation;
- The critical appraisal of the selected method and a personal assessment of its value;
- An analysis and evaluation of the changes that undertaking the exercise has induced in the students thinking processes.

Futures dilemmas

A written presentation or equivalent exploring the ethical issues raised by a specific change, with particular reference to the cultural and political context involved.

---

reflections on events, feelings, resources used and personal circumstances. Students were conscious of the time commitment needed to complete the journal and even more for useful analysis and reflection, but having found it useful in the identification skill levels and the areas for improvement, expressed a wish to extend the exercise to the rest of the course. Comparison of the journals revealed that the frequency and amount they were used varied with individuals and that while some themes grew and recurred, personal feelings were not always readily acknowledged. The free style was a release from demands of writing academic prose but past styles of writing sometimes created a block that needed to be overcome. A variety of media was used: hand-written, word processed, dictaphone, tapes etc. though it was thought that a Hypertext structure would be beneficial for cross-referencing. Consideration of privacy and access of others to materials in individuals' journals was seen as important. (It had been agreed that the journal belonged to the individual who could determine what would be made public and what kept private.) One fact to emerge in the discussion was that all students had felt marginalised from the course or their peers at some point and had used the learning journal to record this. Despite this it was agreed that all students present at the discussion had undertaken and reflected sufficiently on the process and materials to be deemed to have passed the module.

Evaluation of the Introduction and Issues modules was based on the identification of positive features and areas which could be improved. Positive features included: the venue, which enhanced discussion and the scheduling of the two day sessions on Friday and Saturday; the mix of discussion gained from the diverse group and their enthusiasm; the enthusiasm and quality of staff input; the informality achieved in the approach and the programme and the breadth of early modules.

Things to examine and change were mainly related to administrative issues and the clarity of communication about the level and depth of work required. Comment was also made about the gender balance of the course (it was predominantly male). It is likely that these issues were affected by the short time-scale of the development and recruitment processes and they will be addressed in subsequent years.

Staff development and research

The degree was developed by a course team with members from different parts of the University who began working together through the University's Futures Network. This collaboration was a central feature of the course's development and is pivotal to its operation. Each member of the group brings a unique contribution which together provide a rich learning environment appropriate to futures. Examples of these teaching and research contributions include:

- the attitudes of children to the future;
- information technology and in particular experience of a collaborative micro-electronics project funded by the European Union Framework IV;
- arts futures;
- innovation and creativity;
- technology foresight;
- business futures;
- feminist approaches to the future;
- futures methodologies;
- the theoretical issues raised by futures activity;
- sustainable development;
- urban futures.

Members of the team are also active in a variety of international, national and regional organisations relevant to the course. Among them, The UK Futures Group (developed from a joint initiative between staff of the University, British telecom and IBM), which has about 100 corresponding members, and the Futures Mailbase discussion list (an e-mail facility for the exchange of views among academics and others), are both coordinated from the University.

Future developments

Having established the Masters degree, the course team wants to consolidate its position and to increase the profile of futures within the University. Consideration is therefore being given to the creation of an Advisory Group composed of members of the local community to assist the course team in both ensuring the relevance of futures to the community's needs and its development within the University. Among the ideas being pursued are the incorporation of more Futures modules into undergraduate programmes; the floating of combined honours programmes bringing together futures and other themes of the University's activities, such as environment, business and information technology; the creation of a Foresight Centre. In pursuing these ideas, the Futures team has benefited from the support of the University's senior management. This reflects the more positive attitude to foresight in the UK which has developed in recent years. The latter maybe a temporary phenomenon, perhaps related to the imminence of the millennium, but as the MA indicates, it does provide the futures community in the UK with an opportunity to make a greater impact than has been possible for many years.

References

Jupp R and O'Neill G (1994) *Ireland 2000: Reflections on Ireland in the Year 2000*, Dublin: Lansdowne Market Research and Henley Centre Ireland.

Leeds Metropolitan University (1996) *Modular Masters Programme: MA Foresight and Futures Studies: Book II Course Document*, Faculty of Design and the Built Environment, School of the Built Environment.

Orheim O (1992) *The Norwegian Glacier Centre Publicity Pamphlet*, Norwegian Glacier Centre.

May G H (1984) 'Futures Studies in Higher Education – A UK Experience in Course Development', *Futures* 16 (1): 86–93.

Mendell J S (1978) 'The Practice of Intuition', in Fowles J B (ed.) *Handbook of Futures Research*, Westport, CON: Greenwood Press.

Rifkin J (1995) *The End of Work: The Decline of the Global Labour Force and the Dawn of the Post-Market Era*, New York: Tarcher/Putnam.

15. Student responses to learning about futures

Martha Rogers

Summary

There is little disagreement about the severity of global problems we now face or their potential deleterious long-term effects if humanity continues along the path we are now traveling. There is a critical need for people to change fundamentally their perspectives, feelings, value priorities and ways of living. Those changes are dependent on learning. However, learning about futures is a far more complex process than many may realize. It is a process that involves not only the mind, but also the heart and the soul. The aim of this chapter is to draw attention to the subjective responses of students and to illuminate the human experience of learning about futures in its richness and depth. A greater understanding of students' responses to learning about futures can only enhance our abilities to facilitate learning which is necessary for building a bridge of hope for the future.

Introduction

My interest in exploring the nature of learning about futures arose out of my own experience as a learner during my doctoral programme. I was an experienced educator and considered myself to be fairly thoughtful and knowledgeable about the world. Despite this, I was profoundly affected by a course that focused on what I call 'global futures', or the study of alternative futures of human and planetary life. My own experience resonated with those who have written about the intellectual and emotional challenges of learning about global issues and futures (Macy, 1983; 1991; Moore, 1992; Schwebel, 1990). While learning is seen as the key to achieving a positive future, the challenges of this kind of learning can be overwhelming, leading to despair, existential isolation, hopelessness and loss of meaning. In some instances, learning may paradoxically result in paralysis rather than mobilizing the learner toward action. Reflections on my own experience as a learner coupled

203

with a belief in the importance of learning for the future of humanity launched me on a journey of studying the subjective experiences of students as they engage in learning about global futures.

Metaphorically, I have come to see learning about global futures as a rich symphony of human experience. To appreciate the symphony, we need to attend to all of the instruments, the rhythms, cadences and notes as they weave in and out, blending together in a synergistic whole. We need to appreciate the wholeness of this experience and resist any temptation to focus totally or primarily on the cognitive domain. Approaching learning about global futures as if it were solely a content-driven, intellectual enterprise would be like trying to appreciate a symphony by listening only to the violins. While the string section may be important, it is only one aspect of the whole. In the following, I will attempt to illuminate the symphony of the human experience of learning about global futures. In so doing, I will describe the responses of students as they have been conveyed to me through my research endeavors and discuss some possible implications for those of us who are in roles of facilitating learning.

Learning about global futures: a conceptual model

Over the past five years, I have had the opportunity of listening to many stories from students about their experiences learning about global futures. The stories were recounted verbally and/or in writing during qualitative studies of forty adult learners (Rogers and Tough, 1991) and eleven graduate students (Rogers, 1994) all of whom were taking a course on global futures at the University of Toronto. This four month, graduate level course was taught by Dr Allen Tough, professor of futures studies and adult education. The content for each week's class centred around eight questions which were drawn from Tough's book *Crucial Questions about the Future* (1991). The questions were as follows:

- What is most important of all? Is it the long-term flourishing of human civilization? Why should we care about the next 40 years, not just the next few months? How much responsibility do we have to future generations?
- Why do we act in ways that hurt our future? What forces and factors oppose the importance of humanity's future?
- What will our actual future turn out to be? What are our chances? Is pessimism or optimism more appropriate?
- How can we achieve a satisfactory future? Which priorities are fundamental?
- Which catastrophes would be the worst of all and how can we prevent them?

- What sorts of intelligent life and civilizations exist in the universe? What role will they play in our future?
- From which aspects of reality can we gain meaning and purpose?
- How can each person contribute? Can one person make any difference? Why is it worth trying?

Participants in the studies were asked to describe their personal learning experiences which occurred throughout the course as well as changes that had resulted as a consequence of their learning. An analysis of students' accounts provided the foundation for the development of a conceptual model of learning about global futures (see Figure 15.1). Although the model is based on two qualitative studies, there is further evidence to support its validity. Supporting evidence has been provided by students in Dr Tough's subsequent classes who were asked to critique the model based on their own experiences and through numerous narratives that have been offered to me by my own students as well as others in various places around the world, all of whom were taking courses that focused on global futures.

As the model indicates, learning about global futures is a more complex process than many realize. It is a process that has cognitive, affective and soulful aspects which operate to spur learners on to action. These aspects of the learning process are illustrated by the outer arrows of the model. The inner arrows, labeled 'self-helping patterns', refer to the actions taken by students to facilitate or help them cope with their learning. It is important to

Figure 15.1   Learning about global futures: a conceptual model.

note that a model is a representation of reality, it is not reality itself. Thus, is does not convey the fluid and dynamic nature of the learning process which, in reality, is more like a holograph or kaleidoscope rather than a linear or sequential process. It also cannot be said to represent the experiences of all people. There are no doubt variations in the experiences of learners just as there are certainly variations in the intensity of responses to learning. What the model does do is communicate the experiences of students who have shared their stories with me.

Awakening of the mind

'Awakening of the mind' refers to cognitive or intellectual dimensions of learning, including knowledge acquisition, ways of thinking and overall perspective taken. As educators, we would expect knowledge to be increased during learning. In fact, this is often the sole focus of educational endeavors. However, learning about global futures frequently poses deeper intellectual challenges. In part, the intellectual challenge lies in the fact that many students may be exposed, for the first time, to the vast, interrelated problems facing our civilization in the present. In part, the challenge comes from extending the temporal perspective from a past/present orientation to one that embraces images of the long-term futures. The challenge is also associated with accepting one of the main assumptions of futures studies which is that many alternative futures scenarios are possible and that the future is not pre-determined. These are difficult intellectual shifts in thinking which may cause students to question, critique and dramatically change their entire world view or perspective. As difficult as these challenges may be, they are, as Slaughter (1989: 263) noted, necessary reconstructions of our personal paradigms. He argued that without a shift in temporality and without a global view, humans will lack the necessary capacity to see the 'interconnectedness and systemicity that characterizes the global system' which is essential to comprehending and managing the issues we face currently and in the future.

Learning about global futures can challenge students to engage with content and ways of thinking that are quite different from their existing perceptions of reality and ways of thinking. This can create, as many students reported, a sense of cognitive dissonance, confusion, discomfort or scepticism. For instance, students said when they began learning about global futures they thought it was 'nonsense', 'out of touch', 'airy-fairy', 'crazy' and 'garbage'. As the dissonance began to be resolved, in some cases by a conscious letting go of their existing perspectives, students spoke of experiencing an intellectual awakening.

The awakening of the mind stimulated many reactions. The reactions included feelings of being intellectually overwhelmed, incapacitated, paralyzed and pessimistic. One student said, 'It was like a crashing of reality against all my hopes and dreams.' Another said, 'I never thought about the future. Then I started to read about all the complex issues and their solutions, and by the third week of class I was completely incapacitated.' The intellectual challenges of learning can be quite profound as students 'wake up' to the issues of the present and begin to contemplate the alternative futures they may portend.

In order to cope with the cognitive demands of learning, students described the need to take actions to reduce the sense of being overwhelmed, pessimistic and paralyzed. The actions, or 'self-helping patterns' took several forms. In many cases students consciously controlled the type and amount of information they took in. Some completely stopped reading class-related materials, watching television or reading the newspaper where the content had anything to do with global issues or futures. It is noteworthy that coping meant distancing from the content of learning in order to achieve some intellectual relief. Distancing, in these cases, was a manifestation of effective coping and not resistance to learning. Some students also described the need to create mental frameworks to organize new knowledge or re-organize ways of thinking. 'You have to create a way of organizing the whole by breaking the whole down into smaller, more manageable pieces because the whole is just too big and too overwhelming', said one student, echoing the sentiments of many. The self-helping patterns then allowed students to re-engage with learning in a way which reduced or eliminated intellectual overload.

Learning about global futures is challenging from an intellectual perspective. While students are likely to acquire new knowledge, this is less significant than the changes that may occur in ways of thinking, leading to a perspective that is more holistic, inclusive and futures oriented.

Awakening of the heart

One of the characteristics of cognitive or intellectual dimensions of learning was the apparent lack of emotion in the reports from students. However, the heart did not remain still for long. Many students described a point along the learning process where intellectual knowing, or 'knowing out there' shifted to a more personal knowing, or 'knowing in here'. It was at this juncture that the heart began to stir. While the depth of emotional responses varied, many students described learning about global futures as being emotionally intense. The awakening of the heart was repeatedly referred to as being like a 'roller coaster' where emotions fluctuated in an up-and-down cadence, often in a paradoxical way. One student exclaimed, 'My cognitive knowledge was progressing in a steady incline but my emotions were constantly oscillating dramatically, up and down: depression-elation, hopeless-hopeful, anxious-calm'. Another said, 'Every class I entered feeling fairly positive and optimistic, and every class I left feeling depressed and despairing. It was an emotional roller coaster'.

The roller coaster experience included many different emotions. Some people experienced anger; anger at themselves, all people, the professor or God. Many students experienced depression or despair, some to the point that it was nearly overwhelming. One powerful illustration was offered by a student who said, 'The despair was overwhelming and it affected every part of my life. I was frightened by the power of my despair. For weeks I walked around in a storm cloud. It was all I could do just to keep going and not succumb to the overwhelming feelings.' Some people experienced guilt in relation to their perceived 'self-centeredness', anthropocentrism, lack of awareness of global issues or their focus on materialism. Other emotions, such as powerlessness, hopelessness, isolation and fear were also described. Still others experienced a feeling of elation or what one student called a 'learning high'.

Coping with the emotional turmoil demanded the use of 'self-helping patterns'. One of the actions students described was simply to accept the emotional nature of the learning process. Additional coping strategies included finding like-minded people who could understand what they were going through, appreciating beauty in nature and life and consciously controlling emotions. As the turmoil subsided, learners explained that they found themselves experiencing a very deep sense of caring about the planet, humanity and the future as well as a feeling or urgency to do something, anything that would help achieve a reasonably desirable life for future generations.

The emotions experienced by students as they learn about global futures can be profound, as I have indicated. Many of the feelings expressed by students, such as anger, depression, a sense of falling apart, powerlessness and hopelessness, are consistent with a grief response. Grieving has been reported as a common reaction to learning about global threats to human survival (Macy, 1983, 1991; Varguish, 1980; Yeomans, 1988). The loss associated with the disintegration of one's personal paradigm or world view, as reported by some students, or imagining the possible loss of humanity or the planet, are real losses which may trigger a necessary and healthy grieving response. Grief along with all the other emotions reported, is an important aspect of learning about global futures. It is through the heart that deeper learning may occur at the level of the soul.

Awakening of the soul

While many of us might expect that learning about global futures would include cognitive and affective dimensions, we might not anticipate or even consider the possibility that this learning has a soul-level dimension. Generally speaking, educational theory and writing rarely addresses soulful aspects of learning, yet my research suggests that the soul plays a central role in learning about global futures. The term 'soul' is used here to refer to the person's total being, arising from within and suffusing all other dimensions of self. Soul, according to the Merriam Webster's Collegiate Dictionary is the 'immaterial essence; animating principle, actuating cause of an individual life'. Concepts of a similar nature have been described by others and may include references to spirituality, the 'higher self' in psychosynthesis (Assagoli, 1965), the 'mind' (Berman, 1981) or tacit knowing (Polanyi, 1962). For the purpose of this discussion, I will define soul as the 'essence of the human being, the core values one holds, the theistic or secular meaning for existence and the sense of life purpose' (Rogers, 1994).

The path to the soul is through the heart, wrote Zukav (1990) and this appears to be the case in learning about global futures. An analysis of the students' stories revealed that the awakening of the soul occurred as a cons-equence of the emergence of a feeling of deep caring about humanity, the planet and future generations along with the sense of urgency to do something to contribute to a healthy future. Students reported that they began to question their 'total' life including ways of living, relationships with partners or spouses, their children or paid and voluntary work. Some described a feeling that they had drifted away from their 'centre', 'basic values', 'core' or the essence of their being. Some began to question their faith in God. Still others said they became consumed with thoughts about the meaning and purpose of life or the meaning of death. Soul searching was experienced as disquieting. Many learners reported feeling lost and directional, using a metaphor of being in a rudderless boat out on an open and turbulence sea, being tossed about at the mercy of the elements. The awakening of the soul included self-reflection on values, faith, ways of living and on the meaning and purpose of life.

Soul-searching questions about the meaning and purpose of life reportedly led to the emergence of a sense of personal responsibility and commitment. For example, one student said, 'It is my responsibility and it has to do with the purpose of my existence. It's a very personal thing'. Another student, whose awakening came in a dream, explained that she started to resolve her anger toward God when she stopped looking to God to make things better. She said, 'I realized it is not God's responsibility but the responsibility of all. I felt it was my first experience of connection with a higher self – a spiritual, transcendent experience.' A personal sense of responsibility contributed to the experience of being committed or recommitted to actions that would preserve life for the future, although the path of personal action remained elusive for some students. 'I started to feel totally committed to do something but for a long time I didn't know what I could do', remarked one student who continued by saying she needed to find out what one person could do to make a difference to the world. She said, 'It sounds and looks easy, but it's not'. Students related the sense of responsibility and commitment to the exploration of life's meaning and purpose, a proposition that has also been noted theoretically by Yalom (1980) in his work on existential psychotherapy, Varguish (1980) in his classic article on why people struggle to accept 'limits to growth' and by Tough (1986) in his work on secular sources of meaning.

Questions about the meaning and purpose of life, the sense of feeling lost and directionless were struggles that necessitated the initiation of 'self-helping patterns' with respect to the soul. Students argued that they needed to take action in order to 'connect with the soul' which they did through meditation, visioning, renewing faith or dwelling with nature. Many noted the importance of reading books or articles which presented more positive images of the future or that described actions people could take. Learning what others were doing, either through reading or conversations, was important in coping with the soulful dimensions of the learning process.

Finding a path of action

Soul searching with its focus on life's meaning and purpose as well as human responsibilities and commitments prompted students to embark on a journey of searching for and finding personal paths of action. Actions took many forms. Some students decided to reduce consumer spending, buy natural products, determine 'needs' instead of 'wants', recycle or reduce car use. One person decided, after a long teaching career, that she no longer wanted to be a teacher. Another realized that her marriage was no longer satisfactory. Still another decided to have a baby after many years of being resigned to and comfortable with being childless. Most commonly, students said they began to see global issues and futures in everything. At home, work or through involvement in community groups, students said they were 'consciousness raising', 'speaking out' and 'telling the truth' about the world's problems. Students said that it mattered not how great or small the actions were, but it was knowing that one person could do something that would enhance the quality of the future that was important. Once a path of action became known, students experienced relief, a sense of calmness, certainty, lightness and excitement.

Two significant outcomes resulted when students initiated their paths of action. Without exception, students said their actions led to feelings of personal power and hope. Personal power, consistent with Macy's (1983; 1991) definition, was not seen as power over someone or something, but as power arising from within. Some spoke of the power to change, the power to make choices or the power to speak out about the world and to make a difference. Hope was also expressed as an outcome of taking action. As one student put it, 'Once you start to feel committed and you start to search for the ways you can make a difference, you start to feel more powerful, more in control and more hopeful'. Students, both implicitly and explicitly, made distinctions between hope and optimism. Most said they felt less optimistic about the future but more hopeful about people's capacity to change. As one student explained, 'I feel less optimistic but more hopeful. You have to have hope or it will feel like there's no way out'. As is evident, learning about global futures involves the soul. It is through the existential questioning as to the meaning and purpose of life and through an exploration of human responsibilities and commitments that students discover their own paths of action and initiate those actions in a hopeful and powerful way. Although there is a dearth of literature in the field of education that relates to concepts of the soul, it clearly played a pivotal role in learning. In fact, the path to informed and committed action was through the soul. Not only does this raise important questions for further research, but it may also call into question the very purpose of education. When learning has to do with issues of human and planetary survival for the future, some have suggested that there is a need to reconceptualize education's philosophical purpose. Perhaps we ought to consider the notion that the purpose of education be reconceptualized as the facilitation of people's search for meaning, wholeness, transcendence and an understanding of our individual roles in the human evolutionary journey (Moore, 1992; Slaughter, 1991; Swimme and Berry, 1992).

Reflections on educational practice

The stories of students that have been provided to me and described here underscore the complexity and holistic nature of learning about global futures. The processes of learning pose intellectual challenges as students engage with content and ways of thinking that may be discrepant with their existing perspectives. Learning can be emotionally tumultuous and may involve grieving the loss of old ways of knowing or the loss of innocence as people face the enormity of world's problems and consider alternative futures in light of present day circumstances. Learning about global futures can also catalyze deep soul-searching questions. Educators need to appreciate the nature of this learning process – which may mean critically reflecting on our own assumptions about the nature of learning and its facilitation.

As educators, our practice is a reflection of implicit or explicit theories or frameworks. While I would support the notion of theoretical pluralism, not all educational frameworks can be considered useful when speaking of learning about global futures. For instance, the most predominant approach to education today is based on the original work of Tyler (1949). From this perspective, learning is viewed as a linear, systematic process where needs are assessed (generally by educators), discreet objectives are formulated, a plan is 'delivered' and the outcomes are objectively measured. It is a framework which is widely used as the basis of curricula, models of 'training' or programme planning and competency based learning. While this approach may be useful in certain learning situations, particularly those which involve skill development, it has been criticized for being mechanistic and reductionistic, thus denying the wholeness of the learning experience or the dynamism of the process (Brookfield, 1985). Certainly, with reference to learning about global futures, a rigid adherence to pre-determined, behavioural objectives, the 'delivery' of content using didactic methods and a highly structured learning environment might well inhibit, prevent or at least render invisible the deep, holistic learning that was described by students. We need to be critically reflective about the educational models that are operating in our conscious or preconscious minds in order to ensure that the frameworks we select are consistent with the needs of learners and the learning process.

What educational frameworks and strategies can be useful in facilitating learning about global futures? To respond to this question, I will draw upon some theoretical works as well as specific strategies and ideas that were proposed by students who participated in my research.

First, learning about global futures, even at a cognitive level, is not and probably should not be simply a matter of acquiring new knowledge or skills. Many students described the intellectual challenges of learning that brought into question their beliefs, assumptions, perspectives, temporal orientation and ways of viewing the world. Learning that challenges sometimes dramatically changes the personal paradigms of learners, is often broadly referred to as transformative learning. Several people have written about this form of learning including Cranton (1994), Freire (1970) in his discussion of 'conscientization', Mezirow (1978; 1985; 1991) in his work on 'perspective transformation', McKenzie (1991) in describing education related to world view construction and Bateson (1972) in his discussion of 'Learning III'. In all of these works, the personal paradigms of learners, including basic assumptions, are reflected upon critically. Through critical reflection, learners may affirm, modify or dramatically transform their perspectives, world views or paradigms. It is a process of letting go of old ways of thinking, struggling with confusion and taking on a new, more informed and liberated view. As Bateson noted, this kind of learning does not mean the blind acceptance of one paradigm over another, but rather an understanding of the nature of the paradigms themselves. Bateson, Mezirow and McKenzie all suggest that transformative learning fosters a more inclusive, discriminating and integrative understanding of the self and the world, enabling people to better participate in life in an empowered way. Transformative learning is one of the frameworks which can be used to understand and facilitate learning about global futures.

At a more pragmatic level, students may benefit from understanding, conceptually, that learning about global issues and futures can challenge deeply held, unquestioned assumptions or beliefs, possibly leading to a transformation or 'paradigm shift'. When old and new paradigms collide, as was reported by students in my research, there is often a sense of being confused and overwhelmed. Students need to understand that these experiences are part of the process of learning and that they will give way to new insights or possibly a new perspective. Talking about personal experiences of learning about the long-term futures and the intellectual challenges learning creates, was considered to be important by those in my research. Learners also noted that it was necessary to consider many different futures scenarios, but it was essential to balance more optimistic visions with those that were pessimistic. Dwelling on catastrophe scenarios can be frightening and immobilizing. Talking about or reading positive views of the future is not only important in terms of coping with learning, but they also begin the process of building new personal paradigms or perspectives that are positive, hopeful and empowering.

The second major point has to do with the holistic nature of learning about global futures. Educators need not only to understand the cognitive challenges but also the impact of learning on the heart and soul. At a theoretical level, there are some frameworks that may be useful in this regard. For instance, the construct of 'holistic learning' holds that the learner is a holistic being, inter-connected with all other people as well as the broader universe (Miller, 1988). From this perspective, effective learning is that which addresses the whole learner including the cognitive, emotional and physical dimensions as well as the spiritual or transpersonal self and the connection of people with the human community. Another framework which is little discussed but which is potentially extremely useful is one where learning is conceptualized as growth of consciousness. Weiser (1988) and others applied concepts of psychosynthesis in creating this framework. Growth of consciousness, and consequently learning, involves an awareness of and connection with the 'inner self' or 'higher self' and in being inextricably linked to an existential search for meaning and purpose. Of particular note for this discussion is the application of this frame of reference to help people cope with 'global dark times', described by Yeomans (1988). Both of these educational frameworks are holistic in nature and draw attention to the emotional and spiritual aspects of learning.

Returning, once again, to the more pragmatic level, there are strategies which may be considered in order to facilitate learning at the level of the heart and soul. It seems rather obvious to say that the first step is to acknowledge the fact that learning about global issues and alternative futures involves emotions and soul searching. The disintegration of a personal paradigm or consideration of the potential loss of humanity and the planet are real losses that may trigger grief. In fact, Macy (1983; 1991) has argued that grieving is an essential part of the process leading to deep caring about the world. Educators do not need to be transformed into psychotherapists in order to help students who are experiencing the myriad emotions that may accompany this learning. We do need to acknowledge that it is a natural, healthy and positive response. We do not need to 'fix it' or 'make it better', but we do need to create an environment that fosters the expression of feelings, giving them legitimacy as part of the learning process. As students in my research noted, it is important to accept the fact that this learning is emotional, but there are ways of coping by finding support from classmates, friends or family members who can understand the experience and by seeking out the beauty of life through music, poetry, children or nature.

Similarly, if learning about global futures involves soulful questioning of
the meaning and purpose of life and human responsibilities and commitments,
then the first step is to acknowledge that this is a part of the learning process.
As such, it is something that should be discussed and supported. Educators
can facilitate discussions about the sources of meaning and purpose in life or
values. It is also possible simply to raise questions similar to those put forth
by Tough (1991); 'Does the on-going flourishing of human civilization matter?'
'Can one person make a difference?' Questions like these were said to be
extremely powerful, by students in my studies, in terms of helping them reflect
on and talk about issues of the soul. Finally, the soul enjoys and responds to
images. Part of the soul-work of learning is the development of images of
desired futures; images that may be expressed in music, art, words or other
aesthetic venues. Embedded in images of desired futures is hope, commitment
and the path to empowered action.

If we accept that learning about global futures is a truly holistic experience,
then it behoves us to ask the following questions when selecting a theory,
framework or educational strategy:

- Will this approach help learners to become consciously aware of
  their existing perspectives so that there can be critical reflection on the
  basic underlying assumptions, beliefs, values and expectations? Will
  this approach help students understand the intellectual challenges of
  learning?
- Will this approach help learners to express and cope with the many
  emotions that accompany this learning experience?
- Will this approach help learners explore issues related to life's meaning
  and purpose, commitments and responsibilities?
- Will this approach support learners as they search for, explore and initiate
  personal paths of action?

Conclusion

Learning about global futures is a complex symphony of human experience.
It is learning that demands critique of the very foundations of our world views.
It requires that we open ourselves to and effectively cope with the myriad of
emotions that crash into consciousness as we face issues of today and arrive
at a place of caring about humanity, the planet and future generations. It is a
process that asks us to search our souls to find the meaning and purpose of
our own existence and choose actions based on those deliberations. The path
to a hopeful future depends of this symphony for it is one that compels us to
learn about and make choices with respect to the potential destinies of all
human and planetary life.

References

Assagioli, R (1965) *Psychosynthesis*, New York: Viking.

Bateson, G (1972) *Mind and Nature*, New York: Patton.

Berman, M (1981) *The Reenchantment of the World*, Ithaca, New York: Cornell University Press.

Brookfield, S (1985) *Self-Directed Learning: From Theory to Practice*, San Francisco: Jossey-Bass.

Cranton, P (1994) *Understanding and Promoting Transformative Learning: A Guide for Educators of Adults*. San Francisco: Jossey Bass.

Freire, P (1970) *Cultural Action for Freedom*, Cambridge, Massachusetts: Harvard Education Review.

Macy, J (1983) *Despair and Personal Power in the Nuclear Age*, Philadelphia: New Society Publishers.

Macy, J (1991) *World as Lover, World as Self*, Berkeley, California: Parallax Press.

McKenzie, L (1991) *Adult Education and Worldview Construction*, Malabar, Florida: Krieger Publishing Co.

Mezirow, J (1978) Perspective transformation, *Adult Education Quarterly*, 28(2), 100–110.

Mezirow, J (1985) A critical theory of self-directed learning, in: Brookfield, S (ed.), *Self-Directed Learning: From Theory to Practice*, San Francisco: Jossey-Bass.

Mezirow, J (1991) *Fostering Critical Reflection in Adulthood*, San Francisco: Jossey-Bass.

Miller, J (1988) *The Holistic Curriculum*, Toronto: Ontario Institute for Studies in Education Press.

Moore, T (1992) *Care of the Soul: A Guide for Cultivating Depth and Sacredness in Everyday Life*, New York: Harper Perennial.

Polanyi, M (1962) *Personal Knowledge: Towards a Post-Critical Philosophy*, Chicago: University of Chicago Press.

Rogers, M and Tough, A (1991) 'What Happens When Students Face the Future?' *Futures Research Quarterly*, 8(4), 9–18.

Rogers, M (1994) 'Learning About Global Futures: An Exploration of Learning Processes and Changes in Adults', Unpublished doctoral dissertation, University of Toronto. Microfiche from the National Library of Canada.

Schwebel, M (1990) 'The Construction of Reality in the Nuclear Age', *Political Psychology*, 11(3), 521–553.

Slaughter, R (1989) 'Cultural Reconstruction in the Post-modern World', *Curriculum Studies*, 21(3), 255–270.

Slaughter, R (1991) 'Changing Images of Futures in the 20th Century', *Futures*, 23(5), 499–515.

Swimme, B and Berry, T (1992) *The Universe Story: From the Primordial Flaring Forth to the Ecozoic Era: A Celebration of the Unfolding of the Cosmos*, San Francisco: Harper Collins.

Tough, A (1986) 'Gaining Meaning and Purpose from Seven Aspects of Reality', *Ultimate Reality and Meaning: Interdisciplinary Studies in the Philosophy of Understanding*, 9, 291–300.

Tough, A (1991) *Crucial Questions About the Future*, Lanham, Maryland: University Press of America.

Tyler, R (1949) *Basic Principles of Curriculum and Instruction*, Chicago: University of Chicago Press.

Varguish, T (1980) 'Why the Person Next to You Hates *Limits to Growth*', *Journal of Technological Forecasting and Social Change*, 16, 179–189.

Weiser, J (1987) 'Learning From the Perspective of Growth of Consciousness', in: Boud, D and Griffin, V *Appreciating Adults Learning: From the Learner's Perspective*, London: Kogan Page.

Yalom, I (1980) *Existential Psychotherapy*, New York: Basic Books.

Yeomans, A (1988) 'Reflections on Psychosynthesis and Non-Violence by a Therapist Turned Peace Educator and Activist', in: Weiser, J & Yeomans, T (eds.) *Readings in Psychosynthesis: Theory, Process and Practice*, Toronto: Ontario Institute in Studies of Education.

Zukav, G (1990) *The Seat of the Soul*, New York: Simon and Schuster.

Further reading

Rogers, M and Tough, A (1996) 'Facing the Future is Not for Wimps', *Futures*, 28(5), 491–196.

16. Identifying sources of hope in postmodern times

David Hicks

Summary

This chapter begins by reporting on popular images of the future during the twentieth century and in particular their dystopian emphasis. By then looking at the failure of modernity and the clash between deconstructive and revisionary postmodernism it sets these images in a wider social context. The crucial importance of positive images of the future is emphasised and the outcomes of envisioning workshops with students and others described. This then leads to discussion about the significance of hope in combatting pessimism and a growing interest in this phenomenon is identified. A research project which worked with global educators to identify their sources of hope is described with a final comment on the need for socially committed educators to consider the pedagogical implications of this more closely.

Images of the future

One of the abiding concerns of futurists and futures educators has been the nature of people's images of the future. Indeed Dator (1996: 109) argues that this is a central concern of futures studies: 'One of the things futures studies tries to do is to help people examine and clarify their images of the future – their ideas, fears, hopes, beliefs, concerns about the future – so that they might improve the quality of their decisions which impact it.' What then do we know about popular images of the future in the western world during the late-twentieth century?

One of the major studies was a comparative ten-nation survey carried out in the early 1970s called *Images of the World in the Year 2000* (Ornauer *et al.*, 1976). This showed that people's ability to think about the future was not very well developed and that images of the future were most often framed with reference to science and technology. Pessimistic visions of the future were more common than optimistic ones. Livingstone's (1983) survey in Ontario reported more frequent thinking about the future and a focus on a wider array of social issues. He found that corporate capitalists, managers and professional employees claimed the greatest clarity over their images of the future. During the 1980s images of the future tended to be of nuclear winter or environmental disaster (Macy, 1992). More recent studies in the UK still show a widespread disaffection over the future coupled with a sense that things can only get worse (Jacobs, 1996: 1–2).

The literature on young people's views of the future has been reviewed by Hicks & Holden (1995) where similar worries were shown to be present to a greater or lesser degree. Hutchinson (1996) and Eckersley (1995) have written about this in the Australian context, as has Oscarsson (1996) in relation to Sweden. Young people are shown to be interested and concerned about possible futures yet seldom given the opportunity explicitly to explore them in school.

The dystopia addiction

These findings echo a general malaise about the future which, Bailey (1988) argues, pervades most discussion today in western society.

> It is now difficult to be optimistic. In general conversation, in journalism, in popular social commentary, in political argument, in academic social analysis, perhaps in art, literature and general works of the imagination there are few signs of hope about the future (Bailey, 1988: 1).

In particular Bailey argues that we need to make 'implicit pessimism explicit', more open and available for discussion rather than an under-current which we prefer to keep in the background. Everitt (1995) captures these popular feelings of unease in his description of how we approach the millennium, 'we seem to be moving towards 2000 with a head full of fears, to be drifting into a cyberspace populated by monsters from the deep'.

If futurists and in particular futures educators, have an interest in images of the future, then this clearly needs to be more than a casual concern. Such images cannot merely be of passing interest since they seem to express our deepest concerns about the present as well as a fear of the future. Kumar (1995: 207) argues that a sense of 'endings without new beginnings has been more or less constant throughout the twentieth century'. Even utopians such as HG Wells were swimming against the tide and this, he believes, is the dilemma – western society is infused with a sense of millennial endings rather than the utopian visions needed by society to provide a sense of hope.

Postmodernity

This state of society is best understood in the context of a shift from the certainties of modernity to the ambiguities of postmodernity. Modernity had its origins in the Industrial Revolution and the Enlightenment of the late eighteenth century and marked a major transition from the relatively stable culture of 'pre-modern' societies. It was a period marked by wide-scale growth of industrial processes, capitalist economics, the nation state and socio-cultural disruption (Harvey, 1989). In particular the Enlightenment project valorised western rationalism, scientific endeavour, economic growth, control of nature and the inevitability of 'progress'. It was taken as axiomatic that there was one truth and that reason, particularly through the application of science and mathematics, could achieve liberation for all.

The power of modernity lay in its rejection of tradition, particularly religious dogma and authority and thus its power as a progressive force. New scientific techniques and social insights provided the momentum to transform western culture and move societies out of traditional life and into the modern mode. Central to this endeavour was capitalist efficiency and rationality. While the fruits of modernity have been many, critics in the late-twentieth century have increasingly highlighted its damaging and oppressive elements. Two world wars, the growing global gap between rich north and poor south, increasing environmental damage, repressive political regimes and increased social disintegration, are also outcomes of the priorities of modernity. Postmodernism thus mounts a major critique of what are seen as failures of the Enlightenment project (Rosenau, 1992).

Three main dimensions of postmodernity are readily distinguishable. First, the term refers to the temporal period marked by the capitalist transition beyond industrial modernism as a result of computers, information technology and mass electronic communications. Second, postmodernism refers to a cultural style that rejects the privileged position of modernity, preferring pluralistic styles and multiple choices. Third, postmodernity refers to a method of analysis which emphasises the need to deconstruct our conceptions of reality including the very basis of truth and knowledge.

Among the diversity of perspectives that postmodernity legitimises, it is possible to highlight two main tendencies. These have been variously named deconstructive or sceptical postmodernism on the one hand and constructive, affirmative or revisionary postmodernism on the other (Griffin, 1992; Rosenau, 1992; Walker, 1996). Deconstructive postmodernism is distrustful of all meta-narratives, that is it rejects all claims to higher truth or universal explanations, whether those of Marxism, Christianity or science. It turns away from the Enlightenment notion of an overarching truth and celebrates instead local, personal and multiple narratives. This focus demands that attention be paid to all that which has previously been concealed, unnamed or excluded. All knowledge is therefore relative, all 'texts' must be deconstructed. As there is no truth, temporal and spatial relationships fragment and become meaningless, spectacle and consumption are no more or less significant than war or hunger. Such a relativistic and ungrounded view of society not surprisingly gives rein to pessimism and despair, for it contributes to existing social disintegration, a sense of meaninglessness and loss of purpose. Revisionary postmodernism, while accepting the critique of scientific rationalism, does not fall prey to the nihilism of much deconstructive postmodernism. Rather, it seeks to re-invent and go beyond modernity:

> Going beyond the modern world will involve transcending its individualism, anthropocentrism, patriarchy, mechanisation, economism, consumerism, nationalism and militarism. Constructive postmodern thought provides support for the ecology, peace, feminist and other emancipatory movements of our time, while stressing that the inclusive emancipation must be from modernity itself. The term *postmodern*, however, by contrast with *premodern*, emphasises that the modern world has produced unparalleled advances that must not be lost in a general revulsion against its negative features (Griffin, 1992: xi).

Revisionary postmodernism thus offers a way forward and a ground for hope. It is a fertile zone for those who want to think more critically and creatively about the future. It makes possible the recovery of values and wisdom marginalised or discarded by modernism and encourages the re-membering rather than dismembering of ourselves, our communities and the biosphere. Reason takes its rightful place along with intuition, imagination and creativity. The future can be seen again as an interdisciplinary and collective endeavour rather than an elitist patriarchal project aiming at scientific prediction and control through seductive techno-fix solutions to what are at root moral and ethical dilemmas.

Preferable futures

Envisioning the future

So we are in a contradictory situation where, on the one hand, popular images of the future in the West tend to be negative if not dystopian in nature while, on the other, what is most needed are creative and positive images that provide a basis for hope. If we go back to the beginning of this century, when the promise of modernity was at its height, images of the future were more likely to be positive and benign. The triumphs of Victorian engineering, social control, imperialism and colonialism, had placed Britain in a powerful global position. The future indeed promised 'more of the same'. However, as we now know, this was not to be. The horrors of the First World War were followed by the depression and the rise of fascism. This in turn lead to the Second World War, the Holocaust and the atomic bombing of Hiroshima and Nagasaki. The superpower nuclear arms race (1945–89) was punctuated by the Korean war, the Vietnam war and growing fears of environmental destruction.

In the 1950s, Dutch sociologist Fred Polak (1972) carried out a major study of western images of the future. In doing this he explored all aspects of western culture, from Sumer and ancient Greece up to the mid-twentieth century, to see how images of the future had varied. What he found was that such images provided a barometer for the state of society as a whole. Thus, when a society had challenging and creative images of the future it was likely to be in the ascendant. On the other hand, if a society had negative images of the future it was likely to be in stagnation or decline. Looking at western views of the future in the fifties he commented that never had there been such a dearth of positive images (Boulding, 1979). The social capacity for envisioning creative alternatives seemed to have all but disappeared.

Other commentators and activists noted the same thing, knowing that a positive image of self, of community and wider society, is always necessary to generate effective action for change. Thus, beginning in the 60s and 70s with the work of Robert Jungk and going on into the 80s with the work of people such as Robert Ziegler and Elise Boulding, futures workshops became a vital tool in rectifying this deficiency (Hicks, 1996a). More recently such envisioning workshops have been used with community and other groups (Weisbord and Janoff, 1995) and in the development of Local Agenda 21 programmes (Vision 21, 1996). It is important therefore at this point to examine what sort of images of the future emerge from these workshop processes.

Desirable futures

Boulding (1994) has written an interesting account of the outcomes of her work with groups to help participants visualise their preferred future worlds. The main activity involves a guided visualisation followed by the creation of group posters portaying the key elements of these futures. Boulding listed all the images which appeared in her workshops and then clustered them into key themes. These themes are set out in Table 16.1.

Boulding notes that the first seven themes appear regularly in her futures workshops and they make up what she calls the 'baseline future'. In order to

Table 16.1 Key themes in Boulding's futures workshops

- a lack of divisions based on age, race or gender
- a non-hierarchical world with no one 'in charge'
- a strong sense of place and community
- low-profile and widely shared technology
- particularly relating to communications and transport
- people acting out of a more peaceable 'new consciousness'
- education taking place 'on the job'
- food grown locally
- a 'bright, clean, green' world (particularly strong amongst young people)
- a sense of the local community as joyful, nurturing and celebratory
- a 'boundaryless' world with no social, occupational or political barriers

---

Source: Boulding, E (1994) *Preparing for the Future: Notes and Queries for Concerned Educators*

compare and update these findings a pilot study was carried out with students in higher education in the UK using the same workshop procedure (Hicks, 1996b). After using Boulding's visualisation, participants drew posters in small groups to illustrate the key features of their preferred futures. Twelve major themes were identified and these, together with their associated keywords, are shown in rank order in Table 16.2.

Table 16.2   Preferable futures: key themes in rank order (n = 90)

1. Green	79% clean air and water, trees, wildlife, flowers
2. Convivial	74% co-operative, relaxed, happy, caring, laughter
3. Transport	55% no cars, no pollution, public transport, bikes
4. Peaceful	53% lack of violent conflict, security, global harmony
5. Equity	38% no poverty, fair shares for all, no hunger
6. Just	36% equal rights of people/planet, no discrimination
7. Community	36% local, small, friendly, simple sense of community
8. Education	30% for all, on-going for life, holistic, community
9. Energy	26% lower consumption, renewable and clean sources
10. Work	23% for all, satisfying, shared, shorter hours
11. Healthy	19% better health care, alternative, longer life
12. Food	15% organic farming, locally grown, balanced diet

Source: Hicks, D (1996) *Futures*, 28 (8): 741–749

Most of all, over three-quarters of the students want a future in which the natural environment is respected, protected and revered. They want it to be, using Boulding's words, 'bright, clean, green'. Reference is particularly made to clean air, land and water, richness and diversity of species, together with an abundance of trees and flowers. Balancing this prime concern for the planet is a concern for human interaction and quality of life, particularly with respect to a sense of conviviality, social well-being and celebratory interconnectedness with others.

The third quality that just over half of the participants want to see is a more peaceful world. This is expressed in terms of both the local and global community and is an extension of the conviviality they want to experience in their own lives. The most important issue, mentioned by just over half of the participants, is transport. A strong preference is expressed for a future in which cars are much less important than today and in which cheap and efficient transport, particularly trams and bikes, is available.

The baseline future for this group of students is green, convivial and peaceful, with a stress on alternative forms of transport. Other important features mentioned by just over a third of the group are the wish that this future should embody much greater economic equity than today, with no rich or poor, homes for all, fair trading between countries, no hunger and no exploitation of Third

World countries. Allied to this is the wish for justice, an atmosphere of toler-ance, an absence of discrimination, a respect for the rights of all species. Also important is the sense of belonging to a community, and the feeling that small and local is beautiful, whether in respect to agriculture or industry.

Of Boulding's ten key themes (Table 16.1) seven are also present in this UK study: a lack of discrimination; a sense of place/community; food grown locally; technology in relation to transport; peaceable; green; celebratory. It goes some way to support her contention that there may be a 'baseline future' which emerges from such envisioning. Despite the fact that more work clearly needs to be done on the outcomes of such workshops, these findings do show that envisioning desirable futures is both possible and empowering using this process.

The utopian tradition

One of the most enduring traditions in the West, pre-dating the rise of modernity and its notion of history as progress, is that of the 'good' society or ideal world. Thomas More coined the term utopia in 1516 as a pun in Greek: 'eutopia', the good place, was also 'utopia', no place. Utopias have variously been set in other lands, other times or other galaxies, as blueprints of a better society, or even a perfect society, and embracing all aspects of life (Kumar, 1991). Many utopians have presented their ideas in literary form from Thomas More's *Utopia* and William Morris's *News From Nowhere* to Marge Piercy's *Woman on the Edge of Time* and Ernest Callenbach's *Ecotopia Emerging*.

All in their different ways have a double-edged message. On the one hand they critique the existing conditions in society and on the other, they offer a vision of a better world. Marx's condemnation of the utopian socialists of the nineteenth century as 'unscientific' (in contrast to his scientific socialism) led to a gradual devaluing of the term so that today it is often used with a pejorative connotation. This is unfortunate as the current of utopian thought and action has been a constant and vital force in western thinking up to the present day. There is, of course, also a lived tradition of utopian communities from the Diggers in the seventeenth century and the Shakers in the eighteenth to Robert Owen's New Harmony in the nineteenth century and the communes movement of the 1970s.

Most recently the tradition has resurfaced in the form of feminist and ecological utopias reflecting major concerns of the late twentieth century (Starhawk, 1993). The utopian tradition, whether literary or lived, is a major well-spring of creativity and a crucial source of hope and inspiration in troubled times. However, during this century it is the dystopias that are most remembered, whether Huxley's *Brave New World* or George Orwell's *1984*, followed more recently by movies such as *Mad Max, Blade Runner, Waterworld* and *Judge Dredd*. This is but a continuation of what Polak saw in mid-century, an absence of positive images of the future. As Kumar (1995: 207) has pointed out it is the apocalyptic imagination which still rules at this time. What is lacking, he says, is any sense of hope and this of course is what the utopian tradition provides.

Principles of hope

The notion of hope clearly has a crucial part to play in troubled times. Without hope of some sort there can only be anxiety or despair, whether in our personal lives or in wider society. Hope is clearly related to optimism but both of these, depending on the circumstances, can either be realistic or unrealistic. Because in our lives we have often experienced false hopes or undue optimism it is easy to dismiss hope as an impracticality. Yet hope is essential to the human condition, the belief that things can be other than they are. The envisioning of preferable futures and the utopian tradition itself are key examples of hope in action.

A growing interest

The crucial role that hope has to play in these times is increasingly being noted by commentators. Bill McKibben in *Hope, Human and Wild: True Stories of Living Lightly on the Earth* (1995), looks at recent developments in three contrasting areas: the Adirondack Mountains in the US, the town of Curitiba in Brazil, and the state of Kerala in India. He does so, he says, because he wants to use them as stories of hope.

> I no longer think fear is sufficient motivation to make (the) changes, especially since they involve the most fundamental aspects of our economies, our societies, and our individual lives. To spur us on we need hope as well – we need a vision of recovery, of renewal, of resurgence (McKibben, 1995: 11).

Catherine Thick's book, *The Right to Hope: Global Problems, Global Visions* (1995), contains pictures of original artwork on the theme of 'one world' brought together to commemorate the 50th anniversary of the UN and UNESCO. Artists and writers from around the world combined to respond to this theme and some, such as Susan George, specifically commented on the importance of hope:

> I believe that hope *allows* people to struggle for rights, to create, to affirm their dignity. Fortunately for us all, hope is coextensive with the human condition, not an elusive goal to be constantly beaten back yet constantly reaffirmed. Hope is what makes politics possible: collective hope, far more than collective despair, has been at the root of every significant change in human history (George, 1995: 5).

The third example comes from the work of radical educator Robin Richardson, whose book *Fortunes and Fables: Education for Hope in Troubled Times* (1996), chronicles the dilemmas faced by socially committed educators in the UK. In this he writes: 'We need stories – myths and folk tales as well as true accounts – to help us hold the beginnings, middles and ends of our lives together. Without them we shall not have hope: yes, to lose stories is to lose hope, but conversely to construct and cherish stories is to maintain hope' (page 101). Thus, in their different ways, these contemporary writers all identify hope as a subject relevant to the postmodern condition and worthy of deeper exploration.

The study of hope is not new – although the literature is somewhat scattered and fragmentary – and writers approach this subject in different ways depending on their disciplinary backgrounds. For example, Stotland, in *The Psychology of Hope* (1969), is primarily concerned with the role of hope in clinical problems of anxiety, depression and healing. Alternatively, Desroche in *The Sociology of Hope* (1979) focuses on hope as a religious phenomenon, particularly in relation to millenarian movements, while Bloch's *The Priciples of Hope* (1986) brings together a mass of material from the Marxist and Romantic traditions. Moltmann, in his *Theology of Hope* (1967), offers an extensive exploration of hope in both spiritual and secular traditions. He comments:

> Hope alone is to be called 'realistic', because it alone takes seriously the possibilities with which all reality is fraught. It does not take things as they happen to stand or lie, but as progressing, moving things with possibilities of change.... Thus hopes and anticipations of the future are not a transfiguring glow superimposed upon a darkened existence, but are realistic ways of perceiving the scope of our real possibilities, and as such they set everything in motion and keep it in a state of change. Hope and the kind of thinking that goes with it consequently cannot submit to the reproach of being utopian, for they do not strive after things that have 'no place', but after things that have 'no place *as yet*' but can acquire one (page 25).

Some reflections from educators

It was in the light of the above that a recent research project explored the experiences of global educators, ie educators who manage to retain a sense of hope and optimism while yet staying present to global threats on a daily basis. Using taped interviews, autobiographical writing and a focus group weekend, participants were able reflectively to share their stories and experiences (Hicks, 1997). In the interviews and the focus group, participants identified the aspects of life in postmodern times which caused them most concern, viz. environmental degradation, abuse of human rights, nuclear accidents, the power of multinational corporations, hunger and poverty. Within their jobs they often felt stressed, overworked and marginalised.

From the initial interviews it was obvious that some people could readily identify their sources of hope. Here one participant reflects on growing up near his grandparents' farm:

My playground was a beautiful area bounded by rivers, moorland, woods and empty farmland. Both my parents love it, love natural beauty, love wildlife and are great respecters of it. They are as enthralled by the emergence of celandines on a spring morning as some people might be with the birth of a baby. To them its a source of conversation and delight and this they passed on to myself and my brothers. In our early child-hood when we went for walks each weekend, although we didn't know it, we were told what everything was and what the behavior of things were, birds and animals... And we knew all the wild flowers and where they appeared and why and that I absorbed. It's a magical world in the sense that however close you go into it, it sustains its beauty... And nature never lets you down, it is forever beautiful and, best of all, it provides all our needs. Except love, you have to learn to love...

This captures both the writer's childhood awe and wonder at the natural environment and the role of his parents in grounding that experience. When work gets difficult he still retreats to the woods and fields for a sense of renewal and to put things in perspective. Another participant wrote about the impact of living in a developing country:

The year I spent in Vietnam, along with earlier experiences of living in other cultures, continues to provide me with a reference point for measuring what is really important. When you see people coping with privation, with loss or separation, with lives that benefit from few of the luxuries we often take for granted, you are wise to put into propor-tion your own difficulties and discomforts. When you gain some insights into the things that give those people joy or peace of mind: religious belief; love of the family and the land; music and song; dance; poetry, you have to look beyond the every-dayness of your own life to what is at the core.

Participants generally identified several sources of hope. One person's list included: childbirth as a 'renewal of hope in which we routinely acknowledge our hopes, dreams and ambitions through our children'; 'the uncaring consist-ency of nature as a bedrock to restore my hopes in dealings with people and as an energising source of inspiration'; people who under the most terrible duress still never allow themselves to be overwhelmed by tragedy; people who, while economically poor, offer great generosity and hospitality to one; and finally music, 'from the sound of whales singing to Pachebel's Canon which, like art, ennobles human endeavour and compliments the human condition at every level.'

At the end of the focus group weekend participants listed the key sources of hope which they had collectively identified. These are shown in Table 16.3. One of the striking things about the research process was that it became a

Table 16.3   Sources of hope

- *The natural world:* a source of beauty, wonder and inspiration which ever renews itself and ever refreshes the heart and mind.
- *Other people's lives:* the way in which both ordinary and extraordinary people manage difficult life situations with dignity.
- *Collective struggles:* groups in the past and the present who have fought to achieve the equality and justice that is rightfully theirs.
- *Visionaries:* those who offer visions of an earth transformed and who work to help bring this about in different ways.
- *Faith and belief:* which may be spiritual or political and which offers a framework of meaning in both good times and bad.
- *A sense of self:* being aware of one's self-worth and secure in one's own identity which leads to a sense of connectedness and belonging.
- *Human creativity:* the constant awe-inspiring upwelling of music, poetry, and the arts, an essential element of the human condition.
- *Mentors and colleagues:* at work and at home who offer inspiration by their deeds and encouragement with their words.
- *Relationships:* the being loved by partners, friends and family that nourishes and sustains us in our lives.

---

source of hope in its own right. Participants said that they felt nourished, renewed, aware of the 'tapestry of hope', witnesses to faith in the human spirit (Hicks, 1997).

Epilogue

Deconstructive postmodernism not only leaves us 'between stories' (Berry, 1990) but without any possibility of a new story. Constructive or revisionary postmodernism, however, rather than seeking to eliminate the possibility of such world views looks for a new synthesis. Hope has a central role to play in revisionary postmodernism, not in the shallow sense of merely hoping that things will improve but in the accessing of deep sources of inspiration. Thus in his introduction to *Pedagogy of Hope* (1994: 8–9) Freire writes:

> I do not understand human existence, and the struggle needed to improve it, apart from hope and dream. Hope is an ontological need. Hopelessness is but hope that has lost its bearings, and become a distortion of that ontological need... Hence the need for a kind of education in hope.

Part of that education must be to identify our own sources of hope and how to use them to clarify our visions of a more just and sustainable society (Hicks, 1994; Hicks and Holden, 1995). This needs to become a major focus within education and is essential to any definition of, for example, active citizenship.

As Huckle (1990: 159) succinctly states 'If we are not to overwhem pupils with the world's problems, we should teach in a spirit of optimism...build environmental [and social] success stories into our curriculum and develop awareness of sources of hope in a world where new and appropriate technologies now offer liberation for all'.

References

Bailey, J (1988) *Pessimism*, London: Routledge.

Berry, T (1990) *The Dream of the Earth*, San Francisco: Sierra Club.

Bloch, E (1986) *The Principle of Hope*, Oxford: Blackwell.

Boulding, E (1979) 'Remembering the Future: the Work of Fred Polak', *Alternative Futures: The Journal of Utopian Studies*, Fall.

Boulding, E (1994) 'Image and Action in Peace Building', chapter 6 in: Hicks, D (ed.) *Preparing for the Future: Notes and Queries for Concerned Educators*, London: Adamantine Press.

Dator, J (1996) 'Futures Studies as Applied Knowledge', chapter 4 in: Slaughter, R (ed.) *New Thinking for a New Millennium*, London: Routledge.

Desroche, H (1979) *The Sociology of Hope*, London: Routledge & Kegan Paul.

Eckersley, R (1995) 'Values and Visions: Youth and the Failure of Modern Western Culture', *Youth Studies Australia*, 14 (1): 13–52.

Everitt, A (1995) 'The Dredd of 2000 AD', *The Guardian*, January 7th.

Freire, P (1994) *Pedagogy of Hope*, Continuum: New York.

George, S (1995) 'Why Stop Now?' chapter 2 in: Thick, C *The Right to Hope*, London: Earthscan.

Griffin, D (1992) 'Introduction', in Orr, D *Ecological Literacy*, Albany: State University of New York Press.

Harvey, D (1989) *The Condition of Postmodernity*, Oxford: Blackwell.

Hicks, D (1994) *Educating for the Future: A Practical Classroom Guide*, Godalming: World Wide Fund for Nature UK.

Hicks, D (1996a) 'Envisioning the Future: the Challenge for Environmental Educators', *Environmental Education Research*, 2(1): 101–108.

Hicks, D (1996b) 'Retrieving the Dream: How Students Envision Their Preferable Futures', *Futures*, 28(8): 741–749.

Hicks, D (1997) 'Sources of Hope in Postmodern Times', *Journal of Beliefs and Values*, 18(2), 93–102.

Hicks, D & Holden, C (1995) *Visions of the Future: Why We Need to Teach for Tomorrow*, Stoke-on-Trent: Trentham Books.

Huckle, J (1990) 'Environmental Education', chapter 10 in: Dufour, B (ed.) *The New Social Curriculum*, Cambridge: Cambridge University Press.

Hutchinson, F (1996) *Educating Beyond Violent Futures*, London: Routledge.

Jacobs, M (1996) *The Politics of the Real World*, London: Earthscan.

Kumar, K (1991) *Utopianism*, Milton Keynes: Open University Press.

Kumar, K (1995) 'Apocalypse, Millennium and Utopia Today', chapter 9 in: Bull, M (ed.) *Apocalypse Theory and the End of the World*, Oxford: Blackwell.

Livingstone, D (1983) 'Intellectual and Popular Images of the Educational and Social Future' in: *Class Ideologies and Educational Futures*, London: Falmer Press.

Macy, J (1992) 'Planetary Perils and Psychological Responses' in: Staub, S and Green, P (eds) *Psychology and Social Responsibility: Facing Global Challenges*, New York: New York University Press (pp. 30–58).

McKibben, B (1995) *Hope, Human and Wild: True Stories of Living Lightly on the Earth*, Boston: Little, Brown & Co.

Moltmann, J (1967) *The Theology of Hope*, London: SCM Press.

Oscarsson, V (1996) 'Pupils' Views on the Future in Sweden', *Environmental Education Research*, 2(3): 261–277.

Ornauer, H et al. (1976) *Images of the World in the Year 2000*, Atlantic Highlands NJ: Humanities Press.

Polak, F (1972) *The Image of the Future* [E Boulding transl. and abr.] San Francisco: Jossey Bass/Elsevier.

Richardson, R (1996) *Fortunes and Fables: Education for Hope in Troubled Times*, Stoke-on-Trent: Trentham Books.

Rosenau, P (1992) *Post-modernism and the Social Sciences*, Princeton NJ: Princetown University Press.

Starhawk (1993) *The Fifth Sacred Thing*, New York: Bantam Books.

Stotland, E (1969) *The Psychology of Hope*, San Francisco: Jossey-Bass.

Thick, C (1995) *The Right to Hope: Global Problems, Global Visions*, London: Earthscan.

Vision 21 (1996) *Sustainable Gloucestershire*, Cheltenham: Vision 21.

Walker, J (1996) 'Postmodernism and the Study of the Future', *Futures Research Quarterly*, 12(2): 51–70.

Weisbord, M and Janoff, S (1995) *Future Search*, San Francisco: Berrett-Koehler.

Section III:
Educating for a sustainable future

17. The need to envision sustainable futures

Christopher Jones

Summary

This chapter discusses the need for envisioning positive futures and how critical futures studies can empower students of all ages to transform visions into actions – to realize those futures they imagine. Futures studies are crucial for education, especially to help us better understand the essential role of futures images in our thinking, planning and decision making, all of which can lead toward or away from sustainable paths to the future. This chapter covers the evolution and development of various approaches to envisioning sustainable futures including the path-finding work of Jungk, Boulding, Ziegler and others. It looks at approaches derived from and in addition to, the visioning workshops, including the creation of 'future history' (back-casting), 'reversing the negative' (turning fears into hopes) and 'incasting' alternative futures. In order to take control of our futures and to leave a legacy for our children and grandchildren, we must equip ourselves to envision, create and sustain more humane and ecological futures.

Introduction

Poised as we are on the edge of the millennium, the future seems closer than ever. This illusion is amplified by the accelerating pace of technological and environmental changes surrounding us. Once past the millennium the novelty of living in a new century may wear off, but the future will be no less of a force to be reckoned with. It would be surprising indeed if the pace of change slackened from the rising gale forces our species has set in motion, try as we might to ignore them.

Social and political institutions, large and small, continue to bury their collective heads in the sand or engage in vain attempts to recover the past. No wonder institutional behavior is characterized by denial or avoidance given that the individuals who make up those institutions are loath to come to terms with this on-rushing future. One reason may be that there are no compelling popular visions of the future to inspire them to look forward to the future. More broadly, political and social institutions are slaves to the past and present, especially given that their values and basic assumptions are paradigmatic. Critical futures studies is one antidote to the industrial paradigm.

One of the premises of critical futures studies is that a *status quo* future is unsustainable and that society must envision and work towards more sustainable futures (Boulding 1995, 1996; Elgin 1991, 1993; Hicks 1996c; Hicks and Holden 1995; Robertson 1978; Slaughter 1991; Ziegler 1991). This is primarily an attack on the dominant economic paradigm – unconstrained growth – and is also a challenge to western ideas about materialism and reductionism. Slaughter (1991) defines sustainability as something that 'must be able to continue in indefinite use without causing excessive disturbance or damage.' For Duane Elgin (1991), a sustainable future 'is one in which we have confidence in the long-run ability of the Earth's ecosystem and human culture to support continuing evolution at the planetary scale.' He notes Simone de Beauvoir's view of sustainability as a dynamic process where life is occupied in both perpetuating and surpassing itself, thus 'a sustainable future is one where humans are able not only to maintain themselves but also to continually surpass themselves without destroying the ecological foundations upon which all life depends'.

Beyond the physical challenges to modern industrial civilization required to effect a sustainable civilization, Elgin (1993) notes subjective elements which are also requirements including 'a simple and compelling story of the future [and] practical ways to participate in creating that future in our daily lives...' Ultimately, we must be able to imagine what that future might look like.

Slaughter's *Recovering the Future* (1988) makes a strong case for tying general futures education to visions of sustainable futures. He cites several reasons for introducing futures studies into schools and includes a specific rationale for these. His arguments for integrating futures education and visioning into childhood education include the idea:

- that we must move beyond 'crisis management' to proactive thinking;
- that people's images of the future affect their decisions in the present;
- that we exert our will and intentionality on the future;
- that there are strategic consequences of our actions and decisions;
- that education (which is strongly rooted in the past) requires credible futures alternatives to establish appropriate strategies and directions.

Most of these elements are also essential to a broader futures agenda – for adult education and for social institutions. While a range of approaches can be used to draw out and capitalize on the above, alternative futures images and visioning exercises are among the most effective in bringing out the concerns of the present and strategies for realizing hopes in the future.

Few books have been as influential in futures studies as Fred Polak's *The Image of the Future* (1973) which posited that the images of the future in people's minds shape their intentions and color their decisions and actions in daily life. Polak's rich analysis of historical and cultural patterns reveals what he calls an 'ideal type' of image of the future which consists of the balance of two elements: the eschatological (transcendent) and the utopian (immanent). The first element is that which allows the visionary to transcend 'the bonds of the cultural present' and mentally enter the realm of a 'totally other type of society' (Boulding, 1971). The second element is the 'humanistic utopian' or immanent element, where humans are the 'co-partners with nature (or God) in the shaping of the Other in the here-and-now.'

The first element has become an essential component in many futures exercises, a major requirement for visioning and futures workshops and to a lesser degree an important aspect of brainstorming – suspension of disbelief. The second element figures prominently in Polak's conception of a cyclical tension in western culture between the human and supernatural forces at work in the world. At one extreme, God is taking care of everything and at the other, everything is up to humanity (Boulding, 1971). The second element is very pertinent today given the ubiquitous sense of helplessness and apparent lack of control over external forces.

Polak contended that the capacity to transcend or 'breach' time and to create the totally 'other' has evaporated in this century. He also contends that the capacity to image the future is 'a core capacity in any culture that is manifested in every other aspect of that culture' (Boulding, 1971) and argues that the inability to envision dynamic images of the future will lead to the death of that society. His prognosis for contemporary society was not optimistic, based on 'the disappearance of the eschatological sense of a totally other order or reality' in popular art, literature, and culture (Boulding, 1971). Although Polak's book was first published in the 1950s, his prognosis seems to be supported by the ubiquitous images of the future in popular culture featuring the apocalyptic and post-apocalyptic, eg *The Road Warrior, Waterworld*. Although utopian and optimistic visions of the future do exist in modern literature, few if any have been translated into the mass media. Visioning and futures workshops are being used in an attempt to fill the creative void monopolized by 'fashionable worst-case scenarios with their military focus' (Boulding, 1996).

Preferred futures

A common typology for futurists has been the distinction between probable, possible and preferred futures – the latter always coming last as if thinking about preferred futures was the least realistic of the three. Critical futures studies, especially futures workshops, has emerged as a response to 'scientific futurism' (Ziegler, 1991). Jim Dator argues that 'futures studies helps people clarify their hopes and fears about the future in order to move beyond passive forecasting to the generation of preferred futures as a basis for planning and action' (quoted in Hicks, 1996c). Eleonora Masini (1996) notes the importance of Polak's conception of images of the future, 'this is why futures studies have the basic goal of clarifying future choices, and hence also guiding values'. Masini's work has stressed the importance of scenario-building, developed by those who are going to realize the futures described in them – 'This is when the image becomes vision, because it is related to what will make it achievable.'

Beyond the intrinsic need to have dynamic visions of the future to sustain civilization, there are a host of other reasons for envisioning alternative and preferred futures. These include the value of creativity and social invention, the need to adjust psychologically to 'future shock'; the necessity of understanding the fundamental assumptions of the dominant social paradigm; the importance of making decisions and acting in accordance with desirable futures images.

For the late Robert Jungk (one of the early promoters of futures workshops), creativity was an important rationale. Jungk (1976) invoked both John Platt's (1969) call for 'social imagination' to match the preponderance of technological and scientific imagination and Dennis Gabor's (1964) challenge to 'invent the future'. Jungk's concern about the paucity of positive, creative energy in society resulted in *The Everyman Project*, a book premised on the idea that untapped creativity exists within millions of people to supply the 'energy for survival' which we so desperately need (Jungk, 1976). His futures workshops were one way in which he began tap that creativity – to recover the creative potential, the 'derided and trampled dreams' from people's childhoods (quoted in Hicks, 1996a).

Visioning preferred futures is also a way of taking a more active approach to the rapid pace of change. Much popular futurism lends itself to passive assuaging of the traumas of this form of culture shock, while active envisioning demands that the future be adapted and adjusted to the participant's needs, not the other way around. Thus, envisioning aims to transcend the 'muddle through' approach to crisis management. A crucial role for envisioning alternative futures is exposing the fundamental assumptions of the industrial paradigm. By making obvious and explicit what are often hidden or unconscious values in western culture, individuals can stand back and evaluate the strengths and weaknesses of the dominant paradigm. From a social science perspective, this broader framework of analysis helps individuals not only understand society's basic assumptions, but also to see their role in supporting or undermining them. In terms of creating sustainable futures, uncovering these assumptions is critical in confronting their role in creating the global *problematique* – the destruction of ecosystems and the decline of planetary health.

Ultimately, the key to creating sustainable futures is establishing strategies to transform intentions into actions. It is this 'action-orientation' which must be a key component in the envisioning of preferred futures. Without this component the exercise is incomplete and likely to leave participants demoralized and frustrated. It is this element of a futures approach which is the most empowering, particularly in the face of global environmental, economic and social problems. Hicks (1996b) shows that when future visions are linked with case-studies of social change and personal empowerment, students can begin 'to see themselves as potentially proactive rather than merely reactive to change'. As Masini and others have pointed out, this empowerment extends to other marginalised groups, such as women and non-western people, as a mechanism for greater self-determination.

Approaches

Approaches to envisioning sustainable futures are varied, but the concept generally applies to a specific set of procedures, the best example of which is the World Without Weapons Workshops developed by Elise Boulding and Warren Ziegler (1977). Robert Jungk and Norbert Mullert developed a related process in European workshops as did Oliver Markley (1994) and others in and around SRI International (then the Stanford Research Institute) in Palo Alto, California. The use of visioning workshops and their subcomponents has also spread from futures think-tanks such as SRI and the Institute for Alternative Futures in Washington, DC and from the academic futures programs at the University of Houston-Clear Lake and the University of Hawaii at Manoa. Thus, there has been considerable cross-fertilization between individuals and organizations engaged in alternative futures research and visioning workshops have become widely used in futures studies (Hicks 1996a; Jarva, 1996; Jones, 1992a; Masini, 1996; Schultz, 1991; van Steenbergen, 1996).

Beginning in the early 1960s, Jungk's workshops were organized widely across Europe with a range of groups (Hicks, 1996a) and generally more community oriented than other later visioning efforts. His 'future-creating workshops' brought people into the social planning process, especially creative people (artists, poets, and writers) and involved informal, brainstorming approaches (Cornish, 1977). Whether they lasted a day, a weekend, or longer, they were comprised of four main phases: a preparatory phase, a critique phase, a fantasy phase and an implementation phase. Jungk saw futures workshops as a creative, but revolutionary process – seeking to free the intuitive and emotional as well as analytical and rational (Hicks, 1996a). Regrettably, this short description does not do justice to the widespread influence of Jungk and his workshops across Europe and within the field of futures studies. For example, a visioning workshop and day of planning for the World Futures Studies Federation to reconsider its own future and mission, held in Finland in 1993, was named in his honor.

Ziegler has been involved with futures workshops for more than twenty-five years, first at the Educational Policy Research Center at Syracuse University and now at Futures-Invention Associates in Denver. He has been involved in hundreds of workshops with a wide spectrum of government, business, non-profit and civic groups. He has not only worked with a diverse mixture of clients, but compared to Jungk, has had a wider repertoire of processes for envisioning preferred futures (Hicks, 1996a). A visionary futurist himself, Ziegler has been committed to spreading the gospel of visioning, because, 'just as the education of our children is too important to leave solely to educators, the future is too important to leave solely to futurists'.

For Ziegler (1991), the central premise of envisioning workshops is that 'the future is not the domain of knowledge but of action'. It should come as no surprise then that the final stage of his workshops is a strategy and action phase. Another central tenet is that 'the future is a metaphor for the human imagination', discovered and illuminated in the imaging phase. He notes that the greatest challenge in this phase is unlearning. Other keys to success in envisioning workshops include: the formation of a community of learning (with risk-taking, negotiation, and shared visions), ownership in the participatory process and the recognition that it is individuals ultimately who need to take responsibility for transforming their intentions into actions.

Workshops involve five stages: the discerning of concerns; focused imaging; creating shared vision; connecting the future with the present; discovering strategy paths and formulating action (Ziegler, 1991). The first stage delves into what Ziegler calls 'deep questioning and deep learning' – a fundamental confrontation of the role of language in obscuring dissatisfaction, pain, and suffering. The second stage takes participants through different levels of focused imaging. The third stage brings individuals together to negotiate a shared vision 'as the centerpiece of the scenario while maintaining the integrity of their own compelling images'. In what is undoubtedly an understatement, he remarks that, 'This is difficult work'. The fourth stage requires participants, through individual and group work to build a 'future history' connecting their future to the present. The final stage is to engage participants in various groupings to discover strategy paths and appropriate actions to work towards and their envisioned scenarios. 'Out of this work emerge the policies, programmes, innovative actions, institution-building etc, that constitute the attempt to bring shared vision to life in the present.' (Ziegler, 1991.)

Ziegler's more recent work, reflected in detail in *Ways of Enspiriting* (1994), has taken a decidedly spiritual turn. He has been building a network, through his Futures-Invention Associates group, of 'deep-visioning' workshops directed at personal and transpersonal transformation.

Peace activist Boulding, who collaborated with Ziegler in a series of World Without Weapons Workshops at Dartmouth in the early 1980s (Boulding, 1995; 1996), was the translator of Polak's *The Image of the Future* (1973) into English. One theme she emphasizes is Polak's idea of a 'breach in time' which characterizes the leap of imagination into a preferred future (Boulding, 1995).

The World Without Weapons Workshops, modeled after Ziegler's earlier work, were intended to help peace and anti-nuclear activists focus on positive images of the future and work together towards a shared vision of the future. The reality was that anti-nuclear activists could easily agree upon what they were against, but found it much more difficult to visualizing what they were for (Hicks, 1996a). The format for these workshops involved about a dozen steps involving individual, small group and plenary sessions. A workbook was provided to each participant. After an introduction, participants were asked to:

- produce an individual 'wish list' for their desirable future
- 'recall a childhood memory' to help ease them into thinking about a pleasant 'future memory' (the next step);
- 'step into the future' through a guided visioning process (the breach in time);
- 'share images' in small groups where individuals were asked to draw on large sheets of paper what they 'saw';
- engage in two 'world construction' exercises, as individuals and then in a joint, negotiated vision created by small groups;
- 'remember history' by connecting their future visions to the present with a timeline;
- design 'action plans for the present' individually and in small groups.

The World Without Weapons Workshops were not only popular among participants, but also received widespread attention in futures studies (Boulding, 1971; Schultz, 1991; Hicks, 1996a) and components have been adapted for a variety of futures workshop approaches.

Markley has continued doing visioning workshops and is engaged in teaching a 'visionary futures' course at the University of Houston, Clear Lake. He recently proposed (1994) a five-part visioning multimedia, Internet exercise confronting the 'limits to growth.' His proposal is worthy of mention, not only because of its innovative approach, but because of his use of a '100th generation' (ie 2,500 year) imaging stage. This is similar to Elgin in *Awakening Earth* (1993), and while 2,500 years may seem a long time, the linking of envisioning to the needs of future generations is a powerful tool. Given our time/space myopia as a species, we would do well to expand our time horizon as far as possible.

One last related envisioning exercise should be mentioned in relation to sustainable futures and that is the Council of All Beings developed by Joanna Macy, John Seed and colleagues (Seed *et al*.; 1988; Macy, 1993). Perhaps better described as a sequence of rituals rather than a workshop, the central purpose of the Council is to have participants role-play non-humans, eg animals, endangered species, mountains, ecosystems and even Gaia. Such work has been developed for use with both children and eco-activists. Civics teachers could also adapt a model United Nations, for example, to include represent-atives of indigenous peoples, as well as ecosystems and cetaceans.

Beyond the ideal, pure form of visioning exercise which involves using a 'guided-visioning' process to envisage a sustainable future, there are other methods which can augment the goal of taking students into a sustainable mental space. These include: literature reviews and analysis, brainstorming, future generations exercises and alternative futures exercises.

While sustainable futures have not been transformed into film, there are a wealth of science fiction, feminist fiction and utopian/eutopian novels of sustainable futures. A short list includes: Marge Piercy's *A Woman on the Edge of Time* (1976); Ernest Callenbach's *Ecotopia* (1975); Sheri Tepper's *Gate to Woman's Country* (1997); Charlotte Gilman's *Herland* (1915/1990); Dorothy Bryant's *The Kin of Ata are Waiting for You* 1976), Ursula le Guin's *The Dis-possessed* (1974) and short story collections such as Pamela Sargent's *The New Women of Wonder* (1977). These stories are useful tools to broaden the students' frame of reference and allow them, in a comfortable setting, to confront alternatives to the *status quo* future.

Brainstorming is often used as an essential element of visioning exercises or as a stand-alone technique to get people to 'suspend disbelief' and engage in non-judgmental, creative processes. Brainstorming is widely used in the business and broader educational environments for goal setting, mission evaluation, and other strategic planning processes (Boulding, 1971; Jungk, 1976).

The notion of a concern for 'future generations' is persuasive to students of all ages in relating to futures studies generally and sustainable futures more particularly (Kim and Dator, 1994; Moskowitz, 1996; Tough, 1995; 1996). The idea of future generations acknowledges our responsibility to leave behind a world no worse than we found it for the use of our children's children. It also embodies the idea of taking into account the impact of present actions on the 'seventh generation', an idea attributed to the Iroquois Confederacy. Some methods for making the connection with future generations include letters from the future, time capsules and inventing a 'Court of Generations' (Tonn, 1994; Kim and Dator, 1994).

Also inspired by the work of Polak and others is the alternative futures approach developed primarily by Dator (1979) and further elaborated by researchers at the Hawaii Research Center for Futures Studies and the Institute for Alternative Futures (Jones, 1992b; Schultz, 1991; Schultz *et al.*, 1991; 1993).

Their work has also been substantially influenced by Boulding, Ziegler, Jungk, Galtung, Masini, Henderson, and other futurists involved in creating futures workshops and exploring futures images (Jones, 1992b; 1996). The idea developed by Dator was to distill images of the future in popular culture, especially visionary literature and utopian (or dystopian) futurism. These were seen as coherent, discrete images which could be described in terms of their social and demographic characteristics. Thus, he initially identified four popular future scenarios, which he described as: continued growth, collapse, conserver, and high-technology transformation.

Schultz (1991) summarizes the adaption of futures exercises to a number of different groups and venues during the late 1980s. Workshop details and examples of workbooks can be seen in Schultz *et al.* (1991; 1993). *Reinventing Courts for the 21st Century* provides a wealth of workshop strategies and includes sample worksheets, exercises and guidelines for workshop designers drawn from a variety of sources (Schultz *et al.*, 1993). For example, Schultz and colleagues adapted the Boulding and Ziegler idea of 'remembering history' into what they call 'backcasting' (in contrast to 'forecasting') which can be used as a stand-alone futures imaging tool. Given the resistance that workshop organizers often find in more diverse groups, they have worked on various approaches to suspending disbelief. One such is 'reversing the negative' or turning fears into hopes.

Another popular tool is incasting. Incasting 'takes people on a comparative journey across several possible futures' and asks participants to 'logically deduce particulars, specific details' (Schultz, 1991). For example, what would education, health and family structures each be like in a continued growth, road warrior, or green society? Incasting can contribute to envisioning sustainable futures particularly when integrated into a larger visioning and planning project, but may also have something to offer when used by itself. Workshop sessions usually involve small groups, where each 'incasts' societal aspects of one possible future and a plenary session compares and charts the results.

Outcomes

Two ways to look at the outcomes of envisioning sustainable futures are from a practical standpoint and an existential one. Practically speaking, some workshops work better than others (Schultz, 1991). Some images and action plans are integrated into group goal-setting and strategic planning (Boulding, 1995; Ziegler, 1991). There is clear evidence from the Jungk, Ziegler and Boulding reports that at least some short-term group solidarity is achieved. Long-term impacts are a more open question.

There has been an on-going interest in images of societal futures over the last thirty years and much of the literature has been summarised in Hicks

(1996a; 1996b) and Boulding (1995). Boulding describes some of the outcomes of her own work and raises interesting research questions about the relationship between imagery and action. Ultimately, how do individual actions change after they have been exposed to desirable images of the future? For example, a political scientist might ask how efficacious these activities are. For Boulding, one element of such efficacy is image salience, or the 'relevance to one's personal life situation' of the workshop process. Individuals at a 'choice point' in their lives, students for example, may be more inclined to integrate new 'action orientations' into their lives than others. Perhaps more important in an era of despair about the future is 'long-run salience', 'the feeling that there is a future to work for and a generalized affirmation of commitment to that future' (Boulding, 1995).

Boulding's workshops have had a useful role to play in 'promoting positive approaches to peace' and by leaving participants 'empowered to varying degrees by their own imagery.' This 'feel good' aspect experienced by participants is a commonly reported response to futures workshops. But a host of questions remain about the extent to which the imagery is translated into long-term thinking and action.

From an existential standpoint, futures studies students exemplify the potential emotional and psychological crisis which may occur when one's paradigm is seriously confronted. Rogers and Tough (1996) report extensive personal inner and outer change amongst students studying the future. Inner changes include altered consciousness, heightened emotions, new learning, challenged basic values. Outer changes included altered household activities, friendships, community and political involvement. Thus, futures studies can foster serious thinking about both lifestyles and life purposes.

In part because mental images are fleeting, measurement of the impacts of future workshops and futures studies are elusive. To some extent, looking for substantive outcomes may even be the wrong way to look at these processes. For example, Dator (1994) argues that futures studies is to sustainable development what science was to the educational and political system in the Middle Ages.

Visions and sustainability

In the US there has been some allusion to the importance of the 'vision thing' in presidential politics – it is not something that is widely understood, but it seems that people respond to it. This is arguably the reason behind President Clinton's image of a 'bridge to the twenty-first century'. There has been some discussion of the importance of post-cold war imagery as a guiding vision and concern expressed about the consequences of its absence. There are even hints that a decline in 'civic culture' is somehow due to the end of the Cold War.

Polak would probably argue that this simply illustrates the poverty of our visionary capacity, but I am optimistic that the eschatological sense of a totally other order of reality has not disappeared, but is merely weakened. Along with Boulding (1971), I hold on to the hope that this state of affairs can lead to new insights. I constantly see this with my students and as a facilitator in futures workshops. Positive visions are not dead. They just don't improve profit margins, market share, or appeal to institutional investors.

A recent report to the State of the World Forum (Elgin and LeDrew, 1996) attempts to measure the degree to which an 'integral-paradigm' shift is emerging in the world. The report looks at broad thematic areas including:

- global ecological awareness and concern;
- compassionate social values;
- sustainable ways of living;
- global consciousness and the communications revolution;
- experiential spirituality.

The report is cautiously optimistic that there are significant shifts towards an 'integral paradigm.'

This would suggest that there is an audience and a need for more widespread envisioning of sustainable futures. Time and time again I hear from students and workshop participants, 'No one has ever asked me what I want for the future' – as though they had been cheated.

Envisioning sustainable futures is worth doing because it is creative, helps one adapt and adjust to future shock, explodes the dominant paradigm, provides hope in the face of uncertainty and because it is empowering. It challenges fundamental economic assumptions and underscores the need, not simply for lifestyle changes, but for a new way of life with increasing transfers of energy away from the material to the non-material side of life (Elgin, 1991). Envisioning can connect us to the continuity between generations and help us recognize our responsibility to consider future generations when we act.

But it is not a panacea. Sohail Inayatullah (1994) cautions us that we need to go beyond the language of sustainability to the language of fundamental transformation. He suggests that much of the dominant paradigm should not be sustained and that we need to break through our conceptualizations of the secular, of ethics, of democracy and recreate them. 'In the critical view, we also deconstruct the idea of sustainability itself, asking not what will be gained in creating a sustainable world, but what chances for transformation, for creativity, are lost by such a strategy?'

To that end, a continuous, interactive process of creating a 'breach in time' to envision other realities will be required. We owe it to our children and to future generations to encourage and empower them to take that leap and then to take us with them into their futures.

References

Boulding, E (1971) 'Futuristics and the Imaging Capacity of the West', in *Human Futuristics*, Maruyama, M and Dator, J (eds), Honolulu: Social Science Research Institute, 29–53.

Boulding, E (1995) 'Image and Action in Peace Building', in *The Future*, Boulding E and Boulding K, Thousand Oaks, California: Sage, 93–116.

Boulding, E (1996) 'The Cultures and Futures of Peace', *Futures*, 28(6/7), 535–538.

Bryant, D (1976) *The Kin of Ata are Waiting for You*, New York: Moon Books.

Callenbach, E (1975) *Ecotopia*, Berkeley: Banyan Tree.

Cornish, E (1977) *The Study of the Future*, Washington DC, World Future Society.

Dator, J (1994) 'What is (and is not) Future Studies', *Papers de Prospectiva*, May, 24–47.

Elgin, D (1991) 'Creating a Sustainable Future', *ReVision*, 14(2), 77–79.

Elgin, D (1993) *Awakening Earth*, New York: William Morrow & Co.

Elgin D and LeDrew, C (1996) *Global Paradigm Change: Is a Shift Underway?* San Anselmo, California.

Gabor, D (1964) *Inventing the Future*, New York: Knopf.

Gilman, C (1915/1990) *Herland*, New York: Pantheon Books.

Inayatullah, S (1994) 'Empirical, Civilizational and Critical Approaches to Sustaining and Transforming the World for Future Generations', in Kim, T and Dator, J (eds) *Creating a New History for Future Generations*, Kyoto: Institute for the Integrated Studies of Future Generations, 27–42.

Hicks, D (1996a) 'Envisioning the Future: The Challenge for Environmental Educators', *Environmental Education Research*, 2(1), 101–108.

Hicks, D (1996b) 'A Lesson for the Future: Young People's Hopes and Fears for Tomorrow', *Futures*, 28(1), 1–13.

Hicks, D (1996c) 'Retrieving the Dream: How Students Envision Their Preferable Futures', *Futures*, 29(8), 741–749.

Hicks, D and Holden, C (1995) *Visions of the Future: Why We Need to Teach for Tomorrow*, Stoke-on-Trent, Trentham Books.

Jarva, V (1996) 'Developing "the Female Society" Image', *Futures*, 28(6/7), 597–600.

Jones, C (1992a) 'Green Visions: The Goddess, Earth First! and Gaian Futures', in *Linking Present Decisions to Long-Range Visions*, vol. 2, Mannermaa, M (ed.), Budapest: World Futures Studies Federation.

Jones, C (1992b) 'The Manoa School of Futures Studies', *Futures Research Quarterly*, 8(4), 19–25.

Jones, C (1996) 'Conundrum and Vision', *Futures*, 28(6/7), 600–603.

Jungk, R (1976) *The Everyman Project*, New York: Thames & Hudson Ltd.

Kim, T and Dator, J (eds) (1994) *Creating a New History for Future Generations*, Kyoto: Institute for the Integrated Studies of Future Generations.

Le Guin, U (1974) *The Dispossessed*, New York: Harper & Row.

Macy, J (1993) 'Deep Ecology and the Council of All Beings', *ReVision*, 16(2), 72–74.

Masini, E (1996) 'A Future with Dignity', *Futures*, 28(6/7), 626–629.

Moskowitz, M (ed.) (1996), *Thinking About Future Generations*, Kyoto: Institute for the Integrated Studies of Future Generations.

Piercy, M (1976) *A Woman on the Edge of Time*, New York: Fawcett Crest.

Platt, J (1969) 'What We Must Do', *Science*, 166(3909), 1115–21.

Polak, F (1973) *The Image of the Future*, Amsterdam: Elsevier.

Robertson, J (1978) *The Sane Alternative*, St. Paul, Minnesota: River Basin.

Rogers, M and Tough, A (1996) 'Facing the Future is Not for Wimps', *Futures*, 28(5), 491–6.

Sargent, P (ed.) (1977) *The New Women of Wonder*, New York: Vintage Books.

Schultz, W (1991) 'Words, Dreams, and Actions: Sharing the Futures Experience', in *Advancing Democracy and Participation*, van Steenbergen *et al.* (eds), Barcelona: Centre Catala de Prospectiva and Centre UNESCO de Catalunya, 201–6.

Schultz, W, Rodgers, S, Jones, C and Inayatullah, S (1991) *Office of State Planning Scenario Building/Vision Project*, Honolulu, Hawaii: Research Center for Futures Studies.

Schultz, W, Bezold, C and Monahan, B (1993) *Reinventing Courts for the 21st Century*, Alexandria, Virginia: Institute for Alternative Futures.

Seed, J, Macy, J, Fleming, P, and Naess, A (1988) *Thinking Like A Mountain. Towards a Council of All Beings*, Philadelphia, New Society Publishers.

Slaughter, R (1988) *Recovering the Future*, Melbourne, Graduate School of Environmental Science, Monash University.

Slaughter, R (1991) *Futures Concepts and Powerful Ideas*, Kew, Victoria, Australia: Futures Study Centre.

Tepper, S (1997) *Gate to Woman's Country*, London: Voyager/HarperCollins Publishers.

Tonn, B (1994) 'Future Generations, Environmental Ethics, and Global Environmental Change', in Kim, T & Dator, J (eds) *Creating a New History for Future Generations*, Kyoto: Institute for the Integrated Studies of Future Generations, 141–58.

Tough, A (1995) 'A Message from Future Generations', *The Futurist*, March/April, 30–2.

Tough, A (1996) 'My Connectedness to Future Generations', *Futures*, 28(6/7), 687–9.

van Steenbergen, B (1996) 'Looking Into the Seeds of Time', *Futures*, 28(6/7), 679–83.

Ziegler, W (1991) 'Envisioning the Future', *Futures*, 23, 516–27.

Ziegler, W (1994) *Ways of Enspiriting*, Denver: FIA International LLC.

Further reading

Boulding, E (1991) 'The Challenge of Imaging Peace in Wartime', *Futures*, 23, 528–33.

Dator, J (1979) 'The Futures of Culture or Cultures of the Future', in Marsella, A (ed.) *Perspectives on Cross-Cultural Psychology*, New York: Academic Press, 369–88.

Dator, J (1993) 'American State Courts, Five Tsunamis and Four Alternative Futures', *Futures Research Quarterly*, 9(4), 9–30.

Markley, O (1994) 'Experiencing the Needs of Future Generations', in Moskowitz, M (ed.), *Thinking About Future Generations*, Kyoto: Institute for the Integrated Studies of Future Generations, 215–31.

Ziegler, W (1983) *A Mindbook for Imaging/Inventing a World Without Weapons*, Denver CO: The Futures-Invention Associates.

18. Environmental education for a new century

John Fien

Summary

The aim of education for sustainability is to develop the civic or action competencies that can enable all students and institutions to play a role in the transition to sustainability. As such, it encompasses a vision for society that is not only ecologically sustainable but also one which is socially, economically and politically sustainable as well. Thus, education for sustainability encourages those involved in education to activate the socially critical or reconstructionist tradition in education and to promote pedagogical approaches that help integrate the teaching of conservation, social justice, appropriate development and democracy into a clear vision for the future. This chapter seeks to provide an anlaytic framework based upon questions such as: what conceptions of sustainable development are privileged in education for sustainability? What assumptions about knowledge and ways of knowing are privileged? It is important that education for sustainability be conducted in a professionally ethical manner. The chapter concludes with a case for a committed but impartial approach to handling values issues.

Introduction

Over the last 25 years we've gradually become aware of the impact of our species on the rest of life on Earth. This new found awareness has at last provided a corner stone for a fundamental transformation in the way that we manage the Earth's resources and restrict our impact on other species....

Whatever the nature of the changes required, education is of paramount importance. The well-being of all future generations depends on the skill and effectiveness with which we inform and inspire the knowledge base and values of those currently in our schools and colleges. The challenge is daunting, in as much as each and every delay in bringing about the necessary transformation will cost us dear in the future (Porritt, 1990: 1).

Very often, schools and teachers are called upon to address problems that civil society finds intractable – problems such as unemployment, racism, youth alienation and environmental degradation. Very often too, governments establish problem-focused educational programmes as an easy option or as a way of being 'seen' to be doing something – especially if addressing the root causes of the problem is too expensive or politically challenging. Thus, there are demands that school programmes be vocationally relevant when the real problem of unemployment is industrial restructuring; programmes to promote intercultural appreciation and harmony when the real problem is institutionalised racism at all levels in society and programmes to encourage active and informed citizenship when the real problem is the civic paralysis that results from social and economic alienation. Hazlett has described the policy process through which 'social problems' become 'educational problems' and require a response from schools and teachers:

> The nation tends to reduce political, social, and economic problems to educational ones and claims to expect schools to cure present ills and provide for a brighter tomorrow for individuals and the collectivity. (Hazlett, 1979: 133.)

Calls for young people to be educated for sustainable futures may be part of the same process. This may especially be the case given the multiple and often contradictory meanings of sustainability and sustainable development and the cynicism with which some governments and companies have appropriated the terms to justify sustainable economic development. To ascertain any legitimate role for education in the sustainable development movement, it is instructive to trace the origin of the concept.

The UN World Commission on Environment and Development took the concept of sustainable development as the focus of its report *Our Common Future* (1987). Commonly known as the Brundtland Report, this urged governments, industries and families to adopt a sustainable approach to development 'which meets the needs of present generations without compromising the ability of future generations to satisfy their needs' (WCED, 1987: 8). Sustainable development was the theme of the Commission's UN Conference on Environment and Development (the Earth Summit) which was held in 1992. The Commission took the term, sustainable development, from the 1980 World Conservation Strategy published by IUCN, WWF and UNEP.

Being the result of a consensus between parties who come from essentially quite distinctive paradigms or world views, it is logical that sustainable development is one of those terms that cannot have a single, simple and agreed meaning. Many conservationists have argued that ecological sustainability 'should be a goal in its own right, unshackled to development' (Yencken, 1994: 220). On the other hand, some argue that it is necessary to put economic sustainability ahead of ecological sustainability because following environmental regulations and conservation principles is expensive and businesses need to be profitable to be able to afford them.

Thus, we can see that interpretations of sustainability are value-laden but these extreme points of view miss the essential point: the concept of sustainable development requires change and compromise from everyone. Sustainable development is, in the words of Yencken, 'an inspired way in which a bridge can be built between two conflicting paradigms, between the paradigm that has underlain past western approaches to the environment and an emerging new environmental paradigm' (Yencken, 1994: 221). Thus, while it is possible to find many definitions of sustainable development in the literature, the important point to note is that all definitions – whatever their source – serve particular social and economic interests and that they need to be critically assessed.

As a result of the contested meaning of 'sustainable development', one commentator, Jickling (1992), has suggested that education for sustainable development could be anti-educational. He fears that the conflicting meanings of the concept creates the potential for bias in teachers educating for their favoured meanings – or favoured government meanings – rather than helping students become autonomous thinkers capable of participating in the contestation and debate over the nature and processes of sustainable development.

These comments by Jickling indicate two issues that need to be addressed. These are, first, establishing a comprehensive range of meanings for the concept of 'education for sustainability' and its related educational objectives and second, developing a range of pedagogical processes that are professionally ethical and effective to obviate the charge of possible indoctrination. There is a grave risk that the metaphor of education for sustainability may become little more than a slogan (Jickling and Spork, 1996) unless these two tasks are undertaken. Greenall (1981; 1993) has described how the important social transformation rationale and pedagogies of environmental education were diluted or deleted in the first wave of contemporary environmental education in the 1970s, and environmental education was effectively colonised by 'business as usual' in education. This chapter seeks to address these two issues as a contribution to avoiding this possibly happening in the second wave of contemporary environmental education we know as education for sustainability.

Behind the metaphor: towards a model of education for sustainability

Education seeks to provide the intellectual enlightenment and the spiritual emancipation in the search for a better existence for all life on earth…. The sustainability transition is in effect a social and political revolution that hopefully can take place through peace and understanding. This is the challenge for environmental education for the next generation. (O'Riordan, 1994: 8.)

Education for sustainability has been described as the 'missing chapter' (Fien, 1990a) in the Brundtland Report, just as there are fears that education may become the forgotten priority of the 1992 UN Conference on Environment and Development. Nevertheless, *Caring for the Earth: A Strategy for Sustainable Living* (IUCN/UNEP/WWF, 1991: 5) argues that 'sustainable living…will require a significant change in the attitudes and practices of many people. We will need to ensure that education programmes reflect the importance of an ethic for living sustainably'. Similarly, *Agenda 21*, the report of the Earth Summit devotes a whole chapter to the role of education and states that:

> Education is critical for promoting sustainable development and improving the capacity of the people to address environment and development issues.… It is critical for achieving environmental and ethical awareness, values and attitudes, skills and behaviour consistent with sustainable development and for effective public participation in decision-making. (UNCED, 1992, chapter 36: 2.)

Sadly, many mainstream educationalists have carried on their theorising and research as if the crises of sustainability and these demands upon teachers did not exist. Indeed, D'Urso (1990: 2), an educational philosopher, has described the neglect of the environmental crisis and educational responses to it as being 'curiously neglected by socio-cultural theorists of education' and urges researchers to strike 'beyond the bounds of current educational concerns' to establish environmental education as 'a new and vitally important discourse'. The paradox is, as Trainer (1990: 105–7) argues, that while mainstream educationalists ignore the environmental crisis, both the overt and the hidden curricula of schools play a major role in reproducing the socially and ecologically unsustainable values of 'industrial, affluent, consumer society', including the desirability of economic growth and a competitive economy, the importance of self-advancement and the correctness of allowing the market to determine economic and social priorities. Thus, Berberet (1989: 3) notes that the environment has been only 'a minimal factor in mainstream educational thinking', but education has played a key role in perpetuating unsustainable environmental practices:

> Historically, the values of schools and colleges have mirrored those of the larger society. Not only has education uncritically accepted the association of progress and the unfettered growth economy, it has trained the engineers and managers, performed the research, and developed the technologies which in aggregate have had such a devastating impact on the environment. A fundamental reorientation now needs to occur with the development of new assumptions undergirding education which treat the interactions of ecological processes, market forces, cultural values, equitable decision-making, government actions, and environmental impacts of human activities in a holistic, interdependent manner. (Berberet, 1989: 4–5.)

Education for sustainability needs to become mainstream in the thinking of educational theorists, researchers and administrators. As Orr (1992) ironically asks, 'What's the good of a research agenda without a planet to conduct it on?' Issues of environment, social justice and sustainable development pose important questions for the future of human society. They are also important for those who wish to teach for a just and sustainable future and those who are involved in the education of such teachers. This means that those involved in education, at whatever level, need to activate the socially critical or reconstructionist tradition in education and promote approaches to curriculum planning and pedagogy that can help integrate social justice and ecological sustainability into a vision and a mission of personal and social change. As Orr also reminds educationalists:

> The crisis of sustainability, the fit between humanity and its habitat, is manifest in varying ways and degrees everywhere on earth. It is not only a permanent feature on the public agenda; for all practical purposes it is *the* agenda. No other issue of politics, economics and public policy will remain unaffected by the crisis of resources, population, climate change, species extinction, acid rain, deforestation, ozone depletion, and soil loss. Sustainability is about the terms and conditions of human survival, and yet we still educate at all levels as if no such crisis existed. (Orr, 1992: 83.)

Fortunately, environmental educators in many parts of the world have accepted the challenge of education for sustainability in recent years. These deliberations have been published in conference proceedings and journal articles (eg. Fien, 1990b; Huckle, 1991) and books (eg. Benedict,1991; Fien, 1993; Huckle and Sterling, 1996) and, increasingly, they are being translated into professional development programmes (eg. Huckle, 1994; Fien, 1995) and curriculum guidelines and materials (eg. Huckle, 1988–91; Macleod, 1992; Xu *et al.*, 1996).

However a number of problems remain and in general, care does need to be exercised in evaluating the literature on education for sustainability. One of the major problems is that many of the materials accept the unproblematical view of sustainable development in the Brundtland Commission's definition of sustainable development as 'development which meets the needs of present generations without compromising the ability of future generations to satisfy their needs' (WCED, 1987: 8). In not adequately exploring what is involved in such an approach to development, these materials tend not to explore the fundamental contradiction in the Commission's definition: how can continued economic growth solve the problems of global poverty and environmental degradation when even present levels of resource use are unsustainable? Many have also neglected the alternative conceptions of sustainability that have been proposed.

A second problem is that much writing to date on education for sustainability is based on unproblematic assumptions about education and social change. They seem to assume that more environmental education, especially about global environmental problems and strategies for sustainable development, will change global patterns of development. This is an unrealistic expectation of schools and teachers; as Huckle (1993) and Sterling (1993) have argued, while this is, at best, only a long-term strategy for social change, it is also a naive one as it neglects the ethical and structural determinants of individual lifestyle change and the challenge to existing power structures required in the broader social transformation towards sustainability.

A third problem in many works is a neglect of the human dimensions of geographical scale. Very few concentrate on the local environment and the great potential for education to play a part in Local Agenda 21 initiatives. Among the innovative exceptions to this are many of the chapters in Huckle and Sterling (1996) and the excellent curriculum materials in Huckle's units on local environmental democracy in *Reaching Out* (1994), in Unit 9 of *What We Consume* (1988–91) and the case study of student involvement in healthy-city projects in Macleod (1992).

At the opposite end of the geographical scale, few works on education for sustainability have effectively addressed the global dimension, especially the essential social justice core of the concept of sustainable development.

> But respect for the environment alone will not be enough to save our common future. A sense of solidarity with the world's underprivileged will be equally important. There is no way we can win the battle to save the global environment unless we deal squarely with the issue of world poverty. We must teach the next generation that necessity of caring for the poor and the dispossessed, not only because it is morally right, but because it is in our common interest to do so (Brundtland, 1991: 4–5).

Materials which deal with this dimension of education for sustainability especially well include: *Only One Earth* (Beddis and Johnson, 1988), several units in Huckle's *What We Consume* (1988–91 and the UNESCO-UNEP professional development programme for teachers, *Teaching for a Sustainable World* (Fien, 1995).

O'Riordan (1994: 8, 11) is especially insistent that education for sustainability address global (and indeed local) issues of social justice. He argues that it does little good to teach 'about living within the confines of natural replenishability if only a few get the advantages and the rest increasingly suffer'. The result, he foresees, is that environmental education will continue to be marginalised 'as yet another example of middle class guilt foisted on the poor and thwarting the upwardly mobile'.

A related problem in the literature on education for sustainability is that approaches to environmental education which ignore issues of social justice tend to be guided by a technocratic rationality and behaviouristic goals of reductionist, western science and western approaches to development (Robottom, 1989; Greenall, 1993). Ecofeminists such as Merchant (1980), Shiva (1989) and Rodda (1991) have traced the patriarchal assumptions and attitudes to nature, women and development upon which western science is based as a major cause of environmental exploitation and the increasing marginalisation of many of the world's people. Educators need to be aware of this critique of the assumptions upon which environmental education has developed and examine the call made by Shiva (1989) for a new environmental science. In directing us towards a new environmental 'science', she urges us to consider the knowledge base and goals of the women's ecology movement in the south as a model.

> A science that does not respect nature's needs and a development that does not respect people's needs inevitably threatens survival. In their fight to survive the onslaughts of both, women have begun a struggle that challenges the most fundamental categories of western patriarchy – its concepts of nature and women, and of science and development. Their ecological struggles are aimed simultaneously at liberating nature from ceaseless exploitation and themselves from marginalisation. They are creating a feminist ideology that transcends gender, and a political practice that is humanly inclusive; they are challenging patriarchy's ideological claim to universalism not with another universalising tendency, but with diversity; and they are challenging the dominant concept of power as violence with the alternative of non-violence as power (Shiva, 1989: xvii–xviii).

Viewed from this perspective, another important dimension of education for sustainability is an alternative epistemology which values diverse ways of knowing, identifies with the people and communities it purports to serve and respects community-based approaches to social change.

Figure 18.1 is a model that helps conceptualise a resolution to these problems. The top box illustrates the present descending spiral of unsustainable development in which 'business as usual' privileges economic growth and ignores the associated declines in the quality of environmental conditions and human social well-being at all scales from local to global. The bottom box outlines the desired state of sustainability in which economic growth is replaced by a concern for economic welfare and is embedded within concerns for human life quality within (and respectful of) environmental limits.

The middle box shows the complementary need for education and action for the public as well as government and business. This represents the necessity for a transformation of business as usual in the institutions which have the power to create the systems and conditions of life in which individuals, families and communities can learn about the present situation and make individual and group, lifestyle changes for a sustainable future. Note also the role of the formal education system as but a subset of the public for whom education for sustainability is important and the role of intergenerational influence and learning as part of the educational process (Ballantyne, Connell and Fien, forthcoming). Thus, the model envisages multiple approaches to social change, multiple ways of experiencing the crisis of unsustainability and learning about it and how to deal with it and therefore, multiple sites for such learning to occur.

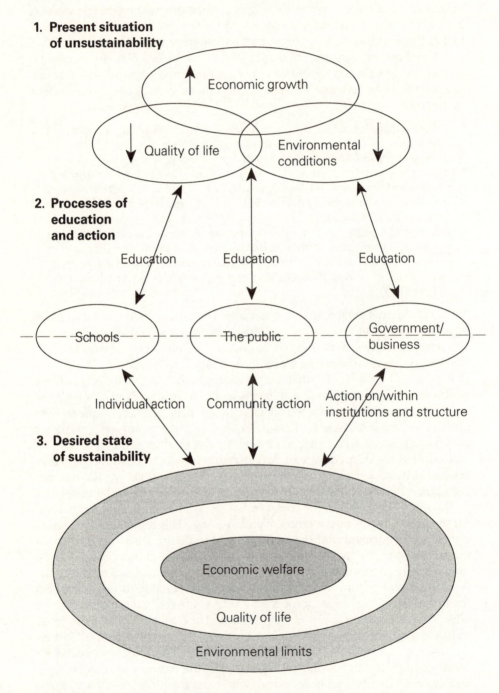

Figure 18.1 Education for sustainability.

As they stand on flat paper in Figure 18.1, the relationships between the three boxes appear linear. However, this is only a function of the limitations of a two dimensional model. Imagine the model cut out and folded in half from top to bottom with the fold going horizontally through the centre of the middle box. What we would see then is that the words 'education' and 'action' are superimposed – this is intentional.

The aim of education for sustainability is to develop the civic or action competencies so that all citizens and institutions can play a role in the transition to sustainability. The civic education aspect of environmental education has been sadly neglected in dominant models of liberal, individualist, environmental education (Robottom, 1995) which focus on individual, lifestyle change (eg recycling and green consumerism). In assessing the importance of the civic dimension in the transition to sustainability, O'Riordan (1994: 10) argues that 'the challenge for education is to connect the responsibilities of the individual as consumer with the individual as citizen'. In thereby linking education and action, or making a case for education through action, O'Riordan states further that 'Environmental education therefore needs to become civic education with a large dose of active community involvement in the processes of change that might restore stability and harmony in an increasingly troubled and disrupted world.'

Pedagogy and sustainability

Appropriate pedagogy is an important aspect of education for sustainability. This is especially so, given the contested nature of sustainable development and the potential for indoctrination in Jickling's warning that some teachers could be tempted to educate for their own or a government's particular meanings of sustainability. It is important that education for sustainability be conducted in a professionally ethical manner.

Jickling (1992) described his recommended pedagogy when he stated that to educate for something is really 'training' as education must be based upon the development of autonomous thinking. Thus, he recommends a form of education about sustainability through the balanced treatment of all positions and the opportunity for students to engage in a philosophical analysis of them. Jickling states that:

> Having argued that we should not educate *for* sustainable development, it is quite a different matter to teach students about this concept. I would like my children to know about the arguments which support it and attempt to clarify it. But, I would also like them to know that 'sustainable development' is being criticized, and I want them to be able to evaluate that criticism and participate in it if they perceive a need. I want them to realize that there is a debate going between a variety of stances, between adherents of an ecocentric worldview and those who adhere to an anthropocentric worldview. I want my children to be able to participate intelligently in that debate (Jickling, 1992: 8).

There is a certain attractiveness in the liberal fairmindedness of this position. However, what Jickling tends not to recognise is that all forms of pedagogy – even liberal-fairminded ones – incorporate a political vision. Pedagogy is more than just a set of teaching methods or instructional practices; it also includes a consideration of the contexts of teaching and learning and the social interests served by teachers' decisions and actions. Thus, pedagogy subsumes a political vision of what education should be and as a result, reflects political decisions by education systems and teachers. Liberal pedagogy ignores the possibility of political bias in its own position. As Shaull (1970: 15) argues in his foreword to Freire's *The Pedagogy of the Oppressed*:

> There is no such thing as a neutral educational process. Education either functions as an instrument which is used to facilitate the integration of the younger generation into the logic and practice of the present system and being about conformity to it, or it becomes the 'practice of freedom', the means by which men and women deal critically and creatively with reality and discover how to participate in the transformation of their world. The development of an educational methodology that facilitates this process will inevitably lead to tension and conflict within our society.

Jickling's liberal prescriptions for education about sustainability seem to ignore this perspective and the reconstructionist critique of values relativity (Huckle, 1983). Therefore, they do not consider approaches to teaching about values-laden issues based upon what Hill (1991, 1994) and Kelly (1986) call 'committed impartiality'. The reconstructionist or critical pedagogy of 'committed impartiality' would provide learning experiences in which students analyse alternative positions on sustainability. However, contrary to the seemingly fairminded approach which would tend to treat all positions equally, irrespective of issues of power and influence, teachers seeking to enact a critical pedagogy would be mindful that balanced teaching might not necessarily result in balanced learning if certain positions are more privileged than others in public discourse. Thus, it would replace values relativity with invitations and guidance for students to:

- identify and challenge the assumptions in all positions on sustainable development;
- imagine, explore and critique alternatives of their own;
- question the influence of context and the social interests served by all positions;
- use the values of ecological sustainability, social justice and democracy as criteria in the evaluation of all positions;
- adopt a reflective scepticism to their own and other people's ideas and actions.

Such a critical framework can help educate for a body politic comprised of 'people able to act to maintain the best of what we have, to challenge the unsustainable, and to build the desirable' (Hoepper, 1993: 36). Thus, along with many others, Orr (1992: 145–46) argues that environmental education is 'unavoidably political' in that we have to choose whether we 'equip students morally and intellectually to be a part of the existing pattern of corporate-dominated resource flows, or to take part in reshaping these patterns towards greater sustainability?' Critical pedagogy has been the subject of much theorising and critique in recent years. Reflecting the views of Dewey, Counts and other early social reconstructionist philosophers of education, it is possible to argue that the social change goals of critical pedagogy are founded upon a view of schools as 'democratic public spheres' in which students can learn how to be both 'critical thinkers and transformative actors' (Giroux, 1987: 120). Giroux argues that the purposes of critical pedagogy are twofold they 'not only empower students by giving them the knowledge and skills they will need to be able to function in the larger society as critical agents, but also educate them for transformative action...in the interest of creating a truly democratic society' (Giroux, 1988: xxxiii).

These two goals of critical pedagogy are reflected in the writings of Feinberg (1989: 71) who states that the purposes of critical pedagogy are 'to help youngsters develop the modes of thinking and critical perspectives which will enable them to make wise choices and to participate critically in the activities of a political community'. What is especially significant in such critical approaches to education for sustainability is the potential to help students acquire and value the skills to be fully active in society.

Extending the sense of community from the local to the global is an important dimension of such education for sustainability. This may involve understanding manifestations of global processes in the local community (what Shor (1980) called 'extraordinarily re-experiencing the ordinary') and critically analysing the consequences of personal choices and local community practices in global patterns of social and ecological sustainability (or the lack thereof). This may involve the investigation of the reasons, dimensions, directions and impacts of flows of goods and services and the development of small-scale alternatives and locally relevant alternatives to them.

In a critical approach to education for sustainability, we may be able to stand with those whom Orr (1992: 145) has described as having refused to 'stand aloof from the decisions about how and whether life will be lived in the twenty-first century', and may be able to say with Kirk (1977: 35) that our work has contributed to the task of education as 'the catalyst that not only saves the human race from extinction, but (which) also...serves to unite all the people of the world in a common effort to find solutions to the perplexing and difficult problems that threaten life on the planet.'

References

Ballantyne, R, Connell, S and Fien , J (forthcoming) 'Students as Catalysts of Environmental Change: A Framework for Researching Intergenerational Influence Through Environmental Education', *Environmental Education Research*.

Benedict, F (ed.) (1991) *Environmental Education for Our Common Future: A Handbook for Teachers in Europe*, Oslo: Norwegian University Press.

Beddis, R and Johnson, C (1988) *Only One Earth: A Multi-Media Education Pack*, Godalming: World Wide Fund for Nature.

Berberet, W (1989) *Education for Sustainable Development*, Unpublished testimony prepared for Globescope Pacific Conference, Los Angeles.

D'Urso, S (1990) 'Editor's Note', *Discourse*, 10(2): 92.

Feinberg, W (1989) 'Fixing the Schools: The Ideological Turn' in Giroux, H A and McClaren, P (eds) *Critical Pedagogy, the State and Cultural Struggle*, Albany: State University of New York Press, 69–91.

Fien, J (1990a) '*Our Common Future* and the Case of the Missing Chapter', *Annual Review of Environmental Education*, 4: 14–15.

Fien, J (ed.) (1990b) 'Teaching for Sustainable Development', Special Issue of *Geographic Education*, 6(2): 15–41.

Fien, J (ed.) (1993) *Environmental Education: A Pathway to Sustainability*, Geelong: Deakin University Press.

Fien, J (ed.) (1995) *Teaching for a Sustainable World*, Brisbane: Griffith University for UNESCO-UNEP International Environmental Education Programme.

Giroux, H (1987) 'Citizenship, Public Philosophy and the Struggle for Democracy', *Educational Theory*, 37(2): 103–20.

Greenall, A (1981) 'Environmental Education: A Case Study in National Curriculum Action', *Environmental Education and Information*, 1(4): 285–94.

Greenall, A (1993) *Founders of Environmental Education*, Geelong: Deakin University Press.

Hazlett, J S (1979) 'Conceptions of Curriculum History', *Curriculum Inquiry*, 9(2): 129–35.

Hill, B (1991) *Values Education in Australian Schools*, Hawthorn: The Australian Council for Educational Research.

Hill, B (1994) *Teaching Secondary Social Studies in a Multicultural School*, Melbourne: Longman Cheshire.

Hoepper, B (1993) 'Seeking Global Citizens in the History Classroom' in D Dufty and H Dufty (eds) *We Sing of a World Reshaped: Readings and Reflections on Global Citizenship*, Brisbane: Social Education Association of Australia, 35–7.

Huckle, J (1983) 'Values Education Through Geography: a Radical Critique', *Journal of Geography*, 82, March–April: 59–63.

Huckle, J (1988–91) *What We Consume*, Godalming: World Wide Fund for Nature (UK) and Richmond Publishing.

Huckle, J (1991) 'Education for Sustainability: Assessing Pathways to the Future', *Australian Journal of Environmental Education*, 7: 49–69.

Huckle, J (1993) 'Environmental Education and Sustainability: a View from Critical Theory' in Fien, J, (ed.) *Environmental Education: A Pathway to Sustainability*, Geelong: Deakin University Press, 43–68.

Huckle, J, (ed.) (1994) *Reaching Out*, Godalming: World Wide Fund for Nature (UK).

Huckle, J and Sterling, S (eds) (1996) *Education for Sustainability*, London: Earthscan.

IUCN/UNEP/WWF (1991) *Caring for the Earth: A Strategy for Sustainable Living*, Gland: International Union for the Conservation of Nature.

Jickling, B (1992) 'Why I Don't Want my Children to be Educated for Sustainable Development', *Journal of Environmental Education*, 23(4): 5–8.

Jickling, B and Spork, H (1996) 'Environmental Education for the Environment: Retained or Retired?', Unpublished paper presented at the annual conference of the American Educational Research Association, April, New York.

Kelly, T (1986) 'Discussing Controversial Issues: Four Perspectives on the Teacher's Role', *Theory and Research in Social Education*, XIV (2): 113–38.

Kirk, J (1977: 35) 'The Quantum Theory of EE', in *Current Issues in EE–III*, North American Association for Environmental Education, Troy, OH.

Macleod, H (1992) *Teaching for Ecologically Sustainable Development: Guidelines for Year 11 & 12 Geography*, Brisbane: Queensland Department of Education.

Merchant, C (1980) *The Death of Nature: Women, Ecology, and the Scientific Revolution*, San Francisco: Harper and Row.

O'Riordan, T (1994) 'Education for the Sustainability Transition', *Annual Review of Environmental Education*, 8: 8–11.

Orr, D (1992) *Ecological Literacy: Education and the Transition to a Postmodern World*, Albany: State University of New York Press.

Porritt, J (1990) 'Introduction' in P Martin, *First Steps to Sustainability: The School Curriculum and the Environment*, Godalming: World Wide Fund for Nature (UK).

Robottom, I (1989) 'Social Critique or Social Control: Some Problems for Evaluation in Environmental Education', *Journal of Research in Science Teaching*, 26(5): 435–43.

Robottom, I (1995) 'Environmentalism as Individualism: A Critique', in B Jensen, B (ed.) *Research in Environmental and Health Education*, Copenhagen: Royal Danish School of Educational Studies, 7–16.

Rodda, A (1991) *Women and the Environment*, London: Zed Books.

Shaull, R (1970) 'Foreword' in P Freire, *The Pedagogy of the Oppressed*, New York: Seabury Press.

Shiva, V (1989) *Staying Alive: Women, Ecology and Development*, London: Zed Books.

Shor, I (1980) *Critical Teaching and Everyday Life*, Boston: South End Press.

Sterling, S (1993) 'Environmental Education and Sustainability: a View from Holistic Ethics', in Fien, J (ed.) *Environmental Education: A Pathway to Sustainability*, Geelong: Deakin University Press, 69–98.

Trainer, T (1990) 'Towards an Ecological Philosophy of Education', *Discourse*, 10(2): 92–117.

UNCED (1992) 'Promoting Education and Public Awareness and Training', *Agenda 21*, Conches: UN Conference on Environment and Development, chapter 36.

UN World Commission on Environment and Development (1987) *Our Common Future*, Oxford: Oxford University Press.

Xu J, Wang H, Yang M and Hao F (1996) *Environmental Education for Sustainable Development – Teachers' Guidebook for Environmental Education in Middle Schools*, Beijing: Normal University Press.

Yencken, D (1994) 'Values, Knowledge and Action', in L Grove, D Evans and D Yenchen (eds), *Restoring the Land: Environmental Values, Knowledge and Action*, Melbourne: Melbourne University Press, 217–36.

Further reading

Giroux, H (1988) *Teachers as Intellectuals: Towards a Critical Pedagogy of Learning*, South Hadley MA: Bergin and Garvey.

19. An MSc in Environmental and Development Education

Aileen McKenzie

Summary

Taking the MSc in Environmental and Development Education at South Bank University, London as a case study, this chapter provides snapshots, from an NGO perspective, of what happens when two very different cultures come together in the design and delivery of a Masters level course. The central message is that educators need to consider how visions and reality are likely to collide in such partnerships and thus, where possible, to learn from the experience of others. In the case study featured there is, on the one hand, the story of a successful, innovative and popular course and on the other, the more difficult subtext of what was involved in reaching such a goal. All integration within the state system is strategically important to futures-orientated education, but it needs to be, as far as possible, on terms that everyone understands and agrees to.

Introduction

The evolution of the MSc in Environmental and Development Education at South Bank University provides an excellent example of what takes place when the initial visions of one group collide with the practical reality of another. The visions in this case came from the Masters Curriculum Project, a three-year, higher-education curriculum development project established in 1992 with funding from the European Community, World Wide Fund for Nature, Oxfam, CAFOD (Catholic Fund for Overseas Development) and Christian Aid. The project grew from the ideas and fundraising activities of a working party comprising representatives from NGOs (non-governmental organisations) concerned with environmental education and development education and a number of interested academics which I had established a year earlier. The reality was provided by South Bank University, the host institution for the project and ultimately, the base for the MSc in Environmental and Development Education. Although the creation of a flexible, modular,

259

distance-learning MSc for a broad cross-section of educators was probably seen by outsiders as the main purpose of the Masters Curriculum Project, the Working Party attempted to build other, strategic, goals into the design of the project such as contributing to the legitimation of environmental education and development education and increasing the quantity and quality of educators committed to these two fields.

This account is a story of how, through the collision of visions and 'reality', the MSc in Environmental and Development Education came into being and has since developed. This is not to say that visions are impractical or that reality is always rational even if it is possible to determine the institutional logic behind what goes on. It might be said that visions and reality will inevitably collide and that it is naive to expect otherwise. Yet while I foresaw the likelihood of this, it was impossible to predict with any degree of certainty where such a collision (or collisions) might take place. With something as innovative as this MSc, anything was possible. The course was, after all, a leap into the dark, involving new ideas, new fields, new methodologies and a new form of partnership. What follows is a story of how this popular and successful course came into being. I believe that innovative educators need as many of these 'stories' as possible to inspire, inform and (most important of all) forewarn. Advancing futures-oriented education need not involve advancing into the unknown if there are beacons of experience from which we can learn.

Visions

It came to me, in the late 1980s, while I was doing doctoral research into the theory and practice of development education, that it was 'timely' to create an initiative which addressed a number of issues critical to the advancement of futures-orientated education: the progressive marginalisation, over the previous decade, of the 'adjectival educations' such as global education and peace education (Giroux, 1989; Chitty, 1991; Sterling, 1990); the role played by higher education in the politics of educational legitimation (Goodson, 1985; 1988), the needs of socially (and globally) conscious educators in a shifting education system where, as the power and resources of local education authorities were being eroded, traditional forms of support and in-service were becoming increasingly unavailable (Dale, 1989; Bowe, Ball and Gold, 1992). Fortunately I was able to find colleagues who agreed with the need to address such issues and were prepared to join a working party to look at what could be done. We came up with the idea of setting up a Masters degree because we felt it would help us address our task in a practical way and if it was successful, could point the way to other contexts where certificated courses involving progressive partnerships could be established.

Our early working party deliberations predated the 1992 Earth Summit and *Agenda 21* (UNCED, 1993) and began just before the launch of the *Caring for the Earth: A Strategy for Sustainable Living* (IUCN *et al.*, 1991) strategy document on sustainable development. This led us to be more tentative about environmental–development and environmental education–development education relationships than we might have been a year or so later, when a literature on the relationships between these fields really began to emerge. We were thus cautious about calling the course a Masters in 'education for sustainability'; did we or indeed anyone know enough about what education for sustainability was and even if we believed that we did, would educators identify with such a term? It was probably better, we reasoned, to put environmental education and development education on the map in a constructive alliance and give the course a title which reflected this.

Looking back, we were probably wise to regard education for sustainability as an emergent field and one that we did not have the time to theorise. We were beginning to perceive the enormity of the task that we had set for ourselves and that parameters were needed to delineate what we could feasibly tackle. As we learnt more about distance learning it was clear that we were approaching the course backwards, ie a course team normally comes together to develop and teach a course on a face-to-face basis and then develop a version of it for distance learning. In the end we chose to introduce our students to what environmental education and development education could bring to education for sustainability and encourage them through the process of the course to develop their own perspectives.

Coming from a development education background I was especially interested in what development education could bring to this new field, because it seemed to me that education for sustainability was increasingly being 'hijacked' by the environmental education lobby. I was troubled by the way that an increasing number of actors from these lobbies appeared to be laying claim to education for sustainability with no theoretical or practical modification of their existing work. When later, more thoughtful environmental educators such as Fien (1993a), Huckle and Sterling (1996) began to put forward environmental education as an approach or 'pathway' to education for sustainability, this seemed to me to be correct. If the course could offer pathways to education for sustainability through deconstructive as well as reconstructive approaches to environmental education and development education, this I believed, would be both helpful and provocative to the students involved. Furthermore, since as a working party we were committed to promoting a reflexive and participatory practice based upon the development and ownership of critical understandings of environment – development – education relations, we sought approaches which would actively encourage our learners to make autonomous decisions about education for sustainability.

The organisation of our course content was similarly led by our ideals. We wanted to stimulate and especially surprise. We believed that environmental educators needed to take development, particularly global inequality, into account and thought that development educators would benefit from the challenge of weighing environmental questions, problems and issues against human needs. We certainly did not want to emulate what was currently on offer in the higher education sector, although we were happy to draw from it. Our funding application and later our validation document in 1994 explained that we believed the NGO sector had insights to offer higher education, especially those based upon practice and fieldwork. The planning stages before our eventual collaboration with South Bank University were lively times and even after this our vision shone through in the course units we eventually offered (see Table 19.1).

Some learning curves

By 1993, the first four units had been commissioned predominantly, but not exclusively, from writers based in environmental education and development education NGOs. By 1994 the next four units had been commissioned and a pilot cohort of almost forty students had been admitted, since South Bank University wanted an overlap between the final year of project funding and the arrival of fee income from students. 1994 was a difficult year not least because the first four units (each comprising a reader and a study guide) were reaching final production only slightly ahead of being sent out to students. At the same time, the delivery systems (the despatch of course materials to students, the organisation of day schools, the various forms of communication between the central course office, tutors and students) were being trialed and work was progressing on the second year units five to eight. During 1992–1995, the Project's decision-making structures were also being adapted to the changing needs of the course. Most of the members of the working party joined the management group of the Masters Curriculum Project when the funding came on stream in 1992 and several management group members also participated in the course development meetings at South Bank between 1993 and 1994. However, as work progressed on the course units and many of the unit writers became tutors when the course was launched in 1994, a course team began to emerge which become increasingly significant. By the time the course was handed over to South Bank the people who could be designated as 'key players' had changed quite substantially, although at each stage there were actors who overlapped from one to the next. The project and later the course called for substantial intra-organisational change, some planned, much improvised. In innovative projects where there is an absence of precedents, learning curves can be very steep.

Today, all the eight 'taught' units are assessed by coursework. Students are able to refine coursework topics to suit their needs and interests with tutors. Because most of the tutors work out of South Bank, the bulk of tutor-student

Table 19.1   Course structure

Unit 1: Introduction to environmental education and development education – the histories, actors, tensions, theories and practices of the two fields.

Unit 2: Environmental education and development education within the formal education system – focusing on curriculum issues salient to practitioners such as the role played by ideology, ways of affecting curriculum change, subject-based and cross-curricular approaches, the interfaces between and specific contributions of such 'adjectival educations' as antiracist and multicultural education, world studies, peace, human rights and futures education.

Unit 3: Issues in participation – comprising a compulsory half unit, (3A) 'equality issues', which takes race and environment and gender and development as its main emphases, and a choice between two largely non-formal sector-focused half units: (3B) youth, community and adult education programmes North/South; or (3C) policy issues in NGO education programmes.

Unit 4: Theories and perspectives on environment and development – which covers such areas as frameworks for understanding the global environment and complementary and competing concepts of development and environment.

Unit 5: Media coverage – focuses upon media coverage of the South and of development issues and on the relationship between science and the media in media reportage of environmental questions, problems and issues.

Unit 6: How local and global factors interact North/South – taking four case studies, examines through the concept of 'social learning' the relationship between new forms of educational and political activity and communities North/South.

Unit 7: Education for sustainability – by working through key considerations for practitioners of education for sustainability this unit enables students to bring together elements from earlier units in a coherently theorised and planned educational strategy or programme.

Unit 8: Research tools and skills – focusing on the likely research needs of a broad range of educators, this unit covers such areas as planning and decision-making, primary- and secondary-data collection, data-quality assessment, research for change (principally action research), examples of research design and the presentation of research findings.

Units 9–12: Dissertation – of 15,000 words.

---

contact takes place by telephone although fax and e-mail are becoming more important as increasing numbers of overseas students join the course. The flexibility of the course has come to be maintained by a paradoxical amount of systemisation in terms of expectations, entitlements, standards and procedures; hence it now has three handbooks: a course handbook, a tutor handbook and a dissertation handbook (containing information about university requirements and the organisation of supervision for students who may never meet their supervisors).

The targeting of the course toward a broad range of educators (teachers, lecturers, youth, community and adult educators, NGO educational personnel) was led by a combination of pragmatism, based on the need to maximise student numbers and the size of pool from which the intake could be drawn, and ideals, based on the value of bringing educators from different phases and sectors of education together to share perspectives and strengthen work across different phases and sectors. All these principles later came to be endorsed by *Agenda 21* (UNCED, 1993). Before we hit the harsh world of the economic imperative (where overseas students seem only to be regarded as important for their extrinsic worth) we regarded the prospect of welcoming continental-European (or overseas) students as immensely exciting. We were right to think this, the presence of continental-European and non-EC students has been of great value to both staff and students; it enables us to circulate and be stimulated by examples of coursework from very different contexts, but even so, such students still remain an under-utilised resource.

What changes would the course team make in the light of experience? Though such aspects as unit content, support and standards score consistently well in course monitoring and examiners' reports, there are a great many things that we would do differently now or change and extend. Developing a distance-learning course at Masters level is difficult enough but all the more so when the proposed course content has not been taught before or is under-theorised – as was and still is the case for development education. Would we have secured our original funding for a different sort of approach? It is very unlikely that the funding bodies supporting the initial project would have put money into a lengthy research and development period and I am doubtful as to whether we could have attracted money from other sources. Most of the project funding came from development education sources which, in fact, rarely support research since they are attracted to product-oriented rather than process-based initiatives (an important contributing factor in the under-theorisation of development education).

During the planning stages we had no real way of anticipating course intake and even now our intake continues to surprise us because we expected to attract only educators. Part of our learning curve has been to find that there are people outside the educational community who want to be able to communicate more effectively about environmental and development issues. At the time of writing, for example, we have an army officer, a police officer, a fire-prevention officer and an engineer doing the course. We are now much more aware of what our students want from the course and while we have addressed immediate needs via a raft of modifications, it would be exciting at this stage to embark upon a second stage of development where more strategic needs could also be attended to. At this broader level, we find that students are greatly concerned with hearing about and testing alternatives to what Fien (1993b) has called the 'dominant social paradigm'. It would thus seem appropriate to enable the students to engage in different ways with a broad array of northern and southern attempts to develop 'constructive postmodern thought' (Griffin, 1992) based upon the interplay of utopianism and practical action. In parallel with the advances that have been made in proposing how an 'alternative social paradigm' might be brought about, we have become much more knowledgeable about how to prepare educators to respond creatively to the task of working toward sustainable development. In sum, if the course were to enter into a second stage of development, we would concentrate less on the realm of the hypothetical and substantially more on the realm of the realisable.

A view of reality

Valuable learning also comes from looking at the broader circumstances in which this initiative took place. As futures-orientated educators, we need to be able to look critically at higher education and implement interventions which skill and inspire learners to confront the world ahead. What is useful, I think, are the insights gained as a result of coming from experience of the environmental and development NGO sector into a culturally contrasting set of academic institutional circumstances. The following is not intended as any sort of comprehensive resumé of the state of higher education in Britain today, it is more a series of snapshots.

Ainley (1994) suggests that tertiary education in Britain has been the subject of three main phases of growth in recent years, a modest period of elitist higher education expansion in the 1960s, the substantial expansion of mediocre further education and youth training from the 1970s through to the 1980s and the rapid and a very mixed large-scale expansion of higher education in 1990s as a product of the social and economic restructuring of the 1980s. Ainley regards this most recent expansion of higher education as maintaining cultural divisions in a society, where the economic changes of recent years have eroded the traditional distinctions between the manual working class and the non-manual middle class. Drawing on Bourdieu et al. (1979), he argues that educational qualifications take on a new significance in the acculturation of working- and middle-class people and hence, the distribution of access to privilege and power. One way it occurs, says Ainley, is through the evolution of a higher-education hierarchy in which research and the more prestigious courses are becoming concentrated in a minority of institutions with teaching and skills narrowly related to employment increasingly becoming concentrated in the rest. It may come as no surprise that Ainley sees the new inner-city universities as predominating in the lower-status group. Ainley paints a dispiriting picture of academic culture, suggesting that while, on the one hand, academics may see the value of breaking the mould, on the other, many are hidebound by what can only be described as the 'Oxbridge ideal'.

Before commenting upon how the MSc course became incorporated into South Bank University, two sets of preparatory remarks are required. First, the two cultures about to be described should not be seen as monolithic but exhibiting generalisable characteristics. In terms of the (environment and development) NGO community, I have a sufficiently broad enough base of experience to appreciate that there are both subtle and rather more apparent differences in ideology and approach among its members. In the case of the higher education community, I can only say that I believe that the South Bank scenario is indicative of an inner-city, new university. Second, my research and experience disposes me towards the view that it is impossible for NGOs and state institutions to be completely equal partners. The organisation of sponsorship (funding) and patronage (legitimation) systems ensure that NGOs remain subordinate in their interactions with state institutions whether schools, colleges or universities. That said, NGOs are not without some cards of their own to play. They can, for example, add democratic respectability to the workings of state institutions, but when the cards are down, state institutions invariably have the upper hand. In an ideal world the NGO and its state partner would be able to perceive their relationship, talk openly about it and agree a code of conduct for their interactions, but as often as not, such discussions simply do not occur, because the parties concerned cannot see the nature of the problem.

At this point the cultures of the two parties concerned become important. While environmental and development NGOs have differences, such differences tend to emanate, not so much from their respective interests in environment and development, but rather from the market niche they have carved for themselves. Billis and MacKeith (1992) talk of the dialectical relationships between the personal world, associational world and bureaucratic world in NGO life and argue that in terms of function, NGOs tend to occupy space in the associational and bureaucratic worlds. In the associational world there is an objective or mission, a name to the grouping and often a membership with rights and duties. Princen and Finger (1994) see NGOs as significant expressions of a 'post-modern politics based upon new forms of social fragmentation and the erosion of the project of modernity', but development NGOs tend not to be extraordinarily different to environmental NGOs in this respect. Hence, the bureaucratic world tends to be regarded with some reserve, especially by those whom Arnold (1987) regards as the 'conscience of the organisation' (notably educators). Most public sector organisations (and this includes higher education institutions), on the other hand, occupy space in the bureaucratic world and are characterised by hierarchical relations and bound together by instruments of accountability and authority (Billis and MacKeith, 1992). Without going into the many reasons why NGOs need, and are often required, to occupy a distinctive space in society, Princen and Finger's (1994) analysis suggests that NGOs are likely to be sceptical of bureaucratisation and especially that which is associated with the workings of the state. In comparison, higher-education institutions tend to be very large bureaucratic structures and while on the one hand academics may be critical of bureaucracy, indeed of many aspects of modernity, on the other the economic imperatives impacting upon such institutions often counteract professed missions. Hence, inner-city new universities which, with their varied styles of course delivery, innovative content, flexible entry and modularisation, would seem to be prime candidates for the crown of 'postmodern learning institution' come to adopt organisational approaches which are contradictorily modernist. Even distance learning, which while often associated with a brave new world of open and lifelong learning can equally be equated with Fordist production, centralisation and managerialism (Raggatt, 1993).

The most striking manifestation of these two cultures comes through comparing the internal life of the Masters course which leans toward the tentative, collaborative and experimental, with the surrounding institutional culture which tends toward the inflexible, combative and procedurally-led. Cultural differences are also apparent when aspirations for the course are examined. As members of the working party, project and then course development team, we wanted the venture to be numerically and materially successful so we could continue to contribute to work in the field. South Bank University, on the other hand, has never been particularly interested in advancing work in the field of education for sustainability, prizing instead the course's substantial development funding, the promise of high student numbers and the fee income to be generated. At one level this might seem like an appropriate division of interest, but the crucial point is that this is not a partnership of interest. The anticipated coming together of NGO verve and imagination and higher education rigour and know-how did not fully come to pass. The lack of university staff we could work with during the development phase who were committed to environmental education and development education was undoubtedly a contributing factor to this lack of partnership. Even now, few staff fully understand the significance of the curriculum development that was orchestrated. The story would probably not have been much different with any other inner-city new university. It might not have been that different if we had selected an older university. It might have been different, however, had we chosen to work with academics who were already active in and committed to the field. Had we selected a more financially secure institution the prognosis for future development might be better. What can be learnt from this is that there were a number of factors governing our choice of host institution and while the choices seemed prudent at the time, and resulted in the establishment of an innovative and exciting course, we may have perpetrated the ultimate irony for futures educators of making decisions that limited the course's future.

Conclusion

In many respects this story is context-specific but we cannot ignore the fact that there is much in the current higher-education system that is not conducive to the advancement of innovative futures-oriented education. Futures-orientated education represents ideologies, practices and goals that are in many ways at odds with higher education's current trajectory. It is important, therefore, that we tell each other our stories with as many warts as is professionally acceptable in order to learn from our experience. I can see no merit in furnishing each other with superficial accounts of our work. Despite this seemingly salutary conclusion the Masters course is extremely popular and has achieved many of its goals. It has certainly been a worthwhile undertaking, not least for our individual and collective learning and what we are now able offer to others. The pleasure of working with the students has made the exercise particularly worthwhile. It should not go unrecorded that at end of the MSc in Environmental and Development Education's five year period of validation we can expect some 150–200 competent and confident practitioners to enter education systems and other learning situations, as far afield as Belize, Brazil, Fiji, Hungary, Kenya, Indonesia, Ireland, Malta, Mexico, Papua New Guinea, the Philippines, South Korea and the United Kingdom.

Here are some student comments after their first year on the course:

> *From a Northern student with an environmental education background:*
> (It has been) generally a stimulating challenging year which has given plenty of scope for further thought around the theory and practice of doing DE (particularly) as well as opening up new areas of thinking

> *From a Northern student with a development education background:*
> My immediate work context involves teaching a short course for grass-roots development workers on Environment and Development. The MSc course has thus been invaluable in providing space for critical reflection and devising strategy…

> *From a Southern student with a development background:*
> About 60% of the material was Northern but it offered great insights I enjoyed reading it…I found the materials relevant. I notice that there is a symbiotic relationship between the North and the South. The balance of materials was excellent.

It is to be hoped that comments such as these will inspire others – both tutors and students – to follow where the initiators of this innovative course have trodden.

References

Ainley, P (1994) *Degrees of Difference: Higher education in the 1990s,* London: Lawrence and Wishart, 23, 25.

Arnold, S (1987) *Constrained Crusaders? British Charities and Development Education,* Washington DC: School of International Service, The American University.

Billis, D and MacKeith, J (1992) 'Growth and Change in NGOs: Concepts and Comparative Experience', in Edwards, M and Hulme, D (eds) (1992) *Making a Difference: NGOs and Development in a Changing World,* London: Earthscan, 122.

Bordieu, P *et al.* (1979) 'The Inheritors, French Students and their Relations to Culture', in Ainley, P (1994) *op. cit.*

Bowe, R, Ball, S and Gold, A (1992) *Reforming Education and Changing Schools,* London: Routledge, 7.

Chitty, C (ed.) (1991) *Changing the Future: Redprint for Education,* London: Tufnell, 21–2.

Dale, R (1989) *The State and Education Policy,* Oxford: Oxford University Press, 115.

Fien, J (ed.) (1993a) *Environmental Education: A Pathway to Sustainable Development,* Geelong, Australia: Deakin-Griffith Environmental Education Project.

Fien, J (1993b) *Education for the Environment: Critical Curriculum Theorising and Environmental Education,* Geelong, Australia: Deakin-Griffith Environmental Education Project.

Giroux, H A (1989) *Schooling for Democracy: Critical Pedagogy in the Modern Age,* London: Routledge, 16–23.

Goodson, I (ed.) (1985) *Social Histories of the Secondary Curriculum,* Lewes: Falmer Press.

Goodson, I (1988) *The Making of the Curriculum: Collected Essays,* Lewes: Falmer Press.

Griffin, D R (1992) 'Introduction to the SUNY Series in Constructive Postmodern Thought', in Orr, D *Ecological Literacy: Education and the Transition to a Postmodern World,* New York: State University of New York Press.

Huckle, J and Sterling, S (eds) (1996) *Education for Sustainability,* London: Earthscan.

IUCN/UNEP/WWF (1991) *Caring for the Earth: A Strategy for Sustainable Living,* London: Earthscan.

Raggatt, P (1993) 'Post-Fordism and Distance Education – a Flexible Strategy for Change', *Open Learning,* 8(1), 23.

Princen, T and Finger, M (1994) *Environmental NGOs in World Politics: Linking the Local to the Global,* London: Routledge, 61.

Sterling, S (1990) 'Environment, Development, Education – Towards an Holistic View', in Abraham, J, Lacey, C and Williams, R (1990) *Deception, Demonstration and Debate,* London: WWF/Kogan Page.

UNCED (1993) *Agenda 21,* New York: United Nations Conference on Environment and Development.

20. The WWF UK Reaching Out programme

John Huckle

Summary

This final chapter explores the construction, delivery and evaluation of Reaching Out, the World Wide Fund for Nature UK's programme of professional development for teachers. It argues that political ecology and critical theory provide sound foundations for understanding our current crisis of environment and development and for determining the aims, content and pedagogy of education for sustainability. This suggests that such education should link with political movements beyond the school and explains why many teachers will reject its introduction at a time of conservative educational reform. The evaluation of Reaching Out offers reasons for its limited success and while there is much scope for revision and improvement, the chapter argues that WWF-UK should not abandon a developing philosophy of education for sustainability which accords with the recent proposals of the Real World coalition. The chapter is a reminder that futures education should be securely anchored in present material and cultural realities and the trends which they display.

Introduction

> The modern educational crisis is a product of the one-sided development of our capacity for rational management of human affairs and rational problem solving. The institution of mass schooling can be either a source of the problem or a possible vehicle for the changes in learning we require (Young, 1989: 23).

In reviewing *A Critical Theory of Education: Habermas and Our Children's Future*, Carr (1992) suggested that the book's author, Robert Young, had constructed a comprehensive critical theory of education. This offers a diagnosis of the modern crisis concerning the role of mass education in society and a response framed around a belief in the potential of education to promote citizenship and sustain a genuinely democratic way of life.

This chapter explores the construction, delivery and evaluation of a programme of teacher education for sustainability based largely on the theory which Young outlines. It begins by locating the programme within the work of the education department of the World Wide Fund for Nature (WWF) and then outlines how critical theory shaped course design. An account of the delivery and evaluation of the programme suggests that its adoption and success have been limited by the increased hold of instrumental reason and ideology on teachers and their 'deep-seated aversion to abstract philosophical thinking' which Carr mentions in his review. Such obstacles will take a considerable time to overcome but, the chapter argues, WWF should not abandon a critical approach to education. This allows the emergence of values which lie at the heart of *Caring for the Earth* (IUCN/UNEP/WWF, 1991), the revised world conservation strategy and facilitates critical consideration of the kind of policy proposals advanced by those environmental and social justice groups, including WWF, who have joined together to form the Real World coalition.

Reaching Out

The World Wide Fund for Nature began its educational programme in the UK in 1981. Peter Martin, its newly appointed education officer, decided that a wildlife club and visiting speaker scheme for schools were having a limited impact and resources were thus switched to the development of curriculum materials. Within the decade, the education department had an impressive catalogue listing materials which enabled environmental education to be introduced through most school subjects to pupils of all ages. These materials were developed and written by an expanding network of teachers, consultants and writers; by 1991 curriculum management and teacher education materials were being added to the list. WWF-UK has done much to sustain environmental education in the UK during a period in which it has been a low priority in the government's programme of educational reform (Smith, 1996).

The publication of *Caring for the Earth*, and the lead up to the Earth Summit in Rio, caused the education officers at WWF-UK to re-assess their aims and strategies. *Education for Sustainability* (Huckle and Sterling, 1996), provided a sharper and more demanding focus than environmental education, with the actions promoted in *Caring for the Earth* and Agenda 21 (Quarrie, 1992), clearly pointing to a greater emphasis on community and citizenship education. The new challenge was to educate teachers and schools to use WWF's curriculum materials, along with others, in ways which encourage democratic change towards more sustainable ways of living. Resources were therefore re-directed to the professional development of teachers and the support of innovative schools. A teacher education officer, Phil Champain, was appointed in 1991 and he invited a team of writers to prepare an in-service teacher education programme.

Reaching Out: Education for Sustainability (Huckle *et al.*, 1995) is the main vehicle for WWF-UK's current teacher education strategy. It consists of a set of workshop materials which make up a comprehensive course in the theory and practice of education for sustainability. It draws on existing WWF materials and is designed to support a wide range of courses from a short professional development session in school, to a thirty-hour module which contributes to a certificate, diploma or higher degree. The workshops enable teacher educators to introduce teachers to the literature of environmentalism, sustainable development and environmental education, and to examine the ways in which this and other factors have influenced curriculum development. A common core of sessions in parts one and three introduces education for sustainability and its implementation in schools and the wider community, while different routes in part two cater for primary school teachers and for a range of secondary subject specialists (english, geography, science and technology). The objectives of *Reaching Out* and the titles of the sessions in parts one and three are listed in Table 20.1.

Meeting the theoretical challenge through political ecology

Asked to suggest a rationale and curriculum framework for *Reaching Out*, which could guide the writers of the materials in the tutor's file, I was much influenced by political ecology and critical theory. During the 1980s writers such as Gorz (1980, 1989, 1994) and O' Connor (1988) had sought to combine political economy and natural economy (ecology) to explain the first and second contradictions of capitalism: that between the forces and relations of production and that between the conditions of production and relations of reproduction. In addition to exploiting human nature and thereby producing alienation and poverty, capitalism (and 'actually existing' forms of socialism) also exploit non-human nature, or such conditions as soil fertility, biodiversity, climate stabilization and freedom from congestion and pollution, thereby accentuating alienation and making economic production and social reproduction more difficult. The labour and new social movements address these contradictions, seeking democratisation of economic production and social reproduction in order to reduce alienation and poverty and improve the quality of people's lives.

Gorz's early writing on political ecology suggested that these movements should be seeking radical economic democracy. If workers gained control over technology, production and working hours, they would be able to introduce socially useful and ecologically sustainable forms of production, distribution and redistribution and use their newly acquired time to discover and satisfy their real needs and revive civil society. The appeal of consumerism and false needs would then decline but such green socialism would require enabling states or governments, at local, regional, and international levels, to provide

Table 20.1   Reaching out: education for sustainability – WWF-UK's teacher education programme

The programme's objectives	The ten sessions in parts one and three
On completing Reaching Out, teachers should be more able to: • outline and justify a professional perspective on environmental education and education for sustainability; • draw on a range of appropriate knowledge, materials and classroom techniques to educate for sustainability in the classroom and local community; • employ action-research techniques to improve their delivery of education for sustainability; • use national curriculum frameworks to educate for sustainability; • help colleagues to formulate and realize whole-school policies on environmental education; • link education for sustainability within their school and community to other relevant initiatives, locally, nationally and globally.	1 Caring for the Earth. 2 Towards a critical environmental education. 3 Education for sustainability as socially critical pedagogy. 4 Environmental education and the national curriculum. 5 An introduction to action research. 11 Towards a whole school policy on environmental education. 12 Linking with the community. 13 Linking with the wider world. 14 Keeping it all under review. 15 Where do we go from here?

appropriate economic planning and political regulation. Such political ecology was admirably presented in the comic book *Ecology for Beginners* (Croall and Rankin, 1981) and along with world systems theory (Wallerstein, 1984), and ideas from the Programme for Political Education (Crick and Porter, 1978), it strongly influenced *What We Consume*, the curriculum materials for older pupils which I wrote for WWF in the 1980s (Huckle, 1988, 1992).

Bowring (1995) suggests that by combining the ecological imperative with a simplistic Marxism, Gorz's early political ecology risks the suggestion that sustainability can be achieved for people by technocratic means. By grounding the politics of ecology in economics rather than the culture, it leaves social movements fighting for an alternative social system rather than a general state of emancipation. His later work takes the cultural turn and argues that at the core of political ecology is protest against the destruction of the lifeworld or culture of everyday life. It is the knowledge, habits, norms and modes of conduct which comprise this culture that enable individuals to interpret, understand and assume responsibility for the way in which they inhabit the world that surrounds them. The 'nature' or environment whose protection the movement demands is the environment that appears 'natural' because its structures and workings are accessible to intuitive understanding; because it corresponds to a need for a flowering of the sensory and motor faculties; because its familiar structure enables individuals to find their way about in it, interact with it, communicate with it 'spontaneously' using aptitudes which have never had to be formally taught (Gorz, 1993: 57–58).

The goal of green socialism now becomes the reduction of those areas of social life governed by forms of economic and administrative rationality which colonize the lifeworld and their subordination to values which allow its revival as a mechanism of social integration. This requires the promotion of work which is performed as an end in itself, or to produce use value which we ourselves consume. By working for ourselves and one another, outside the market, we can collectively re-define our needs and meet them in sustainable ways, while at the same time creating, maintaining and expanding the life-world. Such sustainable livelihood development (Chambers, 1986) is attracting growing support from trade unions, the unemployed, pensioners, new social movements and community groups as the costs of our current forms of development continue to mount.

Meeting the theoretical challenge through critical theory

By taking the cultural turn Gorz and other green socialists were identifying themselves more strongly with the critical theory of the Frankfurt School and its leading exponent, Habermas. Like earlier members of the School, Habermas is anxious to explain the permanence of capitalism and the failures of 'actually existing' forms of socialism to fulfill the promise Marx predicted. In critical theory, the focus shifts from capitalism, human labour, the economy and the democratisation of production, to modernity, communication, language, the democratisation of discourse and the defense of the lifeworld. The starting point is the potential for human emancipation, autonomy, or freedom inherent within the Enlightenment project and the manner in which this is arrested by the limited forms of rationality which characterise modern societies in their current phase of development.

The process of modernisation involves the differentiation of society, into separate sub-systems such as the economy and politics and its organisation by means of rational forms of management and administration. It leads to structural and cultural transformations which involve the abandonment of traditional ethics and a growing demand that morality be rationally founded. Modernity promises moral consensus and universal ethics, through free and open discussion or discursive democracy; yet welfare capitalism (and state socialism) became dominated by technocracy and instrumental reason which separate means from ends, facts from values, truth from virtue and theory from practice. Prevailing forms of rationality, knowledge and politics, serve the interests of minorities who largely control and manage human and non-human nature for their own gain. Such rationality turns thinking into technique, encourages a detached view of the world, cuts us off from the lifeworld, fosters a modern brutalism which tolerates cruelty and ugliness and makes us strangers to a reified world which is nonetheless our product. Only by realizing more advanced forms of rationality, ethics and democracy, will people reclaim the lifeworld, realize their common interest in more sustainable forms of development, and thereby gain their freedom.

By the early 1990s environmental educators were beginning to link critical social theories of the environment and education (Robottom, 1987; Fien, 1993; Huckle, 1993). *Caring for the Earth* and Agenda 21, stress the role of critical and participatory citizenship in realizing sustainable community development (at all scales from the local to the global) and pointed to the need for teacher education for sustainability which would develop 'transformative intellectuals' (Giroux and McClaren, 1986), aware of the current limited nature of democracy, citizenship and citizenship education (Held, 1987; Carr and Harnett, 1996, Lynch, 1992). The challenge was to build *Reaching Out* on a framework of critical theory so that it could foster the professional development of such teachers.

Legitimation crisis

Four themes within Habermas' work influenced the development of *Reaching Out*: legitimation crisis, knowledge-constitutive interests, communicative action and the colonization of the lifeworld (White, 1989; Goldblatt, 1996). Underlying them all is the process of modernisation which, as we have seen, differentiates the economy and state from the public (civil) and private (domestic) spheres and organises more aspects of social life through rational control. The economic and political systems are the domains of instrumental reason and strategic action, mediated through the steering mechanisms of money and power, where aspects of social reproduction are realized largely as a result of decisions taken by elites. Meanwhile civil society and households remain primarily domains of practical reason and communicative action, mediated through influence and commitment, where other aspects of social reproduction are realized through free and open discourse. The public and private spheres constitute the lifeworld which is increasingly invaded by the priorities and values of the economy and state.

In explaining why economic and environmental crises have failed to develop in ways which undermine capitalism, Habermas suggests that the modern state has developed ways of managing such crises which maintain sufficient people's commitment to the system. State planning and regulation of the economy, society and environment, based on instrumental rationality and administration, serves to offset or delay the economic, social and ecological limits to growth by accelerating the treadmill of production and consumption, offering workers and citizens the compensations of consumerism and welfare benefits and developing new forms of 'environmentally-friendly' production and regulation. Nevertheless, crises continue and may result in legitimation, motivational and identity crises if the state is unable to convince citizens, who have an increased capacity for rational discourse, of the efficacy of its actions. To prevent this happening, the cultural economy and education are pressed into service so that consent is manufactured through the mass media and education (Chomsky, 1991). Not all the resulting 'lessons' are ideologically laden but the net effect is to persuade most people that existing forms of undemocratic social and environmental relations are somehow normal, natural or inevitable and that they work in the interests of all.

Legitimation crisis contributed to the break up of social democracy and welfare capitalism from the late 1960s. Overcoming a crisis of profitability involved the restructuring of production, labour processes and modes of regulation, to allow a new phase of capital accumulation. The erosion of social democracy and the rise of the new right was eased by people's disillusionment with technocracy and their desire for greater personal freedom. Deregulation and privatisation have been used to hasten the introduction of new technologies, products and work practices, to quicken rates of innovation and turnover time in production and to dismantle welfare states. Disorganised capitalism (Lash and Urry, 1987) replaces mass production with mass customization, produces a vast new array of cultural goods and services, involves accelerating globalisation as capital, labour and information become more mobile and brings new social divisions along with new interests and insecurities. This is being cast in a dominant weak mode and in the strong mode, of sustainable livelihood development, which we have already examined. As sustainable growth or the greening of capitalism, the weak mode represents an emerging mode of regulation whereby capital seeks to internalise nature by ideologically redefining it (as a condition of production) and subsuming it within capital as a productive asset subject to technocratic management (Reid, 1995; Huckle, 1996). This may ensure a continued supply of natural resources and services for sections of capital and help to ameliorate problems of legitimation, but it is ultimately compromised by the need for capitalists and nation states to compete internationally (Johnston, 1989). In an age of globalisation and deregulation, weak sustainability is likely to take limited and largely imagined forms, functioning more as public relations than genuine change.

The restructuring of capitalism has been accompanied by the restructuring of education and schooling. This renders it less democratic and tightens the correspondence between the overt and hidden curriculum and disorganised capitalism's economic and cultural needs. The national curriculum, introduced in the 1990s, allows the delivery of education about the environment through several subjects, but is largely consistent with an education for weak sustainability which offers no critical challenge to the *status quo* (Ahier and Ross, 1995). The marginalisation of cross-curricular themes, the guidance materials offered to schools, frameworks for school inspections, national tests for pupils and new restrictions on pre-service teacher education, are all aspects of reform which make the introduction of education for strong sustainability more difficult.

Knowledge-constitutive interests

In discussing knowledge-constitutive interests, Habermas helps us to understand how different human interests constitute different kinds of knowledge and how education for strong sustainability should function as a form of ideology critique. He argues that all societies have a technical interest in achieving control over their environment and a practical interest in achieving mutual understanding. These interests arise from the necessities of social labour and communication, are mediated through the media of work and language and constitute the empirical and positivist sciences and the interpretive sciences or humanities. The hold of positivism and instrumental reason on the economic and political spheres largely accounts for our modern crisis, while interpretive knowledge sustains the lifeworld by promoting appreciation and awareness of our environment and one another. A third emancipatory interest constitutes critical science or theory and it is this knowledge that can free people from ideological (and ultimately material) constraints and assist them in building strong sustainability. Critical theory denies the possibiity of a neutral and apolitical science and requires natural scientists and science teachers, to rethink their philosophy so that can 'make the world a better place' (Wakeford and Walters, 1995).

Communicative action

If legitimation crisis and knowledge constitutive interests provide pointers to the content of education for sustainability, communicative action suggests a process of critical enquiry, or action research, which tests the truth of critical theory and offers a unifying model for pedagogy, curriculum development, professional development and sustainable community development. Language is often a vehicle for misinformation, lies, distortion and ideology, but at the same time it offers truth. Habermas maintains that when we speak we implicitly make four validity claims which are unavoidable and reciprocally recognised. We claim that what we say is intelligible (comprehensible), true (matches reality), correct (legitimate and appropriate in context) and sincere (genuinely meant). In situations of open discussion, termed ideal speech situations, these validity claims can be examined and tested discursively in ways which allow participants to arrive at a consensus through argument alone. Provided they have accurate and complete information about the issue; the ability to reason argumentatively and reflectively about disputed validity claims; self knowledge sufficient to ensure that their participation is free of inhibitions, compensatory mechanisms or other forms of self deception, then they should be able to arrive at a common view concerning what might, could and should be done.

Communicative action provides the theoretical model of praxis, or reflection and action, which underpins socially critical pedagogy in the classroom (Shor, 1980), action research as a means of professional and curriculum development (Carr and Kemmis, 1986) and the empowerment of communities through strong forms of sustainable development from below. In seeking to manage legitimation crisis, the state offers citizens an increasing number of what Drysek (1992) terms 'incipient discursive designs'. Environmental-impact assessment, public inquiries, round tables on sustainability and national strategies and guidelines of environmental education all play roles but the local Agenda 21 process is just one example of how seeking change through consensus can expose ideology and bring strong sustainability onto the agenda (Tuxworth, 1996; Wals, 1996).

Colonisation of the lifeworld

Finally, in drawing our attention to the colonisation of the lifeworld, Habermas echoes Gorz in suggesting that everyday culture is being taken over by the priorities of those who seek money and political power. Each of the four subsystems of society is specialized in what it produces and relies on others for what it does not produce. The economy produces money, the state produces power, the public sphere influence and the private sphere commitment. These media of exchange must be traded between subsystems (eg the economy relies on the state to influence cultural reproduction in schools) but they are not equivalent in their instrumental capacity. The superior efficacy of money and power means that they progressively dominate over influence and commitment with the result that the lifeworld becomes increasingly commercialised and state dominated. People increasingly live for immediate and instrumental returns and experience each other as functionaries with the result that their lives are robbed of the symbolic and normative content which provides meaning. Colonisation of the lifeworld is a restatement of legitimation crisis at a higher level of theoretical sophistication, which helps us to explain the new politics, radical environmentalism and the resistance offered by some teachers to current educational reforms.

Disorganised capitalism and postmodernisation

Habermas' four themes were developed to account for the pathologies of late-modern societies and may need revision if they are to guide education in postmodern societies. The changes which many associate with the arrival of postmodernity, can be explained as an extension of the two modernisation processes, differentiation and organisation, to extreme levels (Crook *et al.*, 1992). Hyper-differentiation results in social units, such as firms, schools and churches, differentiating at the level of function as well as structure. As they take on new forms and roles and meet new purposes, they become new sources of media of exchange and can more easily challenge, undermine, or resist the economy and state's monopoly of control. The increased availability and power of culture in all its forms is the key to this process which breaks down the central steering mechanisms of society and suggests that agency can float free from structure.

Postmodernisation accelerates individualisation, secularisation and the erosion of traditional institutions such as the family, social class, politics and community. It relativises, contextualises, deconstructs and demysifies knowledge, values and such grand narratives as science, challenging people to construct their own lifeworlds and life narratives, from the profusion of choices on offer. As the distinction between society and culture seems to disappear, it is vitally important that teachers understand young people's search for identity and a viable lifeworld and combine citizenship education with education for sustainability in ways which counter alienation and offer hope (Klaassen, 1996). In meeting this challenge, they can learn from theorists of reflexive modernisation (Beck, Giddens and Lash, 1994; Giddens, 1994) who suggest that contemporary change arouses a new sensitivity to environmental and other risks, encouraging many to reflect on the social use and construction of nature and how it might be used and reconstructed in more sustainable ways.

Postmodernisation does not represent a rejection of the Enlightenment project of social emancipation which Habermas seeks to restore. Rather, it rejects the totalising arguments with which progress and universal rights and values, are imposed on subservient minorities along with much else. It brings a new sensitivity and tolerance to difference and suggests that as well as seeking universal rights, the rights of minorities, including those of other sentient beings, should be sought where they do not diminish the rights of other minorities. Education for sustainability should therefore accommodate the views of ecological humanists, ecofeminists, deep ecologists, postmodern scientists, and others (Merchant, 1994); learn from those educational philosophers who are currently debating the application of Habermas' ideas to education in postmodern times (Carr, 1995; Blake, 1996) and seek inspiration from those who envision progressive schools in postmodern times (Hargreaves, 1994). It should attempt to build these views into the kind of coherent understanding of nature, society and education which critical realism (Dickens, 1992, 1996; Haywood, 1994) provides and should thereby harness itself to the type of new metanarrative or universe story which Jencks (1996) outlines.

Theory shapes practice

Looking again at Table 19.1 the reader can probably now recognise how critical theory shaped *Reaching Out*'s design and content. Session one uses a video synopsis of *Our Common Future* (WCED, 1987) to encourage teachers to clarify their own beliefs and values concerning the double crisis of environment and development. This is linked in the background notes to the nature of modernity, legitimation crisis and current political debates surrounding sustainability. Three different classroom activities on global warming are used in session two to help them recognize how knowledge-constitutive interests shape environmental education and the need for education for sustainability to incorporate critical understanding. Session three invites teachers to plan a classroom activity around a local environmental issue in a way which incorporates both critical understanding and democratic pedagogy (communicative action). The teacher's developing understanding of critical education for sustainability is then applied to the critique and reconstruction of case studies from national-curriculum documents in session four, before session five introduces critical-action research as a means of professional development. Teachers suggest theory-practice gaps in their working lives as environmental educators which need to be closed and develop action plans for part two: a period of action research and curriculum development based in school.

In applying and refining the insights they have gained from part one, teachers and their tutors are supported by five sessions in part two which aid the identification of research topics, examine the potential of links between subjects and explore the relevance of such cross-curricular themes and dimensions, such as citizenship and equal opportunities. In part three teachers begin by sharing the outcomes of part two as an introduction to session eleven on greening the school. This examines the implications of sustainability for the whole life of the school and links with session 12 on local Agenda 21. It explores ways in which teachers and pupils can work with local government, community groups and local businesses, to develop local sustainability and session 13 encourages them to enrich such initiatives by also linking with communities working for sustainability elsewhere in the world. Session 14 returns to the theme of the management and evaluation of education for sustainability in the self-managing school before the final session encourages teachers to speculate about postmodern futures and their implications.

Evaluating *Reaching Out*

Even with launch seminars and extensive publicity the response to the *Reaching Out* programme has been somewhat disappointing. It has not been as easy as expected to recruit teachers to short courses; the sessions in the tutors' file have been much modified and diluted when used on these courses; few universities have adopted the file as the foundation for longer accredited courses. A primary reason for this response is the increased hold of instrumental reason on teachers, schools and teacher education as a result of recent educational reforms. Teachers and tutors are generally pre-occupied with the effective delivery and assessment of the national curriculum's core and foundation subjects. They give little or no priority to cross-curricular themes and can satisfy the government's most recent strategy and guidance on environmental education (DoE, 1996; SCAA, 1996) with minimal or no reference to the kind of critical education for sustainability which *Reaching Out* promotes. Britain has not seen the new-right backlash against environmentalism and environmental education taking place in the USA (Rowell, 1996), but neither is there yet a strong challenge to current curriculum orthodoxies of the kind being voiced by one of the Labour Party's advisers (Barber, 1996) or those further to the left (Hatcher and Jones, 1996).

While the sessions in the *Reaching Out* tutors' file seek to engage teachers with the ethical, philosophical, conceptual and pedagogical foundations of education for susainability, the first short courses revealed that this was clearly not what some members expected. Their reluctance and difficulty in engaging with the ideas can again be explained in terms of the deprofessionalisation, the social division of labour in schools (Dickens, 1996), and teachers' existing levels of environmental and social literacy, but it meant that tutors had to quickly rethink their content and strategies or risk departing from the programme's democratic ideals. Two days did not allow five sessions to be delivered with sufficient dialogue, supportive reading, and cross-referencing of theory and practice; it quickly became obvious that simpler materials were needed. Thus *Let's Reach Out: Primary* (Symons, 1995) and *Let's Reach Out: Secondary* (Webster, 1995) were produced, retaining some but not all elements of the original rationale.

An evaluation of *Reaching Out: Two Evaluation Reports* (Blakeney and Sterling, 1996) devotes considerable attention to WWF's policy, strategy and administration, and suggests that while the materials are 'a considerable curriculum development achievement and resource', they risk being too academic, fail to balance a socially critical view of education for sustainability with an holistic approach and are difficult to deliver in a democratic manner when faced with time constraints. The evaluators seek a review of WWF policy and strategy; systems for tutor mentoring and quality assurance; more attention to links between personal and professional development; additional material relating to neglected areas of the school curriculum; consideration of CD ROM and the Internet to support distance learning; greater clarity regarding the programme's essential core; continual updating of the file and a new tutors' handbook; research to evaluate long-term effects. They also suggest that the links between theory and practice should be made more explicit on courses.

The evaluators' comments point to the inevitably self-limiting nature of *Reaching Out*. WWF is limited by its charitable status and need to sustain corporate and government funding. Its education officers may welcome and promote *Reaching Out*'s critical rationale and content but they will necessarily have to dilute or ignore these when presenting their work to certain audiences. Similarly *Reaching Out*'s writers and tutors may be self censoring and further accommodations occur when the programme works with university tutors, local government officers and other partners. While there are attempts to agree common principles and an overall strategy, WWF still lacks a coherent philosophy of education for sustainability. Consequently there is a real danger that the key role of critical theory and action research in meeting its mission may be diluted or ignored. That is less likely to happen if the education department learns from the Real World initiative.

Learning from The Real World initiative

In 1996 a coalition of 41 British aid, environmental and social justice groups joined together to present an action programme for the government which would take office in 1997. Real World challenged politicians to debate the environmental and development issues of the real world and to adopt such policies as higher spending on housing, community projects and overseas aid, a Bill of Rights and greener economic, energy and transport policies. There is much in *The Politics of the Real World* (Jacobs, 1996) to welcome. It advocates a new kind of green social democracy with strong regulation of markets by democratic government, constitutional reform and a greater role for civil society. In seeking to restore and redefine democracy and citizenship and create a new culture of participation, its aims and vision are consistent with those of critical theorists and *Reaching Out*. WWF's education department cannot afford to ignore such clear analysis and proposals for as the organisation's director states, on the back cover of Jacobs' book, 'protecting the environment can only be achieved by facing up to the underlying social and economic realities'.

Perhaps environmental education ought to be subsumed within social, citizenship or community education, certainly the more progressive and radical teachers attending *Reaching Out* courses have tended to have a background in social education and/or experience of working for social justice and the environment in contexts within and beyond the school. *Reaching Out* has had limited success in difficult times but there are at last some real signs that times are changing. WWF should hold fast to 'the politics of the real world' and the critical education theory and practice which can provide its agenda with a fair hearing.

References

Ahier, J and Ross, A (eds.) (1995) *The Social Subjects Within the Curriculum*, London: Falmer Press.

Barber, M (1996) *The Learning Game, Arguments for an Education Revolution*, London: Victor Gollanz.

Beck, U, Giddens, A and Lash, S (1994) *Reflexive Modernization: Politics, Tradition and Aesthetics in the Modern Social Order*, Cambridge: Polity.

Blackeney, M and Sterling, S (1996) *Reaching Out: Two Evaluation Reports*, WWF Education Department, mimeograph.

Blake, N (1996) 'The Democracy We Need: Situation, Post-Foundationalism and Enlightenment', *Journal of Philosophy of Education*, 30(2): 213–38.

Bowring, F (1995) 'Andre Gorz: Ecology, System and Lifeworld', *Capitalism, Nature, Socialism*, 6(4): 65–84.

Carr, W (1992) 'Review of *A Critical Theory of Education: Habermas and Our Children's Future* by R Young, R, 1989', *Curriculum*, 13(1): 74.

Carr, W (1995) 'Education and Democracy: Confronting the Postmodern Challenge', *Journal of Philosophy of Education*, 29(1): 75–91.

Carr, W and Harnett, A (1996) *Education and the Struggle for Democracy*, Buckingham: Open University Press.

Carr, W and Kemmis, S (1986) *Becoming Critical: Education, Knowledge and Action Research*, Lewes: Falmer Press.

Chambers, R (1986) *Sustainable Livelihoods: An Opportunity for the World Commission on Environment and Development*, Brighton: Institute for Development Studies, University of Sussex.

Chomsky, N (1991) *Manufacturing Consent: Thought Control in Democratic Societies*, Boston: Beacon Press.

Crick, B and Porter, A (1978) *Political Education and Political Literacy*, London: Longman.

Croall, S and Rankin, M (1981) *Ecology for Beginners*, London: Writers and Readers.

Crook, S, Pakulski, J and Waters, M (1992) *Postmodernization: Change in Advanced Society*, London: Sage.

Dickens, P (1992) *Society and Nature, Towards a Green Social Theory*, London: Harvester Wheatsheaf.

Dickens, P (1996) *Reconstructing Nature: Alienation, Emancipation and the Division of Labour*, London: Routledge.

DoE (Department of the Environment) (1996) *Taking Environmental Education into the 21st Century*, London: DoE.

Drysek, J (1992) 'Ecology and Discursive Democracy: Beyond Liberal Capitalism and the Administrative State', *Capitalism, Nature, Socialism*, 3(2): 18–42

Fien, J (1993) *Education for the Environment: Critical Curriculum Theorising and Environmental Education*, Geelong: Deakin University.

Giddens, A (1994) *Beyond Left and Right: The Future of Radical Politics*, Cambridge: Polity.

Giroux, H and McClaren, P (1986) 'Teacher Education and the Politics of Engagement', *Harvard Educational Review*, 56(3): 213–38.

Goldblatt, D (1996) *Social Theory and the Environment*, Cambridge: Polity.

Gorz, A (1980) *Ecology as Politics*, Boston: South End Press.

Gorz, A (1989) *Critique of Economic Reason*, London: Verso

Gorz, A (1993) 'Political Ecology: Expertocracy Versus Self-Limitation', *New Left Review*, 202: 55–67.

Gorz, A (1994) *Capitalism, Socialism, Ecology*, London: Verso.

Hargreaves, A (1994) *Changing Teachers, Changing Times*, London, Cassell.

Hatcher, R and Jones, K (eds) (1996) *Education after the Conservatives*, Stoke-on-Trent: Trentham.

Haywood, T (1994) *Ecological Thought: An Introduction*, Cambridge: Polity.

Held, D (1987) *Models of Democracy*, Cambridge: Polity.

Huckle, J (1988) *What We Consume, The Teachers Handbook*, Richmond: Richmond Publishing.

Huckle, J (1992) *What We Consume, Our Consumer Society*, Unit 3, Richmond: Richmond Publishing.

Huckle, J (1993) 'Environmental Education and Sustainability: A View From Critical Theory', in: Fien, J (ed.) *Environmental Education: A Pathway to Sustainability*, Geelong: Deakin University

Huckle, J (1996) 'Realizing Sustainability in Changing Times', in Huckle, J and Sterling, S (eds.), *op. cit.*

Huckle, J, Allen, E, Edwards, P, Symons, G and Webster, K (1995) *Reaching Out: Education for Sustainability*, Godalming: WWF Education Department.

Huckle, J and Sterling, S (eds) (1996) *Education for Sustainability*, London: Earthscan.

IUCN/UNEP/WWF (1991) *Caring for the Earth: A Strategy for Sustainable Living*, London: Earthscan.

Jacobs, M (1996) *The Politics of the Real World*, London: Earthscan.

Jencks, C (1996) *What is Post-Modernism?* London: Academy Editions.

Johnston, R J (1989) *Environmental Problems: Nature, Economy, State*, London: Belhaven.

Klaassen, C (1996) 'Education and Citizenship in a Post-Welfare State', *Curriculum*, 17(2): 62–73.

Lash, S and Urry, J (1987) *The End of Organised Capitalism*, Cambridge: Polity.

Lynch, J (1992) *Education for Citizenship in a Multi-Cultural Society*, London: Cassell.

Merchant, M (1994) *Ecology: Key Concepts in Critical Theory*, New Jersey: Humanities Press.

O'Connor, J (1988) 'Capitalism, Nature, Socialism: A Theoretical Introduction', *Capitalism, Nature, Socialism*, 1(1): 11–38

Quarrie, J (1992) *Earth Summit 1992*, London: Regency Press.

Reid, D (1995) *Sustainable Development: An Introductory Guide*, London: Earthscan.

Robottom, I (ed.) (1987) *Environmental Education: Practice and Possibility*, Geelong: Deakin University

Rowell, A (1996) *Green Backlash: Global Subversion of the Environmental Movement*, London: Routledge.

SCAA (School Curriculum and Assessment Authority) (1996) *Teaching Environmental Matters Through the National Curriculum*, Hayes: SCAA Publications.

Shor, I (1980) *Critical Teaching and Everyday Life*, Boston: South End Press.

Smith, P (1996) *Curriculum Vitae the First 15 Years*, Godalming: WWF-UK.

Symons, G (1995) *Let's Reach Out: A Survivors Guide for Curriculum Co-ordinators of Environmental Education in Primary Schools*, Godalming: WWF-UK.

Tuxworth, B (1996) 'From Environment to Sustainability: Surveys and Analysis of Local Agenda 21 Process Development in UK Local Authorities', *Local Environment*, 1(3): 277–98.

Wallerstein, I (1984) *The Politics of the World Economy*, Cambridge: Cambridge University Press.

Wakeford, T and Walters, M (1995) *Science for the Earth: Can Science Make the World a Better Place?* Chichester: John Wiley.

Wals, A E (1996) 'Back-alley Sustainability and the Role of Environmental Education', *Local Environment*, 1(3): 299–316.

Webster, K (1995) *Let's Reach Out: a Survivors Guide for Curriculum Co-ordinators of Environmental Education in Secondary Schools*, Godalming: WWF-UK.

White, S K (1989) *The Recent Work of Jurgen Habermas*, Cambridge: Cambridge University Press.

WCED (World Commission of Environment and Development) (1987) *Our Common Future*, Oxford: Oxford University Press.

Young, R (1989) *A Critical Theory of Education: Habermas and Our Children's Future*, London: Harvester Wheatsheaf.

Current information on WWF-UK's education programme can be found via its homepage: http://www.wwf-uk.org

Index